Church, World and the Christian Life

This book argues that modern ecclesiology exhibits two
unfortunate tendencies: it describes the church in ideal terms,
rather than directly addressing the problems of its everyday,
sinful activity; and it undermines the distinctiveness of the
church and its way of life. The book analyzes the impact of
pluralism and inclusivism upon ecclesiology, and draws upon
von Balthasar's theodramatic theory, MacIntyre's theory of
traditional inquiry, postmodern critiques of humanism, and
postmodern ethnography to develop a more flexible and
concrete ecclesiology that can better address the practical and
pastoral needs of the church. This alternative ecclesiology
strongly affirms the need for the church to debate with those
who challenge its claims and their embodiment, both from
within and externally. The book concludes by discussing how
the church may construct its own theological forms of
historical, sociological and ethnographic analysis of both the
church and society.

NICHOLAS M. HEALY is Associate Professor of Theology
and Religious Studies at St. John's University, New York. He is
a member of the American Academy of Religion, the Catholic
Theological Society of America, the Canadian Theological
Society, and the Karl Barth Society.

Cambridge Studies in Christian Doctrine

Edited by
Professor COLIN GUNTON, *King's College London*
Professor DANIEL W. HARDY, *University of Cambridge*

Cambridge Studies in Christian Doctrine is an important series which aims to engage critically with the traditional doctrines of Christianity, and at the same time to locate and make sense of them within a secular context. Without losing sight of the authority of scripture and the traditions of the church, the books in this series will subject pertinent dogmas and credal statements to careful scrutiny, analyzing them in light of the insights of both church and society, and will thereby practise theology in the fullest sense of the word.

Titles published in the series

1. Self and Salvation: Being Transformed
   DAVID F. FORD

2. Realist Christian Theology in a Postmodern Age
   SUE PATTERSON

3. Trinity and Truth
   BRUCE D. MARSHALL

4. Theology, Music and Time
   JEREMY S. BEGBIE

5. The Bible, Theology, and Faith: A Study of Abraham and Jesus
   R. W. L. MOBERLY

6. Bound to Sin: Abuse, Holocaust and the Christian Doctrine of Sin
   ALISTAIR McFADYEN

7. Church, World and the Christian Life: Practical-Prophetic Ecclesiology
   NICHOLAS M. HEALY

Forthcoming titles in the series

Church, Narrativity and Transcendence
ROBERT JENSON

A Political Theology of Nature
PETER SCOTT

Remythologizing Theology: Divine Action and Authorship
KEVIN J. VANHOOZER

Church, World and the Christian Life

Practical-Prophetic
Ecclesiology

Nicholas M. Healy
St. John's University
New York

CAMBRIDGE
UNIVERSITY PRESS

PUBLISHED BY THE PRESS SYNDICATE OF THE UNIVERSITY OF CAMBRIDGE
The Pitt Building, Trumpington Street, Cambridge, United Kingdom

CAMBRIDGE UNIVERSITY PRESS
The Edinburgh Building, Cambridge CB2 2RU, UK   www.cup.cam.ac.uk
40 West 20th Street, New York, NY 10011–4211, USA   www.cup.org
10 Stamford Road, Oakleigh, Melbourne 3166, Australia
Ruiz de Alarcón 13, 28014 Madrid, Spain

First published 2000

Printed in the United Kingdom at the University Press, Cambridge

Typeface TEFFLexicon 9/13 pt   *System* QuarkXPress® [SE]

A catalogue record for this book is available from the British Library

Library of Congress Cataloguing in Publication data

Healy, Nicholas M.
Church, world, and the Christian life : practical-prophetic ecclesiology / Nicholas M. Healy.
    p.   cm. – (Cambridge studies in Christian doctrine)
Includes bibliographical references and index.
ISBN 0 521 78138 8 – ISBN 0 521 78650 9 (pbk.)
1. Church.   I. Title.   II. Series.
BV600.2.H385   2000
262–dc21   99-089659

ISBN 0 521 78138 8   hardback
ISBN 0 521 78650 9   paperback

For *Owen, Rose,*
Gabriel and Griselda

Contents

Acknowledgments

I thank all of the many people who have encouraged, challenged, stimu-
lated or otherwise helped me during the preparation and writing of this
book. Among those I must mention are Erica Avena; Doreen Healy; Jack
Lessard; Paul Molnar; George Schner; the members of the Kryka 2000
conference at Stockholm, especially Sune Fahlgren, Arne Rasmusson, Ola
Sigurdson, and Roland Spjuth; my colleagues and chair in the old Division of Philosophy and Theology on the Staten Island Campus of St.
John's University; and the residents of Moose-pit Road who, entirely
unchurched, have displayed the virtues of neighborliness, hospitality and
patience over the years far better than I. Particular thanks go to Stanley
Hauerwas, Griselda Healy, George Lindbeck, Rusty Reno and Kathryn
Tanner, all of whom read at least one draft of the whole manuscript; they
were all remarkably kind and supportive, even when they disagreed with
me. Whatever is good in the book comes from or through these people;
whatever bad or mediocre, from me.

I thank St. John's University for granting me a number of research
reductions and a semester's leave. Some parts of the book have appeared
elsewhere in different forms. I gratefully acknowledge the kind permis-
sion of the respective editors to make use of material from *Pro Ecclesia* 4:4
(1995); from *The Toronto Journal of Theology* 12:1 (1996); and from the
Swedish journal, *Tro & Liv* 2 (1999).

In a laughably inadequate acknowledgment of the many ways in
which my wife and family have so wonderfully put up with me over the
years, I dedicate the book to them.

1

Introduction

This book is about ecclesiology, about the kind of critical theological reflection that is centered upon the nature and function of the Christian church. The book is rather more *about* ecclesiology than it is an exercise in the discipline, since much of the time it will be concerned with methodological issues. The aim is not, or not primarily at least, to make a set of ecclesiological proposals. Rather, it is to clear a space within the discipline of theology for some new and more challenging forms of ecclesiology.

However, as Karl Barth never ceased to remind us, theological method should be determined as much as possible by its subject matter if the latter is not to become irremediably distorted.[1] Beliefs about the nature and function of the church on the one hand, and the question of how we should go about doing ecclesiology on the other, bear upon one another so as to determine the kinds of things we can and cannot say about the church. Thus any argument for a methodological proposal about ecclesiology will necessarily involve making some constructive proposals as to what sort of thing the church is and what sorts of things it can and should do. So, too, here. The point is that *what* I say about the church will be said primarily in order to make a case for *how* to do ecclesiology, rather than for its own sake. Some things that would be treated within a comprehensive theology of the church, such as the church's

---

1. See, e.g., Barth's *Church Dogmatics*, trans. G. W. Bromiley, I/1 (Edinburgh: T&T Clark, 1975), pp. 295ff. I make infrequent mention of Barth, but my proposals are meant to be largely compatible with his work outside the area of ecclesiology. Like Barth, as interpreted by John Webster, my "theme," too, is *"God and humanity as agents in relation."* Barth's *Ethics of Reconciliation* (Cambridge: Cambridge University Press, 1995), p. 33 (Webster's emphasis).

ministerial structures, its forms of worship and its relation to Israel, will not be considered.[2]

One cannot start from scratch in these matters. By thinking and acting as Christians we are already in some sense engaged in the practice of theology, whether we actually engage in critical reflection upon our lives as Christians or not.[3] And all "theologians," from the non-reflective to the professional, have their own preunderstandings – sets of beliefs, questions, concerns, aesthetic judgments – about what David Kelsey nicely calls "the Christian thing."[4] Such preunderstandings are manifested when, for example, we kneel rather than stand when praying; when we follow or decide not to follow some penitential exercises during Lent; when we approve or disapprove of last Sunday's sermon or simply ignore it as uninteresting or irrelevant; or when we decide that we need not go to church at all. One Christian's preunderstanding will likely be somewhat different from that of most others. Nobody's preunderstanding should be ignored or simply dismissed. But neither should anyone's conception of Christianity be regarded as unrevisable, as if their expertise or authority or personal experience could render it beyond criticism. Rather, in what follows I will take it as axiomatic that one's theological view is always preliminary, always open to challenge, assessment and partial or radical alteration by means of dialogue or confrontation with other Christians and non-Christians, as well as with Scripture and the Christian tradition more generally. Our theological perspectives are points of departure for growth in the Christian life towards better perspectives and new points of departure. I will offer an argument as to why we should think along such lines in a later chapter.

In this introductory chapter I begin the inquiry into ecclesiological

2. For views of the relation between the church and Israel compatible with the concerns of this book, see George A. Lindbeck, "The Gospel's Uniqueness: Election and Untranslatability," *Modern Theology* 13:4 (1997), 423–450; Robert W. Jenson, *Systematic Theology: Volume I: The Triune God* (New York: Oxford University Press, 1997), esp. chs. three and five; Bruce D. Marshall, "Christ and the cultures: the Jewish people and Christian theology," in Colin E. Gunton (ed.), *The Cambridge Companion to Christian Doctrine* (Cambridge: Cambridge University Press, 1997), pp. 81–100; Kendall R. Soulen, *The God of Israel and Christian Theology* (Minneapolis: Fortress Press, 1996); Kendall R. Soulen, "YHWH the Triune God," *Modern Theology* 15:1 (1999), 25–54.

3. As Kathryn Tanner argues in *Theories of Culture: A New Agenda for Theology* (Minneapolis: Fortress Press, 1997), p. 72. John Howard Yoder makes a similar point with regard to social ethics in *For The Nations: Essays Public and Evangelical* (Grand Rapids: Eerdmans, 1997), p. 91. The notion of starting from scratch in any intellectual or existential endeavor has, I take it, been discredited at least since Heidegger.

4. David H. Kelsey, *To Understand God Truly: What's Theological About A Theological School* (Louisville: Westminster/John Knox Press, 1992), p. 32. Kelsey himself adapts the phrase from G. K. Chesterton.

method by describing some of the relevant concerns and beliefs that are part of my own preunderstanding. This is meant only to give some idea of the point of departure for what follows; I am not trying to establish a secure basis from which to proceed deductively or even especially systematically. Indeed, one of my aims is to show that too much emphasis upon bases and systematization is misguided, especially in ecclesiology. And so the argument to follow will proceed in a cumulative rather than deductive way. What is asserted with little or no support will usually get some backing later on. A charitable reader will therefore suspend final judgment upon both the reasonableness of the point of departure and the cogency of the subsequent argument until the end of the book. Towards the end of this chapter, I give an outline of the argument of the chapters to follow.

I have been drawn to the present inquiry in part by the impression that while the ecclesiology of the last hundred years or so has been sometimes profound, and its impact upon the church also sometimes profound, it has not been as helpful as it could be for the Christian community. As the next chapter will begin to show, in general ecclesiology in our period has become highly systematic and theoretical, focused more upon discerning the right things to think about the church rather than orientated to the living, rather messy, confused and confusing body that the church actually is. It displays a preference for describing the church's theoretical and essential identity rather than its concrete and historical identity.[5] That preference may be one reason why ecclesiological reflection has fallen prey to ever-shifting theological fashions, and why some of it has become quite dull, something it need never be. But whether or not that is so, the concern here is to show how their methodological preference has inhibited theologians from engaging in adequate theological reflection upon the concrete shape of the church.

The organization of the inquiry is informed by this concern. I will analyze the various ways in which modern ecclesiology obstructs adequate reflection upon the concrete church, and discuss some of the resulting problems. I will also make some methodological and constructive suggestions as we go along that will enable us to focus theological attention more readily upon the church's actual rather than theoretical identity. This shift in focus will make it easier to identify ways to respond to some of the challenges presently facing the concrete church. The

---

5. Colin E. Gunton traces this preference to Augustine in *The Promise of Trinitarian Theology*, second edition (Edinburgh: T&T Clark, 1991/1997). See especially pp. 56ff.

methodological proposals that result from the inquiry are not meant to constitute a full-fledged ecclesiological method, nor to replace the present approaches. Rather, the primary goal is to develop broader, more concrete forms of ecclesiological reflection. Such complementary approaches are formulated in order to help improve reflection not only upon the church's concrete identity, but also upon its essential or theoretical identity.

What is the "concrete church"? Two things, to begin with, that it is not. First, the concrete church is not to be thought of reductively as merely the visible or empirical church in contradistinction to its more "spiritual" or "theological" aspects.[6] Rather, the latter "aspects," including most fundamentally the active presence of the Holy Spirit, are constitutive of the concrete religious body. To deny this would be to fall into something like the ecclesiological equivalent of Nestorianism, by splitting the church into a human part and a divine part, or into Ebionism, by thinking of the church as the product of human activity alone. Thus any attempt to reflect upon the concrete church requires much more than, say, a sociological analysis of its empirical identity, although such an analysis may well be useful on occasion, provided that it is properly subsumed within theological discourse.

Second, the concrete church is not, as sometimes even its members reductively assume, to be thought of simply as an institution which is dedicated to handing on to another generation that set of doctrines or moral principles that make up the Christian worldview. The church does not teach a theory that at some subsequent stage is to be put into practice. As Stanley Hauerwas has argued, Christianity becomes distorted if it is treated as a system of beliefs.[7] Rather, it can be summarily described as a distinctive way of life, made possible by the gracious action of the Holy Spirit, which orients its adherents to the Father through Jesus Christ. By schooling its members, the church makes that orientation a present possibility for them.[8] The Christian way of life is distinctive because its Lord

6. See Dale B. Martin, *The Corinthian Body* (New Haven: Yale University Press, 1995), for an account of why, for much of the ancient world, such a binary opposition would have made little sense and cannot be presupposed in Paul's conception of the church.
7. See, e.g., Stanley Hauerwas, *Sanctify Them In the Truth: Holiness Exemplified* (Nashville: Abingdon/T&T Clark, 1998).
8. Nicholas Lash notes how many religions have traditionally understood themselves as schools "whose pedagogy has the twofold purpose . . . of weaning us from our idolatry and purifying our desire." *The Beginning and the End of 'Religion'* (Cambridge: Cambridge University Press, 1996), p. 21. See also L. Gregory Jones, *Transformed Judgement: Toward a Trinitarian Account of the Moral Life* (Notre Dame: University of Notre Dame Press, 1990).

is a particular person and because its God is triune. Its life takes concrete form in the web of social practices accepted and promoted by the community as well as in the activities of its individual members.[9]

It is thus not unreasonable to describe the concrete church, at least initially, more in terms of agency rather than in terms of being. Its identity is constituted by action. That identity is thoroughly theological, for it is constituted by the activity of the Holy Spirit, without which it cannot exist. But it is also constituted by the activity of its members as they live out their lives of discipleship. It is therefore not enough to discuss our ecclesial activity solely in terms of its dependent relation upon the work of the Holy Spirit. The identity of the concrete church is not simply given; it is constructed and ever reconstructed by the grace-enabled activities of its members as they embody the church's practices, beliefs and valuations.[10] We must indeed insist that the only adequate form of reflection upon the concrete church is that of theology. But if ecclesiology is to contribute to the health of the church – and by "health" I do not mean, of course, merely success in terms of numbers or prestige – it must examine our human activity as it concretely is: thoroughly human. To do so, it needs to find ways to make theological use of those forms of discourse that critically examine the complexities and confusions of human activity, such as sociology, cultural analysis and history. For, as Stephen Sykes contends, in the face of what he sees as Barth's occasional tendency towards ecclesiological abstraction, "the language of sociology and the language of theology may be separate, but the reality of divine and human power is not. It is not parallel or merely coordinated; it is inevitably, and dangerously, mixed."[11] My concern here, then, is to rule out both theological and non-theological reductionism in descriptions of our ecclesial identity by developing ways in which ecclesiology can appropriate a wide range of critical tools.[12]

9. I follow David Kelsey's definition of "practice" in his To Understand God Truly, p. 118: "A practice is any form of socially established cooperative human activity that is complex and internally coherent, is subject to standards of excellence that partly define it, and is done to some end but does not necessarily have a product." Kelsey's definition is based upon Alasdair MacIntyre, After Virtue: A Study in Moral Theory, 2nd ed. (Notre Dame: University of Notre Dame Press, 1984), p. 187, but it is perhaps more in accord with Charles Taylor's "vague and general" usage defined in Sources of the Self: The Making of the Modern Identity (Cambridge, MA: Harvard University Press, 1989), p. 204.
10. My language here reflects my indebtedness to William A. Christian, Sr., Doctrines of Religious Communities: A Philosophical Study (New Haven: Yale University Press, 1987).
11. Stephen Sykes, The Identity of Christianity: Theologians and the Essence of Christianity from Schleiermacher to Barth (Philadelphia: Fortress Press, 1984), p. 207.
12. James M. Gustafson argued against such reductionism some time ago in his Treasure in Earthen Vessels: The Church as a Human Community (Chicago: University of Chicago Press, 1961).

We will find that in order to reflect theologically upon the concrete life of the church we will need to take a thoroughly catholic (i.e., ecumenical) perspective. Throughout what follows, then, except in obvious instances, the word "church" refers to all those diverse Christian groups who accept what is sometimes cumbersomely called the Niceno-Constantinopolitan creed.[13] That this book is written by a Roman Catholic will no doubt be evident at times from its selection of theological examples. But a particular perspective has to be taken, otherwise the discussion becomes intolerably general or else interminable in treating all possible confessional responses to a given question. Thus, for example, when I discuss the issue of ecclesial arrogance, my primary reference is, as it must be, to the Roman church, although the problem clearly arises in different forms within other denominations. My hope is that the proposals to follow will be useful for every confession and denomination, and that they can help to clear away a few of the many obstacles in the path towards greater communion within the one Christian church.

Wherever we begin, we need some norms and criteria. If we begin with what the church does, looked at from a theological and ecumenical perspective, one of the things we must say about it is that it has been entrusted with the apostolic task. The church's responsibility is to witness to its Lord, to make known throughout the world the Good News of salvation in and through the person and work of Jesus Christ. Correspondingly, whatever else one must say about the individual members of the church, they too have been given a task: to be disciples of Jesus Christ.[14] The effectiveness of witness and the truthfulness of discipleship both depend entirely upon the Holy Spirit. But they are no less *our* tasks, so we must try to do them as well as we can. Although the two tasks are distinct,

---

13. "Church" is not capitalized either. The reason, admittedly not a very forceful one, will be evident in a moment when I discuss the church's sinfulness. Since it concretely is on a par in so many ways with other religious and non-religious bodies, it seems reasonable to reflect this in however minor a way.

14. Robert W. Jenson also begins with the apostolic mission in his *Systematic Theology*. Werner G. Jeanrond has used similar criteria, too, though to a somewhat different end, in his *Call and Response: The Challenge of Christian Life* (Dublin: Gill and Macmillan, 1995). Considering the church as agent could begin somewhat differently by focusing on the central task of worship (which I take here as an integral and partly formative element of discipleship). Significant arguments for that focus have been made by Geoffrey Wainwright, *Doxology: The Praise of God in Worship, Doctrine and Life* (New York: Oxford University Press, 1980); and more recently by Daniel W. Hardy, for whom worship "is the central means whereby human beings are called to their proper fullness in society and the world." *God's Ways with the World: Thinking and Practising Christian Faith* (Edinburgh: T&T Clark, 1996), p. 8. See also, in a different mode, Catherine Pickstock, *After Writing: On the Liturgical Consummation of Philosophy* (Oxford: Blackwell, 1998).

they are usually mutually conditioning and cannot be treated entirely separately. The church's task of witness includes the pastoral function of helping individual Christians become better disciples. This function is accomplished, for example, by developing suitable practices and institutions that help form the dispositions of its members and guide them in their activities.[15] And correspondingly, the individual's task includes contributing to the church's witness by embodying it in her life of discipleship.

These two normative tasks can function as criteria for assessing the identity of the concrete church in terms of the adequacy of its witness and pastoral care. They make it appropriately difficult to avoid consideration of a number of problems, two of the most significant of which I want to focus on here. There is a saying of Saint Paul's that encompasses them both: "far be it from me to glory except in the cross of our Lord Jesus Christ" (Gal. 6:14). Paul, of course, made the statement in the context of a polemic against relying upon the law and circumcision. But the rule has wider application. One part is proscriptive: that apart from Christ crucified, *we should not glory or boast in anything*. The other part is prescriptive: that *we should boast in Jesus Christ crucified*. Evidently the prescription has to do with witness and discipleship. But before we discuss that, let us see how the proscription could apply to the church, using the two criteria. To do so, we need to consider the church's sinfulness.

It is not unjust to say that the concrete church has frequently failed in its task of witness and pastoral care. The power of sin is manifested not only in the actions of individuals but in the Christian communal body, when the latter fosters practices, valuations and beliefs in its membership that are incompatible with the gospel. One of the more obvious examples of this is the failure of the church's leadership to avoid the corruptions of power. A classic illustration of this failure are the Papal Bulls, *Clericis Laicos* (1296) and *Unam Sanctam* (1302), of Boniface VIII.[16] Boniface's teaching does not necessarily reflect actual sin on his part, for he may well have acted with good intentions and in ignorance. But his Christian character was formed within a church whose concrete identity at the time was

---

15. It is Stanley Hauerwas who, perhaps, has most helped us to retrieve this conception of the church's function. See, e.g., his earlier work, *A Community of Character: Toward a Constructive Christian Social Ethic* (Notre Dame: University of Notre Dame Press, 1981). For a more recent sustained discussion of Christian and non-Christian virtue theories, see Stanley Hauerwas and Charles Pinches, *Christians Among the Virtues: Theological Conversations with Ancient and Modern Ethics* (Notre Dame: University of Notre Dame Press, 1997).
16. *Documents of the Christian Church,* ed. and trans. H. Bettenson (New York: Oxford University Press, 1943), pp. 159–161.

flawed, its witness corrupted by the ideology and practices of worldly power. Another, quite different example of malformation can be found in the church's relation to the Jews in Germany and in some occupied lands during the Second World War. A recent apology for the Holocaust by Pope John Paul II spoke only of the sins of individual Christians. No one doubts that many individuals committed actual sins. But, as many Jewish groups have pointed out, the Pope seemed to ignore the corporate failure of the church to witness to its Lord and to help its membership in their task of discipleship by developing appropriate counter-practices to those of the fascist and racist culture.[17]

It might be argued that we cannot blame the church for its misuse of power and authority, its tolerance of slavery, its treatment of women, Jews and non-Christians, and its other failures to conform to its Lord. Perhaps these failures are for the most part simply manifestations of the church's finitude rather than its sinfulness. An analogy could be drawn between the failures of the ecclesial body and an individual's wrongful actions and flawed character. People, we say, who act wrongly in ignorance of moral truth are not guilty of sin. Nor do we blame them for what we know to be unchristian character traits when they live in cultural and ecclesial environments that consider such traits to be laudable. Accordingly, one might contend that the church can also be ignorant, blinded by its location within a corrupt, and corrupting, cultural environment. By historical-cultural contextualization, the church would be absolved from guilt.

There is something to this, to be sure. But some blame may well be involved since the church was often able, even when it was small and weak, to distance itself, sometimes at great cost, from a number of "worldly" cultural practices that it recognized to be sinful. At other times the church was such a powerful moral force within society that it could reasonably be held responsible for at least some of the flaws of its concrete identity. A more significant issue, though, is that Christians believe sin to be an unavoidable and pervasive aspect of our existence. Sin is a fact that has been revealed to us in the work of Jesus Christ. This belief is a doctrine, not something that can necessarily and straightforwardly be discerned from historical experience.[18] Whether or not it does so in ignorance, when the church fosters sinful practices and beliefs among its membership, its concrete identity displays the confusions and stupidities

17. Vatican Commission for Religious Relations with the Jews, "We Remember: A Reflection on the 'Shoah,'" Origins 27:40 (1998), 669–675.
18. See Hauerwas, Sanctify Them, ch. 3, pp. 61–74.

of our sinful state. The church knows that we cannot escape from this state by our own actions but only through the saving work of the triune God. It is thus reasonable to hold that the acknowledgment of ecclesial sinfulness is an essential part of Christian witness to the Cross and Resurrection of Jesus Christ.

Yet it remains the case that the church – especially the Roman – has been rather unwilling to acknowledge that it is part of the fallen world. Until very recently the Roman hierarchy, for example, would admit that only the members of the church sin, not the church itself. Charles Journet's formula, asserting that "the church is not without sinners, but she herself is sinless," has been accepted as if it were doctrine.[19] While the church does not regard itself as immune from some kinds of mistakes it continues to display, as Gregory Jones has noted, a "surprising . . . tendency to self-deception, to a lack of penitence."[20] This cannot be due to lack of familiarity with the concept of social sin. Many judgments have been made by theologians and the church leaderships against various non-ecclesial bodies and societies. But little has been said theologically about how, where and why the Christian social body has succumbed to temptation. Nor, as I will argue in the next chapter, has the acknowledgment of ecclesial sin had much effect upon the way in which ecclesiology is done.

One reason why the church is unwilling to acknowledge its sinfulness has to do with the Christian doctrine that the church is unlike any other religious or non-religious body. The church is distinctive in two ways, sociological and theological. It is sociologically unique because it alone is manifestly orientated towards a particular person, Jesus Christ. That distinguishes it from Islam, for instance, which is distinctive in its own way, since its life is orientated, one might say, around obedience to Allah, who reveals his will through his prophet, Mohammed. This kind of distinctiveness seems obvious enough.[21] But the church claims, in addition, that it is unique in a theological way. As the Creed implies, the church's activity and being are dependent in some fundamental and special way upon the activity of the Spirit of Christ in its midst. It is the Spirit who makes the church's witness true and effective, and who upbuilds the church in a way

19. Charles Journet, *Théologie de L'Église* (Paris: Desclée de Brouwer, 1958), p. 236. The *Catechism of the Catholic Church* (Liguori, MO: Liguori Publications, 1994) still focuses on individual sinfulness. See the section on the church's holiness, pp. 218f.
20. L. Gregory Jones, *Embodying Forgiveness: A Theological Analysis* (Grand Rapids: Eerdmans, 1995), p. 67.
21. I will be discussing some of those for whom it may not be so obvious in chapter 4.

beyond the possibility of human activity. It is this theological uniqueness that is implied in describing the church by means of such phrases as the Body of Christ, *Creatura Verbi*, Temple of the Spirit, and the like.

From this unexceptional Christian doctrine some have drawn further, more problematic conclusions. It has been argued that when the church is truly itself, or when considered at its most profound level, it is something that is fundamentally free of sin.[22] On this view, which in various guises is one often found in contemporary ecclesiology, to deny the perfection of the theological identity of the church would be to raise the possibility that it is distinctive only in the first, sociological way, but not in the theological way. Perfection and theological identity are thus inextricably linked; what is truly special about the church is its essence, which is perfect. The consequences of this move are either that ecclesial sin is simply ignored as incompatible with ecclesial perfection, or else it is rendered of secondary account, as merely an empirical distortion of the church's true theological identity. Either way, ecclesial sin retains little theological significance.

Is it necessary to make such a move? Not, I think, for a theological view of the *concrete* church. It goes without saying that the Holy Spirit is perfect. And some strands of the tradition, such as the Roman Catholic, believe that the members of the church have been so transformed that they are in some real sense no longer sinners. But both Scripture and tradition indicate that ecclesial activity can at times be sinful, however dependent it is upon the Spirit, or however transformed by grace its members may be. The eschatological "not yet" reminds us that until the end of the church's time it remains imperfect and sinful, always *ecclesia semper reformanda* or *semper purificanda*.[23] Although the church at Corinth was evidently not of the highest quality, its members are still "called to be saints," and are "sanctified in Christ Jesus" (1 Cor. 1:2). And for Augustine, the church is *corpus permixtum*, a body in which sinner and saint are commingled, yet it is truly the (pilgrim) church in spite of its present imperfections.[24] As Christians, then, we have not only to fight against the power of sin in the fallen world, we must fight against it in the midst of our ecclesial body and within ourselves. This fact should be reckoned with in every ecclesiology as an unavoidable aspect of the church in its

22. I discuss these claims more fully in the next chapter.
23. See *Lumen Gentium* 15.48, and *Unitatis Redintegratio* 3.6. in *Vatican Council II: The Conciliar and Post Conciliar Documents*, ed. Austin Flannery, O.P. (Northport, NY: Costello, 1975/1986).
24. Augustine, *City of God*, trans. H. Bettenson (London: Penguin, 1972/1984), Book 1, chapter 35.

pilgrim state. Such a reckoning (in both senses of the word) is evident in the book of Revelation, where judgments are made about, and at times against, the seven churches of Asia (Rev. 2 and 3). Jesus Christ is not only Lord of the church, he is its Judge.

Sin and error, in short, are part of the church's theological and concrete identity prior to the eschaton. As Bonhoeffer remarked, "the community which is from God to God, which bears within it an eschatological meaning . . . has fallen into guilt; it must seek repentance."[25] Of course, those who maintain the claim of essential ecclesial perfection may agree that the church is concretely a sinful body, and in that respect more or less like any other. But they may still insist that theology should focus on the pure, essential church, for it is that which can and should be seen only by the eyes of faith. It will take much of the remainder of the book to show that such a move is not a necessary one and that, if it is used as a systematic structuring principle in ecclesiology, it can undermine the church's performance of its tasks.

At this point, though, I want only to suggest that the move is one example of the various ways in which the church runs the risk of failing or, minimally, of giving the appearance of failing to follow Paul's negative rule, namely to glory in nothing other than Christ crucified. Needless to say, all good ecclesiologies are careful to set up blocks against glorying in the church rather than in Jesus Christ crucified. The problem is that the move requires more blocks than are usually provided. Claiming an essential perfection suggests too easily, to those within the church as well as to those looking on from outside, that the church thinks there is something deep down within itself – something about who we are – that is worth at least a little bit of glorying. We can say all we like about our dependence upon grace; it may still appear as though *we* (through grace, to be sure) are a shade better than the rest of humanity. Even if we claim only that membership in the church enables us to be truly human, we may give the impression, to a society that glories in humanity, that we glory in something other than Jesus Christ.[26]

---

25. Dietrich Bonhoeffer, *The Communion of Saints: A Dogmatic Inquiry into the Sociology of the Church* (New York: Harper and Row, 1960), p. 83.

26. The problem and its possible consequences are admirably summed up by Samuel Taylor Coleridge: "He who begins by loving Christianity, better than truth, will proceed by loving his own sect or church better than Christianity, and end in loving himself better than all." Coleridge, *Aids To Reflection* (London, 1825), p. 101; quoted by Daniel Hardy in his essay, "God and the Form of Society," in Daniel W. Hardy and P. H. Sedgwick (eds.), *The Weight of Glory: A Vision and Practice for Christian Faith: The Future of Liberal Theology: Essays for Peter Baelz* (Edinburgh: T&T Clark, 1991), p. 132.

Another way in which the church risks failing to follow Paul's rule can be found in the rhetoric of its preaching and its addresses to the world. Karl Rahner noted towards the end of his life how the church – he was, of course, thinking of the Roman church – gives the impression of knowing all the answers, of not needing to listen to others.[27] The church's representatives talk sometimes as if all that the world has to do for it to be healed is to submit to the church. But it is not the church that is the Light of the World, except in a very derivative sense. A little thought reminds us of the power of sin within the church, of the way in which it has frequently had to be dragged, almost as if it were against its collective will, into better forms of witness by developments in those areas of society or culture that were not specifically Christian. We recall, too, that the Holy Spirit is itself free, not at all tied to the church. In the simplest terms: God is the solution to the problems of the world, not the church. The church, although orientated to, and governed by, the solution, still remains part of the problem.

The church readily acknowledges failures among its discipleship, and responds pastorally to them by, for example, instituting individual or general confessional practices and by inculcating in its members a sense of sin. However, there are few social practices which embody and make public the church's belief in its corporate sinfulness, whereby it could witness to its dependence solely upon the Cross of Jesus Christ. There is nothing, for example, corresponding to the social practice of Yom Kippur. In acknowledging its sin, Israel proclaims to itself and to the world its reliance upon God's forgiveness and reconciliation. What may be the closest analogy to Yom Kippur, Ash Wednesday, is orientated towards the individual, as, for the most part, are General Confessions.[28]

Thus it is reasonable to say that, while the church has not ignored the implications of Paul's rule for its self-understanding, it has not been particularly industrious in applying it to itself. The church sometimes gives the impression, at least, of something rather like spiritual pride. To glory in anything other than Jesus Christ crucified can result in idolatry or, if one glories in something of which one is a part, in sinful pride. That pride

27. *Karl Rahner In Dialogue*, ed. and trans. Harvey Egan (New York: Crossroad, 1986), p. 331. I owe the reference to Karen Kilby's brief but excellent introduction to Rahner's thought, *Karl Rahner* (London: Fount/HarperCollins, 1997), pp. 63f.
28. There are exceptions. Some denominations, such as the Presbyterians, have a place for communal confession in the Sunday liturgy in which they acknowledge their failings as a congregation. I am grateful to Revs. Carol and Wayne Smith, of Cookstown, Ontario, for this information.

is manifested in ways that can also be more or less idolatrous: biblicism, triumphalism, or integralism, as well as in more subtle ways. Its pride may be much more apparent than real. Even so, it is still detrimental to the church's witness and discipleship. It draws attention away from the one to whom the church is to witness and follow in discipleship. It thereby creates unnecessary obstacles to the activity of the Spirit in making that witness effective.

One aim of the following inquiry is therefore to find ways by which ecclesiology can foster those practices that work against ecclesial pride, real or apparent. Ecclesiology has the difficult task of having to talk rather a lot about us, as well as about God. Talking about the two together can confuse them in our understanding so that God's attributes get too closely associated with ourselves. I hope to show that, by expanding its scope to include reflection upon the concrete, ecclesiology itself can become part of a set of Christian social practices which help to conform the church to Paul's rule. By talking about the church in ways that acknowledge its failings, even drawing attention to them, what we say about God becomes less easily confused with what we say about ourselves.

Before we turn to consider the positive application of Paul's rule, this is perhaps the place to stress that, in dwelling upon the church's sinfulness, my interest is entirely constructive. As far as one can know about such matters, I have no animosity towards the church; quite the contrary. I take it to be the task of every theologian to foster the church's witness to Jesus Christ and improve the pastoral care of its members. Constructive criticism of the church is a necessary part of that task since sin and error should be anticipated there as a matter of course. However, my own sinfulness and blindness place me right in the middle of the mess and confusion, so it may well be that part or all the following is misguided, distorted by the power of sin within me. I try to discern the speck in my church's eye so that it may pluck it forth and then more readily help me discern the beam in my own.

The positive rule implied in Paul's phrase is, we recall, to glory *in the cross of Jesus Christ*. This rule requires of us the response of courageous witness and discipleship. Neither is ever easy and they have, of course, on occasion resulted in violence against the church and its members. It is arguable that, in the course of the twentieth century, glorying in the Cross of Jesus Christ has become difficult in a somewhat different way than before. The problem has to do with increasingly pervasive cultural assumptions about the nature and origin of religion, about how to construe the relations between religions, and about the concept of truth as it applies in religions.

These cultural assumptions (I will get to them in a moment) conflict with certain of the traditional premises for witness and discipleship, as well as with central practices of the church such as baptism. Witness to Jesus Christ as the way, the truth and the life involves the claim that what one witnesses to is true.[29] "Truth" here means, minimally, something independent of the subjectivity of the witness or witnesses. The goal of Christian witness is to mediate the activity of the Spirit, and it is the Spirit who makes the church's witness effective by calling those whom it enables to hear to become disciples of Jesus Christ. One vital aspect of this mediation is to show how, through the work of the Spirit, Jesus is followable. That is, the church is called to witness to the fact that in Christ God is indeed forming a covenant people.[30] Thus if it could be shown to be impossible to follow Jesus Christ within the communal life of the church, the church's witness would be demonstrably false.

That is not at all to say that discipleship must be perfect; nor is it the case that, to the extent that the church or its members are sinful, Christianity is untrue. The truth of the gospel does not depend upon our righteousness; it would not be Good News if it did. On the contrary, as we have already noted, Christians believe that the power of sin is strong and pervasive, and following Christ requires us to acknowledge this fact. Thus Gregory Jones argues that true discipleship involves practices that witness to the costliness of what Christ has done and does for us in the Spirit, practices that confess our failures – individual and corporate – and embody our need for forgiveness.[31]

Knowledge of Christian truth and the practices of Christian discipleship have a reciprocal relation. Not only is truthful discipleship dependent upon the person and work of him to whom we witness, our understanding of him, and thus our witness, is dependent upon how well we follow him. This is the point of George Lindbeck's image of the crusader shouting, "*Christus est Dominus*" while hacking off the infidel's head. The words as such are true, and could be used by better Christians to

---

29. See Bruce D. Marshall, "'We Shall Bear the Image of the Man of Heaven:' On the Concept of Truth," *Modern Theology* 11:1 (1995), 93–118.
30. See Richard B. Hays, *Echoes of Scripture in the Letters of Paul* (New Haven: Yale University Press, 1989); N. T. Wright, *The New Testament and the People of God* (Minneapolis: Fortress Press, 1992).
31. Jones, *Embodying Forgiveness*. Jones has an excellent discussion of Bonhoeffer on costly grace in chapter one, and an interesting analysis of the cultural assumptions that make it difficult to embody such beliefs in chapter two.

describe reality truthfully. But the crusader misuses the phrase because his discipleship is inadequate. He demonstrates his lack of understanding of the words by making them part of an intentional action with which they are inconsistent. The phrase is, so to speak, mispracticed; the claim it could have made truthfully is denied by its location within a practice inconsistent with good discipleship.[32]

It is by the sacrament of baptism that one commits oneself to good discipleship and truthful witness. The Christian turns away from other possible ultimates to give himself over, in the power of the Spirit, to a way of life that is true because it is dedicated to Christ as the ultimate truth, as the *nonpareil* way by which one can be incorporated into the life of the trinitarian God.[33] The baptismal claim, then, includes the belief that the way of Jesus Christ, embodied in and taught by the concrete church, is, all things considered, better than other ways of life. It is better because, while other ways of life may have as their goals penultimate truths, the way of life mediated by the church has ultimate truth and goodness as its goal, namely the Father revealed in the Son through the Spirit. The church is thus the created means by which we can turn towards ultimate truth. On that account (alone), the church enables its membership to live what is potentially a more truthful way of life than any other. Therefore insofar as it is the embodiment of that way of life, the church claims, to put it boldly, that it is superior to all other religious and non-religious bodies.[34]

Many in Western cultures find such claims to be intolerable. It is easy to see why. We have just been considering the perception (at least) of arrogance and spiritual pride in the church. The church's past is filled with instances where it has arrogantly and sometimes violently maintained its superiority. Though claiming knowledge of ultimate truth, it seems to

---

32. George A. Lindbeck, *The Nature of Doctrine: Religion and Theology in a Postliberal Age* (Philadelphia: Westminster, 1984), p. 64. Stanley Hauerwas has explored this issue thoroughly. Besides *Sanctify Them,* see his *Christian Existence Today: Essays on Church, World and Living In Between* (Durham, NC: Labyrinth Press, 1988). A not dissimilar point is made from a sociological perspective by Roberto Mangabeira Unger, *Social Theory: Its Situation and Its Task* (Cambridge: Cambridge University Press, 1987); see esp. pp. 41f.

33. Applying the word *nonpareil* to Jesus Christ is a usage borrowed from William M. Thompson, *The Struggle for Theology's Soul: Contesting Scripture in Christology* (New York: Crossroad, 1996).

34. I realize the word "superior" may be an unnecessary stumbling-block to some. Paul Griffiths' sketch of a theory of religion as an "account" says something similar, but uses the words "comprehensive" and "unsurpassable," and perhaps these could be substituted, though they are more difficult to use with regard to the concrete church. See Paul J. Griffiths, *Religious Reading: The Place of Reading in the Practice of Religion* (New York: Oxford University Press, 1999), pp. 3–21.

have failed to live in ways commensurate with it. To many the church appears to be, at best, merely on a par with other religious bodies; to others, it appears to be substantially below them, reflecting out-dated, even morally wrong notions of human flourishing. How could the church be so arrogant, even self-idolatrous, as to claim superiority?

Not only does the Christian claim seem arrogant, it appears to many modern people (including not a few Christians) to be quite obviously irrational. According to one sociologist, about half of baby boomers believe that "[a]ll the great religions of the world are equally true and good."[35] It is often assumed, both popularly and by certain kinds of theories of religion, that the different religions (like moralities and cultures, too, sometimes) are too diverse really to conflict with one another. Religions are incommensurable and thus equally reasonable perspectives upon an ultimate reality that cannot be described. Truth, indeed, is not a category that applies to religion in the same sense that it does elsewhere (i.e., as more or less realist and falsifiable). It would be illogical, then, for one religion to claim to be better, more truthful, than another. Religion, indeed, is often thought of as a rather private affair, with little or no bearing upon those matters that affect the general public. As Stephen Carter puts it, with only a little exaggeration, one's religion can now be thought of as having the same truth status as one's favorite hobby.[36] You spend your summers playing basketball while I prefer instead to go fishing. Our respective decisions are aesthetic and entirely subjective. It would be utterly irrational for me to claim that my decision for fishing rather than basketball is one that everyone should follow. Religious decisions are roughly similar. To live a life of witness to Jesus Christ as if his Cross *really* had universal significance is irrational and fanatical. Needless to say, such thinking makes it more difficult than it already is to give oneself over with total commitment to discipleship.

I will discuss a theoretical version of these challenges to what I have taken to be the traditional claims for the church at some length in later chapters. I will also make a cumulative case for the traditional view, or something rather like it, as the book proceeds. For the traditional premises for witness and discipleship can be maintained rationally, critically and without arrogance. Indeed, without them, it is difficult to see how we could satisfy the two criteria and conform to Paul's rule. To forestall

35. Statistics cited in Wade Clark Roof, *A Generation of Seekers* (New York: HarperCollins, 1993), p. 72.
36. Stephen L. Carter, *The Culture of Disbelief* (New York: Basic Books, 1993), p. 22.

unnecessary misunderstanding, it is useful to make a few more preliminary remarks here about what I mean by the church's superiority.

The traditional claim is, minimally and formally, that there is something about the church that is of paramount importance, and that it can be found only there. The church is unique, and what makes it unique also makes it superior. What that thing is, however, is not necessarily so obvious. At times in its history the church has explicitly claimed or has assumed without reflection that this thing is salvation. On this view, supported by one interpretation of Cyprian's dictum, *extra ecclesia nulla salus*, it is the availability of salvation for its members that constitutes the church's uniqueness and superiority. But contemporary theological inquiry does not support the view that the *concrete* church is uniquely the location of salvation. To begin with, as Francis Sullivan has shown, the tradition is not at all clear on the matter.[37] Vatican II seems to say that salvation is possible outside the church, at least for individuals. Furthermore, it may be that religious bodies other than the church are salvifically significant to some degree.[38] Perhaps, then, the thing that is unique about the church is the presence of the Spirit in its cult and its preaching? But most Christians now acknowledge explicitly that the Spirit is at work outside the concrete church. To be sure, that the Spirit is present within the church in a unique way could be used to support a claim for the church's superiority over other religious bodies. But this only pushes the question further back, for we then have to consider what is distinctive about the Spirit's ecclesial presence.

I suggest that what renders the church unique and superior to all other religious and non-religious bodies is what I have already noted in passing, namely its Spirit-empowered *orientation* to Jesus Christ and through him, to the triune God. The church claims that it is orientated towards the ultimate goal of all humanity, indeed, of all creation. All other religious and non-religious bodies are not orientated to that truth, or not concretely and explicitly anyway. All other bodies do not appreciate the ultimate significance of Jesus Christ; they do not attempt to shape their identities around him. They are not on that account simply wrong, for they may be orientated to other, penultimate truths and they may have much to teach the church. But since they do not attempt to follow Jesus Christ in the Spirit, and since Jesus is the *nonpareil* and

37. Francis A. Sullivan, S.J., *Salvation Outside the Church?* (New York: Paulist Press, 1992).
38. See, e.g., *Lumen Gentium* 8.16. Regarding the salvific significance of non-Christian religions see Sullivan, *Salvation Outside the Church?*, pp. 196f.

unsurpassable revelation of God, those ways are not finally as good and true as that way fostered by the community – when it truly and directly follows him, that is. Indeed, the church must confess (and more often and more loudly) that it and its members often fail to orient themselves truly towards Jesus Christ. They often turn away from the ultimate truth to treat other, penultimate truths as ultimate, or they turn directly to untruth. The church can therefore be as immoral and as untruthful as any other body, at times maybe more so.

The claim, then, can be put this way: To the extent – and only to the extent – that the church, in the Spirit, orientates itself to the Father through Jesus the Christ, it is superior to all other religious and non-religious bodies. Its orientation, whether successful or not, to what it believes to be the ultimate truth makes the church unique. Its declared goal is unique, for it alone of all religious bodies is made up of those whose desire is to participate in the life of the triune God though incorporation into Christ's Body. To help them understand and achieve this goal, as well as to respond to Christ who made it possible, the church has developed practices and institutions that foster the appropriate dispositions and decisions. Hence the means to the goal make possible a way of life that is, in significantly concrete respects, distinctive. The church is guided by the Scriptural witness and by the Spirit to be the uniquely explicit witness to Jesus of Nazareth.

These are not unusual claims in that most other religions and world-views seem to claim that they are orientated towards ultimate truth, too. Nor are they necessarily arrogant claims. The church has nothing of its own to glory in. It is not a particularly (morally) good body, though it has been at times. Nor has it got a monopoly on truth. It must often rely upon others to help it understand and embody the truth it seeks, though its orientation gives it possibilities for knowledge and action that are unavailable to others. There is nothing special about the concrete church that it should expect automatic respect and love from the world. So the claim to superiority is hardly about the church at all. It is about that to which the church witnesses, often indifferently and sometimes quite badly, namely Jesus Christ crucified.

It is, I take it, an essential part of the church's witness to proclaim the particular person Jesus of Nazareth to be the presence of God in a unique and unsurpassable way, and his suffering, death and Resurrection to bring about the salvation of the whole world. That witness, however, often comes into conflict with the claims of other bodies, religious or non-religious. As far as is fitting, our witness should respond to their counter-claims. This is, of course, the function of apologetics, which is therefore an integral part of any theological reflection upon the concrete church. Paul J. Griffiths formulates the apologetic requirement of Christian witness in the form of what he calls the NOIA principle (Necessity Of Interreligious Apologetics):[39]

> If representative intellectuals belonging to some specific religious
> community come to judge at a particular time that some or all of their
> own doctrine-expressing sentences are incompatible with some alien
> religious claim(s), then they should feel obliged to engage in both posi-
> tive and negative apologetics vis-à-vis these alien religious claim(s) and
> their promulgators.

Challenges to the church's witness from any counter-claims cannot simply be passed over in silence. Griffiths takes the example of the doctrine of the self in Buddhism and Christianity, noting that "[m]uch of traditional Christian metaphysics and soteriology cannot stand if the Buddhist account of what constitutes a human person should turn out to be correct."[40] Accordingly he mounts an argument against Buddhist anthropology. For to say that Christian doctrines about the self are true also requires one to maintain that Buddhist and other challenges to that doctrine do not falsify it.[41]

For it to be useful within ecclesiology, the scope of Griffiths' principle needs to be expanded in two ways. First, it will apply not only to doctrinal challenges as such, but also to the practices that embody the doctrines. As Lindbeck's crusader example suggests, the credibility of Christian witness can be undermined by its lack of coherence with Christian practices. Moreover, the very meaning of doctrinal statements can be affected, for good or ill, by the way they are incorporated into particular forms of discipleship. Second, Christian ecclesiological apologetics should include, though it should not privilege, engagement with the claims about religion held by societies and cultures that do not consider themselves explicitly religious.[42] The apologetic challenge for ecclesiology is

39. Paul J. Griffiths, *An Apology for Apologetics: A Study in the Logic of Interreligious Dialogue* (Maryknoll, NY: Orbis, 1991), pp. 99f.   40. Ibid., p. 94.
41. An excellent example of such an engagement from a Reformed perspective can be found in Hendrik Vroom, *No Other Gods: Christian Belief in Dialogue with Buddhism, Hinduism, and Islam*, trans. Lucy Jansen (Grand Rapids: Eerdmans, 1996).
42. The distinction may be moot anyway, since it may be that most secular philosophies are, at root, theologies. Robert Jenson points out how "Greek philosophy was simply the theology of the historically particular Olympian-Parmenidean religion, later shared with the wider Mediterranean cultic world." *Systematic Theology I*, p. 10.

sometimes more general, arising from the pervasive assumptions of modern Western societies regarding the very possibility of making religious truth claims, like those of Buddhists and Christians. If the reasonableness of making such claims (whether or not they are true) is denied, the witness of the church is undermined from the very start. To help the church perform its tasks effectively and fulfill the positive side of Paul's rule, ecclesiology needs to find ways to show that it is reasonable to witness to the ultimate truth and to claim that the church, in spite of its evident sinfulness, can be orientated to it. These claims are clearly vital, too, for supporting a committed discipleship. Furthermore, the truth of Christ is not simply a "religious" matter. As ultimate truth it has implications for society and the world. Christianity cannot permit the exclusion of its own (and other religions') claims by a wrongful denial of their universal application.

Apologetics has acquired a bad reputation in various quarters. For some (Roman Catholics especially) it is associated with a naive form of rationalism, as if one could construct knock-down proofs for basic Christian beliefs. Apologetics has manifested an intellectual arrogance that would seem, perhaps, to betray ecclesial pride.[43] In other quarters (those influenced by Barth, for example) apologetics has been castigated for its tendency to distort Christianity by making it conform to what Christianity's cultured despisers take to be universal and foundational truths. It has been far too timid or defensive in its response to counter-claims.[44] It is possible, however, to develop an ecclesiological approach, the goal of which is to serve the witness of the church, which is neither arrogant nor timid in supporting the church's claim that its beliefs and practices are of universal significance, and which rescues its discipleship from a fideistic commitment to a way of life that is merely "true for me."

The indispensable feature of such an ecclesiological approach, I will argue, is that it maintain the tension between claims for the church's orientation to the ultimate truth on the one hand and, on the other, acknowledgment of ecclesial sin and of the church's dependence upon the challenges and insights of those religious and non-religious bodies that

---

43. Francis S. Fiorenza discusses Roman Catholic apologetics and its history in his *Foundational Theology: Jesus and the Church* (New York: Crossroad, 1985). For a good example of apologetics in manual theology see Ioannes Perrone, S.J., *Praelectiones Theologicae* (Augustae Taurinorum, 1877), Pars I: Adversos Incredulos and Pars II: Adversos Heterodoxos.

44. William C. Placher discusses the issue of apologetics with such concerns in mind in his *Unapologetic Theology: A Christian Voice in a Pluralistic Conversation* (Louisville: Westminster/John Knox, 1989). Barth's mature conception of apologetics can be found in his *Church Dogmatics*, II/1, p. 92ff., and in relation to ethics, in II/2, 520ff.

are orientated primarily to other truths. By means of this tension, we can avoid falling into rationalism, foundationalism, and sundry other philosophical errors, as well as avoiding ecclesial pride and timidity.[45] To maintain this tension will require a theory of truth and religion that effectively counters popular and theoretical challenges to the reasonableness of the church's witness and discipleship. One cannot, of course, provide a timeless or universally applicable theory; nor is it ecclesiology's business to attempt to do so. Theories of truth and religion come and go, but the truth of the gospel does not. The church need only develop a way of thinking that is amenable to its own program, yet can be appealing to at least some of those whom it addresses. One aim of the following chapters is to outline and defend such a low-level theory.

One central aim of this inquiry into ecclesiological method is thus to seek to maintain the necessary yet tensive relation between what, *prima facie,* might seem to be opposing concerns. One concern is to enable ecclesiology to be able to reflect upon the concrete church in ways that explicitly acknowledge, and practically and theologically respond to, its evident weaknesses and sinfulness. Another concern is to find ways by which ecclesiology can help the church respond to a society that finds it irrational and arrogant to claim that the church's witness is true and that the orientation it makes possible for its discipleship is superior to all others. These two concerns are mutually dependent, yet they should not be harmonized or unified. Acknowledging sinfulness without also maintaining the truthfulness of its witness and the superiority of its way of life, or vice versa, would harm the performance of its tasks and risk breaking Paul's rule.

The next chapter begins the argument proper with a critical analysis of modern ecclesiology. The constructive aim is to expand the scope of ecclesiology so as, in effect, to reconfigure the discipline. The thesis is that ecclesiology is better thought of as more of a practical and prophetic discipline than a speculative and systematic one.[46] The church's response to its

---

45. These remarks reflect the criteria for ad hoc apologetics laid out by William Werpehowski in "Ad Hoc Apologetics," *Journal of Religion* 66 (1986), 282–301.

46. "Speculative" can be used in two ways. First, in contradistinction to practical inquiry, speculative inquiry is ordered primarily to truth for its own sake, rather than action. See Thomas Aquinas, *Summa Theologiae* (Turin: Marietti, 1962), Ia, 14.16. This is the meaning here, though it is relativized by my earlier remarks on the relation between discipleship and truthful witness. Second, it can refer to that deductive kind of theology that draws conclusions from the articles of faith understood as premises. This is in contrast to positive theology, which attempts to clarify Scripture and traditional texts. This usage is somewhat less applicable here. The latter distinction is found among Roman Catholic scholastic theologians, such as Reginald Garrigou-Lagrange, O.P., *Christ the Savior: A Commentary on the Third Part of St. Thomas's Theological Summa* (St. Louis: Herder, 1950), pp. 6–11.

ever-shifting contexts should not first-and-foremost be to formulate theoretical constructions, be they doctrinal or moral systems, but should be to reconstruct its concrete identity so as to embody its witness in truthful discipleship. Not incidentally, "context" here does not mean anything like "culture" or "situation" in a Niebuhrian or correlationist sense of something that one can place theoretically over against Christianity. The ecclesiological context is everything that affects the life and work of the church, including its history and its present concrete form. Within the context, then, there is much that is Christian as well as non- or anti-Christian. Ecclesiology's main function is to help the church respond as best it can to its context by reflecting theologically and critically upon its concrete identity. This indicates the need to include a contextual criterion in theological reflection upon the church. Like the other criteria, this one has an ecclesiological correlate: we can assess any ecclesiological proposal by how well it helps the church respond to its context. The critical aim of this chapter is to argue that certain key traits of modern ecclesiology make it hard to satisfy this criterion, and thereby to satisfy the other two as well. As they are commonly used, the method of models and the prevalent abstract and idealistic approaches undermine the practical and prophetic effectiveness of modern ecclesiology.

In the third chapter I draw upon one element of the theology of Hans Urs von Balthasar – his theodramatic theory – to develop an alternative and corrective ecclesiological horizon that makes possible a theological description of the context. A theodramatic horizon or metanarrative is particularly appropriate for reconfiguring ecclesiology as a practical-prophetic discipline. This is because it can hold together in tension a number of elements that otherwise may be confused or separated or treated one-sidedly. These tensive elements include the following: the church's identity is *fully* constituted by *both* divine and human agency, permitting *theological* reflection upon the *concrete* church; the church's role includes the *formation* of the individual disciple's *distinctive* identity; the church's orientation renders it *superior* to others, yet it is *dependent* upon others and is always more or less *sinful*; the church claims to be orientated to *ultimate* truth, yet it must acknowledge that our view of that truth is *limited* by our location within the ongoing drama.

The theodramatic horizon permits ecclesiology to expand its scope considerably and, at the same time, to mount an effective apologetic defense against challenges to the church's life and work. The remaining chapters set out to show this by developing the horizon's ecclesiological

potential in relation to possible alternatives. In the fourth chapter I critically examine the pluralist horizon insofar as it has been developed into a
form of modern ecclesiology that offers a quite different response to the
challenges of the contemporary context. I argue that it fails to satisfy the
three criteria, in part because it cannot respond effectively and coherently
to contextual developments, especially those associated with postmodernism's critique of modernity. Pluralism's failure to engage with non-
Christian traditions as genuinely other, together with the consequences
of this failure, suggest that we should include fostering genuine plurality
as one of the tasks of the church in the present context. This is for the
church's own sake, in that it needs others with whom to engage as it witnesses to, and searches for, the truth. But it is also for the sake of those
religious and non-religious bodies that are occluded by the oppressively
totalizing discourse of theoretical pluralism.

The fifth chapter outlines a theodramatic approach to truth and religious bodies that is meant to counter some of the more pressing challenges
of pluralism and postmodernism. The apologetic strategy here makes use
of some of the work of Alasdair MacIntyre, suitably modified for absorp-
tion into a Christian theodramatic horizon. I appropriate especially his
arguments against perspectivalism and relativism, sketching a theory of
religions as traditions of inquiry that make genuine truth claims. The
fundamental claims of one tradition may well conflict with those of
others, for their differences can be genuine and radical. Yet they are not so
incommensurable that they cannot engage with one another and attempt
to demonstrate their superiority. Indeed, engagement is a necessary part
of making a truth claim. Such engagement, however, must be undertaken
in a Christian fashion. It may occur in abstract ways, in terms of beliefs
and doctrines. But more significant for practical-prophetic ecclesiology is
the possibility of engagement at the concrete level, in the form of competing ways of life that reflect each religious (or non-religious) body's
attempt to orient itself towards the truth that it claims is ultimate.

The sixth chapter then completes my critical examination of modern
ecclesiology by turning to its inclusivist version. As with pluralism, I
discuss inclusivism as a horizon within which to do ecclesiology rather
than as a soteriological theory. Karl Rahner is the main focus here. While
Rahner can be read as moving towards a practical-prophetic form of ecclesiology, his approach forces him away from the concrete. The main
problem here, as in most modern ecclesiology, is the move that postulates
an essential perfection at the heart of the church. This not only relegates

the concrete to secondary status, it spiritualizes and universalizes the church to the extent that it becomes too easily identified with the humanist project in general. While Rahner's context may have led him to make such moves, our context is one that more clearly requires ecclesiology to insist upon genuine plurality. The chapter concludes with some theodramatic suggestions about how to interpret certain ecclesiological and soteriological doctrines so that the issues Rahner had in mind can be addressed without recourse to his inclusivist solution. A theodramatic ecclesiology permits the church to absorb the world into its own horizon. It can do so without having to postulate an already-realized eschatological harmony among what are genuinely diverse traditions of inquiry.

The final chapter then discusses some of the ways in which practical-prophetic ecclesiology could be done. After some consideration of theological forms of history and sociology, I draw upon developments in postmodern ethnography to sketch the elements of what should perhaps, to avoid misunderstanding, be considered a new discipline. Thoroughly theological yet oriented toward the concrete church, I call this mode of critical and constructive reflection, "ecclesiological ethnography." In one of its many possible forms, it can become a confessional social practice, one that would parallel the practice of individual confession in Roman Catholicism or render more expansive and explicit the Presbyterian congregational confession. In another form, it can become ecclesiological history, i.e., a theological (and therefore critical) narrative of the concrete identity of the church over time. In all its forms, this practical-prophetic ecclesiology enables the church to engage self-critically with other religious and non-religious traditions of inquiry at the level of their respective concrete identities.

2

Blueprint ecclesiologies

The previous chapter discussed some of the issues that arise when we focus ecclesiological attention upon the church as a concrete, apostolic agent. The church presently faces significant difficulties in performing its central tasks of witnessing to its Lord and helping its members in their task of discipleship. The church's witness and its pastoral care are compromised when it fails adequately to acknowledge and respond to its sinfulness. The church also needs to respond to the pervasive relativism of contemporary society by constructing and embodying arguments that show the reasonableness of devoting oneself wholeheartedly to the way of life that it makes possible. Ecclesiology can aid the church's efforts by reflecting theologically upon its concrete identity and by supporting what may appear to be somewhat contrary claims: that the church is prone to breaking Paul's rule yet, even as a concrete body, the church can be in some significant way superior to all other religious bodies.

These issues have not, of course, gone unnoticed by theologians, and they have made a variety of proposals as to how to deal with them, some of which we will look at below. The present chapter begins to make the case that the ways in which theologians usually go about developing their ecclesiological proposals make it considerably harder for them than it need be to make an effective response to such challenges. Contemporary ecclesiology comes in many forms, of course, but there are enough common elements and trends amid the diversity to justify the general label, "modern ecclesiology." The label is apt not only because it applies to the ecclesiology of the present day, but also because it applies to certain traits that some have suggested are characteristic of modern forms of inquiry more generally. William Placher, for example, has argued that many theologians of the modern period have followed their colleagues in other disciplines in moving away from the premodern preference for metaphor and analogy toward univocal language. Modern theologians have tightened up their argumentation, making it more linear and rigorously systematic. And their seemingly greater confidence in human cognitive powers has led them into areas that premoderns, who were more willing to acknowledge the mystery at the heart of all theological inquiry, preferred to leave unexplored.[1]

The bearing of modernity upon ecclesiological method should not be exaggerated, however. Nor is modernity necessarily a bad thing, since it may be that some aspects of modernity are not unreasonable responses to the failures and sinfulness of the church. The distinctions between premodern, modern and postmodern forms of inquiry can easily be overdrawn. I will introduce a different, less historically based distinction in the next chapter that is, I think, more fruitful theologically. Yet it remains the case, as I hope to show, that some characteristically "modern" moves can be correlated with some of the methodological difficulties of contemporary ecclesiology. This is not to say that the ecclesiologies discussed below are products of a modern mindset *tout court*; quite the contrary. Many who are cited have rejected, at least implicitly, many elements of modernity. But where these elements *are* at work in these ecclesiologies, they inhibit an effective contribution to the upbuilding of the church.

If we generalize from the wide range of ecclesiological styles of the last century or so, it is possible to detect five key methodological elements. One is the attempt to encapsulate in a single word or phrase the most essential characteristic of the church; another is to construe the church as having a bipartite structure. These two elements are often combined, third, into a systematic and theoretical form of normative ecclesiology. A fourth element is a tendency to reflect upon the church in abstraction from its concrete identity. And one consequence of this is, fifth, a tendency to present idealized accounts of the church. We will begin by discussing the first three elements.

1. William C. Placher, *The Domestication of Transcendence: How Modern Thinking about God Went Wrong* (Louisville, KY: Westminster/John Knox Press, 1996). Placher cites some key non-theological works on modernity on p. 1. The move towards literalism has been discussed in terms of a theory of religious language by Janet Martin Soskice, *Metaphor and Religious Language* (New York: Oxford University Press, 1985). Louis Mackey has approached the topic more historically in his *Peregrinations of the Word: Essays in Medieval Philosophy* (Ann Arbor: University of Michigan Press, 1997). Mackey argues that the "products of thinking are fragile" so that when "thinking becomes literal-minded, then the metaphoric vision collapses," p. 227. Modernity is discussed from a "radical-orthodox" position by Catherine Pickstock in her *After Writing: On the Liturgical Consummation of Philosophy* (Oxford: Basil Blackwell, 1998).

Reflection upon the church in recent years has usually followed something like the approach that Avery Dulles has described, and has developed further and more systematically, in his *Models of the Church*.[2] There he discusses and assesses five concepts or images commonly used in ecclesiology. One model frequently used is "sacrament," favored by Karl Rahner and by Dulles himself when he wrote the first edition of *Models*.[3] Another is "herald," which Dulles believes was used by Karl Barth and Hans Küng.[4] "Institution" was a common model in nineteenth- and early twentieth-century Roman Catholic ecclesiology.[5] A fourth model, "mystical communion," used by Emil Brunner and Emile Mersch,[6] has recently evolved into a somewhat different concept, that of "communion."[7] The model of "servant" was also sometimes favored, for example by Dietrich Bonhoeffer.[8] And in a later expansion of his book Dulles develops a sixth model, his own "community of disciples."[9]

Working with a single primary model permits theologians to develop highly systematic accounts of the implications of a biblical or traditional image or concept for our understanding of the church. They tend to use the model in two ways: in an explanatory way, to synthesize what is already known about the church; and in an exploratory or heuristic way, to lead to new insights about its nature and activity.[10] Occasionally, too, they may also adopt something along the lines of Dulles's own comparative approach, whereby the theologian uses a model to summarize a particular kind of ecclesiology in order to assess its relative merits and drawbacks by comparison to other models. In such a case, the idea is to propose a suitable modification of the model or else to propose a new model that does justice to all the ecclesiological needs reflected in other

2. Avery Dulles, S.J., *Models of the Church*, expanded ed. (New York: Image/Doubleday, 1974/1987).   3. See ibid. pp. 197ff.

4. Dulles relies largely on Barth's *Church Dogmatics* I/1 (Edinburgh: T&T Clark, 1975), ch. one. The later volumes of the *Dogmatics* make it clear, however, that Barth's model is "Body of Christ." I discuss Barth below. Dulles refers to Hans Küng's *The Church* (New York: Image Books, 1976), esp. p. 120.   5. Dulles, *Models*, pp. 34–46.

6. For a Protestant example of the "mystical communion" model, see Emil Brunner, *The Misunderstanding of the Church* (London: Lutterworth, 1952); for a Roman Catholic example, see E. Mersch, *The Whole Christ* (Milwaukee: Bruce, 1938).

7. The literature on communion ecclesiology is rapidly growing. I discuss some examples later in the present chapter. Besides the citations there, the centrality of this model in much ecumenical ecclesiology is noteworthy. See, e.g., the article, "Church," in Nicholas Lossky, *et al.* (eds.), *Dictionary of the Ecumenical Movement* (Geneva: WCC Publications/Eerdmans, 1991), pp. 159–167.

8. Dulles cites Bonhoeffer's *Letters and Papers from Prison*, rev. ed. (New York: Macmillan, 1967), pp. 203–204.

9. *Models*, pp. 204ff. This model is also discussed in Dulles's *A Church To Believe In: Discipleship and the Dynamics of Freedom* (New York: Crossroad, 1982/1987), pp. 1–18.

10. Dulles, *Models*, pp. 24f.

models. The latter approach is taken by Dulles himself in the first edition of his book.[11]

In spite of the diversity of their models,[12] theologians often agree about the second key element, namely a particular construal, at a purely formal level, of the kind of thing the church is. According to this construal the church is something that has a twofold ontological structure. One of its aspects, the primary one, is spiritual and invisible, often described as the church's "true nature" or its "essence." The other aspect is the everyday, empirical reality of the church, its institutions and activities. The relation between the two aspects is often described by saying that the primary one "realizes" or "manifests" itself in the subsequent one, or that the visible church is the "expression" of its invisible aspect. Thus a genuine understanding of the expression is contingent upon a grasp of the basic, primary core.

The twofold structure of the church is formal and flexible enough to be described in markedly different ways, and to serve quite diverse agendas.[13] Three examples illustrate this flexibility. One theologian whose description has been very influential within Roman Catholicism is Karl Rahner. His model, that of "sacrament," addresses the twofold structure of the church directly. According to Rahner, the church is the "fundamental sign or sacrament" of God's gracious presence in the world. The language of Roman Catholic sacramental theology, with its distinction between the reality, the *res*, and that through which it is signified and made present, the *sacramentum,* permits Rahner to distinguish the church's "divine interiority" (i.e., its primary aspect) as something that is "essentially different" from the church's "bodily nature," the visible, "earthly reality" of the church (i.e., its secondary aspect).[14] Drawing a parallel with the most basic sacrament, the Incarnation, Rahner contends

11. An example of the former approach is Yves Congar's critical account of the relative merits of the models, "Mystical Body" and "People of God," in *Concilium*, vol. I (New Jersey: Paulist Press, 1964), pp. 11–37. For further discussion of Dulles's own comparative approach, see Dulles, "From Symbol To System: A Proposal for Theological Method" and George A. Lindbeck, "Dulles on Method," both in *Pro Ecclesia* 1:1 (1992), 42–52 and 53–60 respectively.

12. Other phrases could be cited, of course. For example, Paul Tillich uses "Spiritual Community" in his *Systematic Theology*, vol. III (Chicago: University of Chicago Press, 1963), pp. 149ff.

13. Besides the examples discussed here, see also, e.g., Hans Küng, *The Church*, p. 24; Paul Tillich, *Systematic Theology*, vol. III, pp. 162–165; Dietrich Bonhoeffer, *The Communion of Saints: A Dogmatic Inquiry into the Sociology of the Church* (New York: Harper and Row, 1960), p. 115.

14. Karl Rahner, S.J., *Theological Investigations*, vol. II, trans. Karl-Heinz Kruger (New York: Crossroad, 1975), pp. 73ff. See also Rahner's *The Church and the Sacraments*, trans. W. J. O'Hara (London: Herder, 1963).

that while the two aspects are not to be confused, neither should they be divided. In spite of sin and human finitude the visible church is indeed a true sacrament or *Realsymbol,* for it makes present in history the *res* that is hidden within it. Thus Rahner can say that the church is both the sign of the "real, permanent and ever valid presence of God in the world" as well as that which effects this presence.[15]

Karl Barth also construes the church as a twofold entity, and uses a model, "Body of Christ," that explicitly reflects the church's ontological structure. His concerns in doing so, however, are somewhat different from Rahner's. Barth wants to avoid the kind of sacramental understanding of the church whereby the human activity constituting the visible aspect contributes to the making present of that which is invisible. He insists, on the contrary, that it is the activity of Christ and the Holy Spirit *alone* that creates the church, and that this activity, since it is gracious, is entirely free. Thus he contends that Jesus Christ is the "identical and universal and continuing essence of the church," while the visible group we call the church, on the other hand, is only a church-in-appearance, a *Scheinkirche.*[16] Only when "it is gathered and lets itself be gathered and gathers itself by the living Jesus Christ through the Holy Spirit"[17] does the latter take on a likeness to its inner reality so as to become the "earthly historical existence-form [i.e., the body] of Jesus Christ."[18] Thus the being of the true church (and Barth leaves it open as to how continuous such "events" of gathering by the Holy Spirit may be) is twofold, its visible aspect a witness to that which is its "invisible being."[19]

Although these two theologians have obviously different concerns that guide their descriptions of the relation between the two aspects, and use different models to do so, the formal similarities in construing the ecclesial object are evident. Both theologians use their model to describe the relation between the primary aspect (respectively the self-communication of God and the presence of Jesus Christ) and the secondary aspect, which is the manifestation of the primary aspect in visible ecclesial form. Other models that have been used in much the same way include "People of God" and "Temple of the Spirit." In all such cases, the two terms of the phrase reflect the relation within the twofold structure of the church.

15. Rahner, *Theological Investigations*, vol. II, p.76.
16. Karl Barth, *Church Dogmatics: The Doctrine of Reconciliation* IV/1–IV/3.2, trans. G. W. Bromiley (Edinburgh: T&T Clark, 1956–1962), p. 712. Hereafter cited as CD and volume number. The discussion of the *Scheinkirche* is in *Kirchliche Dogmatik: Die Lehre von der Versöhnung* IV/2 (Zurich: Evangelischer Verlag, 1955), p. 698 (CD IV/2, p. 618).
17. CD IV/1, p. 650.   18. Ibid., p. 661.   19. CD IV/3.2, p. 729.

There are other ways to model the twofold structure. One of the more significant is exemplified in Jean-Marie Tillard's *Church of Churches*, a book devoted to "a revival of the entire vision of the church around *communion*."[20] Tillard believes that the church is most itself when it celebrates the Eucharist as a community gathered about its bishop. At such a time the community's fellowship realizes in visible form the essential reality of the church, which is its participation in the trinitarian communion (koinonia).[21] Here, then, Tillard uses his model to describe the relation between the two aspects of the church by a single analogous term rather than a two-term phrase. However they are used, the combination of the twofold construal and its encapsulation in a single systematic principle has proven quite useful for ecclesiological reflection. The notion that the church has a hidden primary reality manifested in diverse ways can conceivably contribute to ecumenical efforts, since it suggests that underneath concrete denominational differences there lies a shared substratum of what is most essentially ecclesial.[22] Another role for the twofold construal is to provide a way to reconcile the church's ideal primary aspect with its frequently sinful realization, its secondary aspect. The latter can be understood as a distortion of the former. Moreover, as I noted in the previous chapter, the same move has been used to affirm the uniqueness of the church at the essential level. In spite of appearances to the contrary, the concrete church is a realization of something hidden within it that is more basic and perfect, something constituted by God's gracious and saving presence. Thus we might claim that the church is, in spite of its evident sinfulness, *really* unlike other institutions, since they do not have this reality at their core. The church is then both unique and superior, for it is the one religious body that cannot be adequately described in purely sociological terms. Only a theological perspective can access its primary reality.

Another significant move in modern ecclesiology is the third noted above, namely to combine the systematic principle and the twofold construal to develop normative descriptions of the church. The logic of this move is something like the following: If the fundamental reality of the

20. Jean-Marie Tillard, O.P., *Church of Churches: The Ecclesiology of Communion*, trans. R. C. De Peaux, O.Praem. (Collegeville: Glazier/Liturgical Press, 1992), p. xi. For an Orthodox version of communion ecclesiology, see John D. Zizioulas, *Being as Communion: Studies in Personhood and the Church* (Crestwood, NY: St. Vladimir's Seminary Press, 1985).

21. See, e.g., *Church of Churches*, p. 195.

22. "Conceivably" since, as Ephraim Radner has argued, the twofold construal can be used to avoid facing the critical theological issues of division. See Radner, *The End of the Church: A Pneumatology of Christian Division in the West* (Grand Rapids: Eerdmans, 1998), p. 6.

church is some particular thing, namely model x, then x must be realized in the visible forms of the church, which can then be described systematically and normatively in its light. Where x is not evident, or where elements that are counter to x are found, the church should be suitably altered to fit in the area of y. Thus, for example, if the essential reality of the church is "communion," where the visible church is disunited or contentious, we must say that it is realizing itself in a distorted way and should be reformed. This move can be seen in Rahner, for example, who believes that "a knowledge of the church's abiding nature" can exercise "a critical function" in determining its form and actions within a particular historical and cultural situation.[23] Barth, too, focuses upon the Body of Christ as part of his effort to recover the Christological center in the life of the church.[24] And Tillard moves from his definition of the primary aspect of the church to normative proposals about how "communion" should be realized in all aspects of its life.[25]

These three moves of modern ecclesiology do, however, have certain demonstrable limitations and drawbacks. One of the more obvious is that to date no agreement has been reached as to which model of the primary reality is the definitive one. Instead, throughout the twentieth century there has arisen a succession of models, for some of which very strong claims have been made, yet none has been found to be adequate in every significant area. Thus the "Body of Christ" model, popular in Roman circles especially in the 1950s, was relegated to secondary status by some theologians of the next decade or so, who preferred the model "People of God." This in turn has been replaced, again especially in Roman circles, by "sacrament," and more recently and generally, by the model of "communion." Such changes in the tides of ecclesiological fashion would seem to break down the normativity of modern ecclesiology's proposals. The

---

23. Karl Rahner, *The Theology of Pastoral Action* (New York: Herder, 1968), p. 56. Hans Küng makes much the same formal move, though one that is materially quite different, in *The Church*, pp. 43–46.

24. For a more detailed and critical analysis of Barth's version see Nicholas M. Healy, "The Logic of Karl Barth's Ecclesiology: Analysis, Assessment and Proposed Modifications," *Modern Theology* 10:3 (1994), 253–270.

25. With regard to the ministry, see Tillard, *Church of Churches*, pp. 169ff. For normative moves in the same area but within a somewhat different understanding of communion, see Zizioulas, *Being as Communion*, pp. 209ff. Zizioulas's trinitarian grounding of the relation between bishop and people has been effectively criticized by Miroslav Volf, *After Our Likeness: The Church as the Image of the Trinity* (Grand Rapids: Eerdmans, 1998), pp. 109–116. Tillard's less systematic approach renders him less liable to Volf's criticisms. In the same work, Volf also presents a critical analysis of the communion ecclesiology of Joseph Cardinal Ratzinger, and he develops his own Free Church version. Zizioulas's conception of the Trinity is also critically analyzed by Alan J. Torrance, *Person in Communion: An Essay on Trinitarian Description and Human Participation* (Edinburgh: T&T Clark, 1996), pp. 283–306.

argument that "the church is x, therefore the church should look like abc and reform y must be initiated" loses its force if others say "x is not the model that most definitively determines the essential characteristic of the church, but rather z is, and z does not normatively require shape abc nor reform y."

In spite of the lack of consensus, the rhetoric of theologians often seems to suggest that the particular model of the church they have selected is something like the "right" one. Thus Karl Barth claims that, while other images or concepts can be applied to the church only "symbolically or metaphorically," "Body of Christ" is denotative and should structure all theological talk about the church.[26] Similarly, we find in the earlier work of Rahner a number of strong claims for his model of the church as *Ursakrament*.[27] And for Tillard, "communion" constitutes the church's "very essence," the concept that sums up the understanding of the church in the early tradition, and it is this concept "alone" that is the key to further ecumenical progress.[28]

Such strong claims seem to imply that the particular model advocated is to be understood as the fundamental principle of any and all ecclesiology. It may be, though, that theologians use such rhetoric only as an effort – albeit a fruitless one unless all agree on what constitutes the church's primary aspect – to bolster their proposals for the shape of the concrete church. Theologians such as Barth and Rahner might well have agreed, if pushed, with Avery Dulles's assertion that ecclesiology can never discover what he calls a "supermodel," i.e., an image or concept of the church that is entirely adequate and that relativizes all other models.[29] Dulles's rule is based on two considerations. First, his analysis of the various models shows that each of them has been found to be deficient in some way. Second, such inadequacy is due, he believes, to the theologoumenon that since the primary aspect of the church is penetrated by the activity of God it must be understood as a theological mystery and, as such, is essentially indefinable.[30]

Dulles's rule needs a bit more support, however, since those who want to insist that their model is the supermodel could counter it by arguing that the inadequacies of other models are not present in the one they have selected and developed. Furthermore, they could point out that theology

26. CD IV/1, p. 666; see generally §§ 62, 67 and 72.
27. E.g., *Church and Sacraments*, pp. 22f., 34; *Pastoral Action*, p. 34. For the development of Rahner's ecclesiology, see Richard Lennan, *The Ecclesiology of Karl Rahner* (Oxford: Clarendon Press, 1995).   28. *Church of Churches*, pp. 8, 29, xii.   29. *Models*, p. 206.
30. Ibid., pp. 9f.

always has to do with divine mystery, yet the essential elements of many doctrinal *loci* have been defined. Thus, to take an obvious example, they could contend that, although the doctrine of the Trinity cannot comprehend the essence of God, it still says something true about God, and it says it in a way that should structure all our thinking and doing in relation to God. Similarly, their model should structure all further theological reflection upon the church.

Something like this is the argument of Herwi Rikhof who, in his *The Concept of Church*, explicitly rejects Dulles's appeal to mystery.[31] He is also unhappy with the ambiguity he finds in the Vatican II documents on the church; they make use of too many images.[32] Rikhof argues that we need a "central and basic" definition of the church in order to "legislate a more strict use" of the concept "church."[33] He believes that *congregatio fidelium* is the "real definition" that establishes the essence of the church in words that are denotative rather than merely metaphorical or figurative.[34] From this most basic concept, then, Rikhof expects us to be able to make some progress in ecclesiology by means of systematic deductions from a firmly established premise.

Yet is such a rationalistic form of ecclesiology really feasible? If it were, the "right" ecclesiological model would function in some respects like the doctrine of the Trinity, and more deductively than the latter doctrine has traditionally been used. The doctrine of the Trinity is, I take it, implicit in the Scriptural understanding of God[35] and is both the hermeneutic key for reading Scripture as well as the primary rule governing Christian discourse about God. For an image or concept to be a supermodel, something similar would have to be the case, though of course in an appropriately more restricted way. Yet the tradition to date has not found it necessary or even fitting to develop an ecclesiological doctrine parallel to that of the Trinity. Certainly there are a number of doctrines about the church that have been developed over the centuries, such as the four marks of the church, that it is one, holy, catholic and apostolic; the rule against Donatism (*corpus permixtum*); that in some significant, yet doctrinally underdetermined way, salvation can be had only within the church (*extra ecclesia nulla salus*); that the church is not simply an invisible

31. Herwi Rikhof, *The Concept of Church: A Methodological Inquiry into the Use of Metaphors in Ecclesiology* (London: Sheed and Ward, 1981), p. 231.   32. Ibid., pp. 49, 65.
33. Ibid., pp. 3, 231.   34. Ibid., pp. 213, 225, 235.
35. See David Yeago, "The New Testament and Nicene Dogma" in Stephen E. Fowl (ed.), *The Theological Interpretation of Scripture: Classic and Contemporary Readings* (Oxford: Blackwell, 1997), pp. 87–101.

entity; that it is indefectible, and the like. But none of these doctrines requires or relies upon a particular model. Various models have been proposed at one time or another but, to repeat, none has been defined or received as the most basic and fully adequate model.

There are at least two reasons why no single model of the church's fundamental reality has become doctrinally definitive. One is that there seems to be an irreducible plurality of ways of talking about the church within the New Testament.[36] Each ecclesiology there reflects the context and concerns of a particular community: that of Matthew, for example, is clearly different in important respects from that of Luke or Paul. Admittedly, one can also find a not dissimilar plurality of Christologies, but the tradition seems to have decided that the Scriptural parameters for fitting descriptions of Jesus Christ are considerably narrower that those for the church.[37] Throughout the tradition, a variety of ecclesiological models can be found, many of which were considered quite legitimate and useful for some particular context and need. Thus there are simply too few parameters in Scripture or tradition to support strong claims for a single supermodel; quite the contrary. Although we may find that certain models are essential to any good theology of the church ("Body of Christ," "communion," and "People of God" would be obvious candidates), it would be difficult to argue from Scripture or tradition that one of these should be considered the primary one in a way that relegates all others to secondary status.

A second reason for the lack of a basic doctrine about the church has to do with the doctrine of the Trinity itself, the preeminent rule for Christian discourse. A number of theologians have noted how this doctrine requires us to keep shifting our perspective so that we view a theological *locus* like the doctrine of the church in relation to one and then another person of the Trinity, as well as to the Trinity as such. Nicholas Lash has pointed out that no one perspective can be adequate; each will need the "corrective pressure" of another.[38] Thus theological reflection upon the church in its relation to Jesus Christ is inadequate without further reflection from the perspectives of the Father and the Holy Spirit. We cannot

36. See Raymond Brown, *The Churches the Apostles Left Behind* (New York: Paulist Press, 1984).
37. See James D. G. Dunn, *Unity and Diversity in the New Testament*, 2nd ed. (London: SCM Press, 1990).
38. See Nicholas Lash, *Believing Three Ways in One God* (Notre Dame: University of Notre Dame Press, 1993), p. 93. Karl Barth of the CD would agree: see George Hunsinger, *How To Read Karl Barth: The Shape of His Theology* (New York: Oxford University Press, 1991), pp. 53, 107f. The chapter below discusses Hans Urs von Balthasar's similar contention.

combine three such ecclesiological perspectives into a single system, since each perspective reflects upon the whole from a single viewpoint. To adopt another viewpoint must be systematically to begin again. Nor can we make the internal relations of the Trinity into a systematic principle, as some contemporary communion ecclesiologies do, using a social analogy of the Trinity.[39] Describing the Christian community in terms of a formal doctrine abstracts the concrete church from the complex and concrete actions of the three persons made known to us in Scripture. Moreover, such a move founders on the disruption of history by the Cross.[40]

The doctrine of the Trinity supports Stephen Sykes's contention that Christianity itself is too rich and multifaceted a way of life to be fully comprehended within a single system. As an "essentially contested concept," it needs to be described from a variety of perspectives, none of which can be adequate alone.[41] To treat Christianity as if it has a definable essence, a single principle in terms of which one could systematically map the whole, is inevitably to distort it. This is not to say that the attempt to do systematic theology is wrong, only that the limits of the genre should be acknowledged and be incorporated somehow into the system.[42] The point applies *a fortiori* to the Christian life and its embodiment in the concrete church. As Dulles rightly insists, "[m]uch harm is done by imperialistically seeking to impose some one model as the definitive one."[43]

Let us summarize more assertively the main points made thus far in this chapter. To the extent that theologians imply, by their rhetoric or by the structure of their argumentation, that the model they select is the supermodel, their claims are untenable and unfitting. And so, to the extent that they deduce a complete and normative systematic description of the church from the definitive model of the church's essence, their argument fails. To suggest that we abandon such efforts, though, is not to say that we should abandon any and all use of models. We are likely to

39. Examples include Zizioulas, *Being as Communion*, and Volf, *After Our Likeness*. Colin E. Gunton comments on Zizioulas in *The Promise of Trinitarian Theology*, 2nd ed. (Edinburgh: T&T Clark, 1991/1997), p. 198.

40. See Gunton, *The Promise of Trinitarian Theology*, pp. xixf. The move is also a particularly clear example of blueprint ecclesiology, discussed shortly.

41. Stephen Sykes, *The Identity of Christianity: Theologians and the Essence of Christianity from Schleiermacher to Barth* (Philadelphia: Fortress Press, 1984), pp. 251ff. Sykes discusses the question of the essence of Christianity from Schleiermacher through Troeltsch and Harnack to Barth in Part Two, pp. 81–208.

42. For a convincing account of why we should continue to engage in systematic theology, see Colin Gunton, "A Rose by Any Other Name? From 'Christian Doctrine' to 'Systematic Theology,'" *International Journal of Systematic Theology* 1:1 (1999), 4–23.   43. *Models*, p. 32.

find that there are certain things that must be said about the church that
are best said by means of a certain image or concept, so that some models
may be necessary ones. But if different perspectives on the church are necessary as well as permissible, then not only are claims for a supermodel
unwarrantable, the very search for them unwarrantably contracts our
ecclesiological horizons. Models should instead be used to discover and
explore imaginatively the many facets of the Christian church.

We recall that the two remaining tendencies of modern ecclesiological
method are to reflect upon the church abstractly and in terms of perfection. All the systematic ecclesiologies cited thus far in this chapter display
to some degree a tendency to concentrate their efforts upon setting forth
more or less complete descriptions of what the perfect church should look
like. They present blueprints of what the church should ideally become.
This is due in part to the method of models and the twofold construal, for
the images and concepts used to model the church are almost always
terms of perfection.[44] But it also reflects the widespread lack of explicit
and careful analysis of the church's present practices and institutions and
how they might bear upon that description. The impression is given – no
doubt in many cases a false one – that theologians believe that it is necessary to get our *thinking* about the church right first, after which we can go
on to put our theory into practice. It is as if good ecclesial practices can be
described only after a prior and quite abstract consideration of true ecclesial doctrine. The method of modern ecclesiology thus exemplifies the
disjunction between doctrinal and moral reflection, between theoretical
and practical reasoning, which Stanley Hauerwas has argued is a characteristic of modern theology.[45]

One problem with this approach can now readily be seen. Blueprint
ecclesiologies are dependent for their normative force upon agreement
regarding the fundamental starting point, upon the model. If, however,
that agreement is absent, their force is diminished. So it may be better to
interpret a blueprint ecclesiology as more of a rhetorical strategy, something intended to convey an ideal "vision" that will spur efforts towards
some concrete goal. Again, though, if that vision is unappealing, it and its
proposals may be rather easily dismissed by privileging some other
element of Scripture or tradition.

44. A significant exception is Hans Urs von Balthasar's retrieval of the image of the "chaste
harlot." See "Casta Meretrix" in *Explorations in Theology II: Spouse of the Word* (San Francisco:
Ignatius Press, 1991), pp. 193–288.
45. Stanley Hauerwas, *Sanctify Them In the Truth: Holiness Exemplified* (Nashville:
Abingdon/T&T Clark, 1998), pp. 19–36.

Another significant difficulty with the blueprint approach is that its systematic and ideal use of models of perfection does not make a sufficient distinction between the church militant and the church triumphant. The characteristics of the heavenly church are described as so thoroughly present within the earthly church that there is little that needs to be said about the latter except to describe how those characteristics are realized. The church's sinfulness can be considered as no more than a rather infrequent and finally insignificant distortion of the church's abiding fundamental reality, rather than an ever-present aspect of the church's concrete identity. And this can lead to a naive, complacent or worse attitude in those quarters of the church that subscribe to the view that "underneath" our visible flaws there lies the ideal heart of gold if only those carping critics had sufficient "faith" to see it. While there is indeed an ontological relation between the two forms of the church, the tendency of the blueprint approach to focus upon the eschatological form overstresses that relation. The church *in via* has characteristics of its own that are quite different from the church triumphant and which prevent it from being described predominantly in terms of perfection. The pilgrim church is concrete in quite a different way from the heavenly church. It exists in a particular time and place, and is prone to error and sin as it struggles, often confusedly, on its way. If these characteristics are ignored, or relegated to a secondary concern, the temptation arises to set up false goals that cannot be realized, which may lead to depression for those who try to realize them, and cynicism in those who compare the ideal vision with the reality.

Blueprint ecclesiologies thus foster a disjunction not only between normative theory and normative accounts of ecclesial practice, but between ideal ecclesiology and the realities of the concrete church, too. They undervalue thereby the theological significance of the genuine struggles of the church's membership to live as disciples within the less-than-perfect church and within societies that are often unwilling to overlook the church's flaws. As a consequence, blueprint ecclesiologies frequently display a curious inability to acknowledge the complexities of ecclesial life in its pilgrim state. To take just one instance, we noted how Tillard believes that the Eucharist is the most perfect expression of "communion." While that may well be true, Eucharists are concretely and frequently divided by race, class, gender and political ideology, to say nothing of denominational divisions. Does not the presence of such flaws so obscure the expression of perfection that it becomes the contrary, namely an expression of the *loss* of communion?[46] Should we not understand the very brokenness of the Body of Christ as an expression of the church's true reality prior to the eschaton? Tillard, furthermore, believes that we should "reflect calmly" (with "serenity" in the French edition)[47] upon the status of women in the church. Yet the history of the church indicates that serene reflection is the perquisite of those in power. Reforms, like doctrinal agreements, are usually the result, not of serenity, but of struggle and eventual compromise.

In sum, these five methodological traits of modern ecclesiology conspire to distort theologians' reflections upon the church *in via*. To the extent that the blueprint method is used – and, to repeat, we are dealing here with discernible tendencies found in varying degrees in most modern ecclesiology – it can lead to reductively abstract and theoretical views of the church. It provides few tools with which theologians can critically reflect upon the concrete identity of the church. On the contrary, it seems to direct their attention away from it.

Such difficulties with the blueprint approach indicate the need for an alternative that better reflects the proper function of ecclesiology. Ecclesiology is not about the business of finding the single right way to think about the church, of developing a blueprint suitable for all times and places. Rather, I propose that its function is to aid the concrete church in performing its tasks of witness and pastoral care within what I will call its "ecclesiological context."

To introduce the word "context" may be to prompt a misunderstanding that should be cleared up directly. As I conceive it, the ecclesiological context is not something that is separate from the church, such that it and the church could be usefully described independently and then considered in relation to one another. Nor does the term refer to something, like "liberal culture" or "European society," that does not properly belong within the scope of theological inquiry. Hence the term "context" here does not indicate an alignment with those forms of theology which attempt to correlate the church or Christianity on the one hand with its secular and cultural context on the other. That method makes the assumption that the two entities can be described independently of one another, often by means of different disciplines, prior to their being

---

46. Tillard himself seems to be able to consider this as a real possibility, at least outside the Eucharist. See his "Was the Holy Spirit at Canberra?" *One In Christ* 29:1 (1993), 34–64, cited in Radner, *End of the Church*, p. 26.

47. Tillard, *Église d'Églises* (Paris: Cerf, 1987), p. 130; *Church of Churches*, p. 97.

"correlated." The following chapters amount to a cumulative argument against that assumption and the coherence of such a method in theology.[48] Instead, the term is used here simply to point to the fact that the concrete church lives within and is formed by its context. Its context consists of all that bears upon or contributes to the shape of Christian witness and discipleship and its ecclesial embodiment. It therefore includes many churchly elements, such as (a far from exhaustive list): the church's history, both local and worldwide; the background beliefs and the economic and social status of its members; recent developments among its leaderships; styles of argumentation in theology (sapiential, scholastic, modern, postmodern); styles of worship, and the like. The context also includes the whole range of things, including the past and present shape of the church and its theology, that can be described and analyzed by such disciplines as philosophy, history, the social sciences, even the hard sciences. The ecclesiological context, then, is highly complex, so much so that consensus as to its best description is unlikely, not only among theological and non-theological forms of inquiry, but also within a single discipline.

The concrete church, living in and for the world, performs its tasks of witness and discipleship within particular, ever-shifting contexts, and its performance is shaped by them. Critical theological analysis of those contexts, and the present shape and activity of the church within them, should therefore be one of the central tasks of ecclesiology. This is not to suggest that we should simply abandon more traditional forms of ecclesiological inquiry. Rather, it is to propose that we broaden their scope and change their orientation so that they include *explicit* analysis of the ecclesiological context as an integral part of properly *theological* reflection upon the church.[49]

The ecclesiological context is a significant factor influencing the construction of ecclesiology, including the selection of a model. How that

48. The distinction between two correlatable poles is of course the basis of H. Richard Niebuhr's classic, *Christ and Culture* (New York: Harper and Row, 1951). Perhaps the most sophisticated correlation theology to date remains that of David Tracy, *The Analogical Imagination: Christian Theology and the Culture of Pluralism* (New York: Crossroad, 1981), see esp. ch. one. Tracy himself seems not to rule out non-correlationist approaches; see his Foreword to Jean-Luc Marion, *God Without Being* (Chicago: University of Chicago Press, 1991), pp. ix–xv.
49. I find Robert Jenson to be uncharacteristically glib in remarking, in his *Systematic Theology: Volume 1: The Triune God* (New York: Oxford University Press, 1997), p. ix, that "[r]ecent clamor for 'contextual' theology is of course empty, there never having been any other kind." The point of the clamor, "of course," is that it should become far more explicit and careful. Jenson no doubt has in mind correlational forms of contextual theology.

context bears upon ecclesiological proposals is itself a complex process, working through a number of media. It will be helpful for later constructive purposes to give a simple account of some of the factors that prompt theologians to select one model rather than another, setting aside for the moment their explicit theological reasons for doing so.

One key factor that bears upon one's ecclesiology is the theological imagination. Everyone who constructs a theological proposal makes, in David Kelsey's well-known phrase, a "single, synoptic imaginative judgment" as to what the Christian thing is fundamentally all about.[50] Since no theologian who is interesting has quite the same imagination as another, they each make a somewhat different judgment, reflecting their ecclesiological context, their character, life history, status within the church and society, and the like. Notwithstanding such variables, distinctively Christian beliefs, valuations and practices are, of course, the central ingredients of the theological imagination, in keeping with an orientation to Jesus Christ as ultimate truth. These ingredients are mediated to prospective theologians by socialization within their often quite diverse Christian communities.

As theologians mature they may find that the concrete church as they experience it is not entirely consistent, either with Christianity as they have come to understand it, or with some aspects of the ecclesiological context in which they find themselves, or both. Thereby an agenda arises: they seek to affect present Christian discourse and practice so that it more fully accords with their judgment about Christian identity and/or more adequately responds to the present context as they construe it. A specifically ecclesiological agenda will be especially concerned to alter the self-understanding of the church in order to bring about an appropriate change in the community's concrete identity. The kind of change desired can run the gamut from more or less radical reform to the restoration of past beliefs and practices, or simply the preservation of some threatened element of the church's status quo.

An important factor influencing the judgment and the agenda is the theologian's interpretation of the church's historical identity. Theologians construct narratives which situate the contemporary church in the context of history-in-general as well as ecclesiastical history. They develop these interpretive narratives as their answer to questions that include: When and where was the church at its best or at its worst, and

---

50. David H. Kelsey, *The Uses of Scripture in Recent Theology* (Philadelphia: Fortress, 1975), p. 159.

why? What events or patterns of practice and belief are especially constitutive of, or counter to, its authentic identity? What resources and obstacles for ecclesial reform have arisen in the ecclesiological context in recent years, both within and outside the church? What trajectories can be discerned that may bear upon present difficulties and opportunities? For many theologians the narrative remains largely implicit or worked out in comparatively little detail. For others, such as Augustine in the *City of God* and Eusebius in the *Ecclesiastical History*, the narratives are quite explicit and in their particular case somewhat opposed.[51]

The theologian develops her interpretive narrative within the overarching conception of reality by which she makes sense of her world. This conception has been given various names, such as a framework, a horizon or a metanarrative.[52] Although a Christian theologian's horizon will naturally be informed by Christian beliefs, there is no single horizon shared by all Christians.[53] This was the case even during those parts of the premodern period when such horizons were more likely than now to be unthematized, taken for granted, and largely shared among people of a particular time and place. Compare, for example, Thomas Aquinas and Martin Luther who, according to Otto Pesch, develop their theologies within sapiential and existential horizons respectively.[54] Christian horizons may vary, in part because the Christian thing is so multifaceted that it may legitimately be construed in different ways, and in part because every horizon includes non-Christian-specific elements. At present all such horizons, Christian or not, are problematic and so, as they are forced to respond to challenges, they have sometimes become more explicit.[55]

51. Eusebius, *The Ecclesiastical History*, trans. Kirsopp Lake (Cambridge, MA: Harvard University Press, 1926). Augustine, *City of God*, trans. H. Bettenson (London: Penguin, 1972/1984). On the tradition of ecclesiastical history, see R. A. Markus, *Saeculum: History and Society in the Theology of St. Augustine*, rev. ed. (Cambridge: Cambridge University Press, 1970).
52. See Charles Taylor, *Sources of the Self: The Making of the Modern Identity* (Cambridge, MA: Harvard University Press, 1989), Part One, for a discussion of the inescapability of frameworks and their necessity for human life. The term "metanarrative" comes from postmodern commentators, see especially Jean-François Lyotard, *The Postmodern Condition: A Report on Knowledge*, trans. G. Bennington and B. Massumi (Minneapolis: University of Minnesota Press, 1984). The three terms can have different connotations, but they are sufficiently similar that they can be used synonymously here.
53. See Bernard J. F. Lonergan, *Method in Theology* (New York: Seabury, 1972), pp. 131f.; see also pp. 235–237.
54. See Otto Hermann Pesch, O.P., *Theologie der Rechtfertigung bei Martin Luther und Thomas von Aquin: Versuch eines Systematisch-theologischen Dialogs*, 2 Aufl. (Mainz: Matthias Grünewald, 1967/1985), esp. ch. XVI, pp. 918–956.
55. I shall be sketching a Christian horizon in the next chapter that is one of the more fitting.

The interpretive narrative and the horizon are closely related to a key element of the imaginative judgment, namely a decision as to how to construe "the mode of God's presence to the faithful."[56] Barth, for example, understands God to be with us primarily in and through the biblical stories about the particular person Jesus of Nazareth.[57] His judgment can be correlated with his interpretation of the recent history of the church as one of progressive loss of the salvific significance and material decisiveness of the particular person Jesus Christ. This was traceable, he believed, to the rise of liberal Protestantism and subsequently manifested in the inability of the German church to withstand militarism and fascist ideology.[58] Tillard, we noted, considers God to be present to the faithful primarily in Eucharistic communion, in and through which they participate in the trinitarian koinonia. His judgment can be correlated with his interpretation of church history. Accordingly, the emphasis upon communion in the patristic period provides an effective counter to contemporary Western individualism.[59] And, to note another example, liberation theologians judge God to be present particularly in the struggle of the poor and oppressed for liberation. Their interpretation of church history lends weight to their contention that the voices of the marginalized in the third world must be heard if theology is to avoid distortion by an overemphasis upon first-world preoccupations, which are often capitalist and middle-class.[60]

Judgments about the primary mode of God's presence and about the church's history and its present shape will help to determine the way in which we interpret Scripture[61] and tradition and, if we use the models method, how we select our model of the church. If, like Barth, our agenda is to recover the centrality of Jesus Christ, we will require a model that permits us to develop our description of the church accordingly, and will select an image such as Body and/or Bride of Christ. Or if, like Tillard, our

---

56. Kelsey, *Uses of Scripture*, p. 160.   57. So Kelsey, *Uses of Scripture*, p. 162.

58. For an account of Barth's development during the crucial early years, see Bruce L. McCormack, *Karl Barth's Critically Realistic Dialectical Theology* (Oxford: Clarendon Press, 1995). The material decisiveness of Jesus Christ is not thoroughly worked out, though, until later volumes of the *Church Dogmatics*; for which, see Bruce D. Marshall, *Christology in Conflict* (New York: Blackwell, 1987).

59. Tillard, *Church of Churches*, p. 17. I will discuss Rahner's agenda in chapter 6.

60. See, e.g., Gustavo Gutiérrez, *The Power of the Poor in History*, trans. R. R. Barr (Maryknoll, NY: Orbis, 1983), chapter four; Leonardo Boff, *Church: Charism and Power: Liberation Theology and the Institutional Church*, trans. J. W. Diercksmeier (New York: Crossroad, 1992), chapter one.

61. I follow Stephen E. Fowl in holding that interpretations of Scripture can be legitimately diverse, and that there is no "single determinate theory of interpretation." See Fowl, *Engaging Scripture: A Model for Theological Interpretation* (Oxford: Blackwell, 1998), p. 59.

agenda is to recover a way of being church that was most evident in the patristic period, we will be likely to select a model prevalent in that era and interpret it in a more or less patristic way. Or if, like Leonardo Boff, our agenda is the liberation of the poor, then we may follow him in selecting a model of the church developed with an emphasis upon the liberative work of grass roots churches.[62]

This account of some of the background factors involved in ecclesiological proposals is admittedly quite rough-and-ready, but as such it is in keeping with the rough-and-ready way these things actually happen. If it is not too far from the mark, it suggests that, contrary to the implied logic of models and blueprints, there is a thoroughly multidirectional movement in ecclesiological argumentation. While a blueprint ecclesiology may be presented as if it were a normative and systematic deduction from a single model, in fact any ecclesiological proposal, systematic or otherwise, depends for its cogency upon appeals, explicit or tacit, to complex relationships among a wide range of factors. Besides Scripture and tradition, construed within a particular horizon, these include an interpretation of the history of the church, a construal of Christianity and the mode of God's presence to the faithful, and a construal of the present ecclesiological context. Each of these construals may be related to the others in different ways and in different sequences for each theologian. Every theologian who reflects on the church deals with these factors at some stage, either by thinking them through explicitly or else by accepting the view of one or more of them that prevails within her particular ecclesiological context.

To illustrate the multidirectional logic of ecclesiology we return once again to examples of the method of models. At the same time we can note another limitation of the method. Not only is the selection of a model the result of contingent factors, but such factors also affect decisions about how to use the model or, in other words, about what concrete ecclesiological meaning to give it. Certainly images such as "Body of Christ" or theological concepts such as "sacrament" have some specifiable meaning apart from their location within a particular ecclesiology. Thus the Pauline texts inform the use of "Body of Christ," indicating that the church is dependent upon the grace of Christ and is a visible and corporate entity. "Sacrament," too, has an accepted meaning within Roman Catholic circles, and "communion" is informed by trinitarian doctrine. However,

62. See Leonardo Boff, *Ecclesiogenesis: The Base Communities Reinvent the Church* (Maryknoll, NY: Orbis, 1986).

when any one of these is used as a model of the church, its meaning is surprisingly underdetermined.

To show this, let us take the example of the model of "communion," perhaps the most popular model in contemporary ecclesiology. Besides its use by resourcement theologians such as Tillard, and the Orthodox theologian, Zizioulas, the model can be found in liberation theologians such as Leonardo Boff; the feminist, Elisabeth Schüssler Fiorenza; the liberal Protestant, Peter Hodgson; and the Free Church theologian, Miroslav Volf. All six theologians relate the concept to the doctrine of God in such a way that, apart from its ecclesiological implications, the word is used in approximately the same way. One might assume, then, that these six theologians have achieved a consensus that "communion" is the primary model of the church, at least for the contemporary context. However, that consensus, if indeed it exists, would be largely vacuous, since when they explicate the meaning of "communion" considerable differences in the usage of the word become apparent. For Tillard and Zizioulas, communion is expressed in the visible unity of the church when, gathered about the bishop, it celebrates the Eucharist.[63] For Boff, communion is realized at the parish or even smaller level, in the solidarity of the poor as they struggle against oppression.[64] For Volf, communion is described in terms of the metaphor of "sibling friends" within a voluntary association.[65] Used by Fiorenza, the model is used to support far-reaching proposals for a non-discriminatory church order.[66] And for Hodgson, as we will see in more detail in a later chapter, communion (koinonia) indicates the need for a new way of being church that is "nonprovincial, nonexclusionary, nonhierarchical [and] noncultic."[67] In all cases, the concrete meanings of "communion" are analogous at best and, say in the case of Tillard and Hodgson, quite possibly in conflict.

It would be difficult to demonstrate to everyone's satisfaction, and by

63. See Tillard, *Church of Churches*, p. 105. He draws upon patristic ecclesiologies to argue that communion is realized primarily in the local church, whose center is its bishop; see chapter three. Zizioulas says something not dissimilar; see *Being as Communion*, e.g., pp. 250f.
64. Boff argues that communion is "the main definition" of the church in his *Trinity and Society* (Maryknoll, NY: Orbis, 1988), pp. 153f. In his *Ecclesiogenesis* he describes these local forms.
65. Volf, *After Our Likeness*, pp. 180f. Volf's critical discussion of the communion ecclesiologies of Ratzinger and Zizioulas supports my point here.
66. Elisabeth Schüssler Fiorenza, *Discipleship of Equals* (New York: Crossroad, 1993), pp. 269–274.
67. Peter C. Hodgson, *Revisioning the Church: Ecclesial Freedom in the New Paradigm* (Philadelphia: Fortress, 1988), pp. 24f.

means of an analysis of the model itself, that any one of these uses is simply wrong or that one of them is sufficiently basic to relativize the others. This is because what governs the usage of "communion" is not so much the model as such but the respective imaginative judgments and agendas of the theologians. Thus Fiorenza invests her use of "communion" with meaning accorded it by her feminist reading of the church's history and her agenda for reform.[68] Tillard invests his model with meaning accorded it by patristic theology and his concern for ecumenism and community. Volf's model is used to develop a trinitarian ecclesiology for the Free Churches.[69] Boff's model supports an understanding of the church as an agent of liberation in solidarity with the poor. Hodgson's notion of koinonia is filled out with many of the values and concerns of Western modernity. Each theologian, given her or his agenda and construal, arguably uses the model in the "right" way, and so perceives the flaws in other formulations. Thus, if we agree with their agenda, we will likely agree with their use of the model; if not, not.

This does not condemn us to talk past one another endlessly. It means that, if we want to challenge one or other of these ecclesiologies, our argument would best be directed, not against the model itself, but against the construals that govern its use. For what is in dispute among these theologians is *not* the word "communion" but *everything that guides its use*. And without that guidance, it would seem that there are few concrete ecclesiological implications of the "communion" concept beyond ruling out ecclesial structures and practices that foster blatant individualism. A similar indeterminacy is evident in the other images and concepts we have mentioned. The model of "institution" clearly requires some kind of ecclesial structure; but it does not specify its form nor that it be any more than minimal. An institutional model could conceivably be used to advocate a view of the church as a democratic institution as much as a hierarchical one. "Body of Christ" only requires that the church, however conceived concretely, be understood as visible and in a dependent relation to Christ. "Community of Disciples" says nothing of itself about what constitutes discipleship, except that it will involve coming together as a community in some undetermined fashion.

It is therefore not the image or concept itself but how it is used within

---

68. Schüssler Fiorenza presents her understanding of early church history in *Discipleship of Equals*, pp. 151–179; see also her "Missionaries, Apostles, Co-workers: Romans 16 and the Reconstruction of Women's Early Christian History," *Word and World* 6:4 (1986), 420–433.
69. See Volf's two introductions in his *After Our Likeness*, pp. 1–25.

a complex of interpretation – of the church's history and its present concrete shape, of the contemporary context and agenda, of construals of
Scripture, and the like – that gives it its ecclesiological meaning. Of itself,
a model can offer few answers to ecclesiological questions. The model
cannot function logically as a normative principle, but only in a much
weaker way, as a concept summarizing the ecclesiological proposals a particular theologian is advancing or analyzing. An image or concept is not
the starting point for ecclesiological inquiry so much as the reflection of a
decision as to how best to explicate that inquiry's conclusions. This is not
to deny a model's heuristic function, but what among its findings is
accepted or not is determined by the agenda rather than the model itself.
Models may indeed function systematically, but only by gathering
together and organizing everything else that is finally more significant
than the model is itself.

In contrast to the structure and rhetoric of blueprint ecclesiology,
then, theological reflection upon the church is in fact from the very outset
a matter of practical rather than theoretical reasoning. The practice of
ecclesiology arises out of ecclesial practices, and is ordered directly
towards them. Moreover, judgments about the concrete church, however
incipient or implicit, are necessarily a factor in the construction of every
ecclesiology. Thus not only is the search for the supermodel misguided,
the method of models itself focuses attention on the wrong place. The
primary concern of ecclesiology should not be to explicate a particular
model but to make sound judgments upon the "everything else." Putting
it boldly, ecclesiologists have something rather like a prophetic function
in the church. They reflect theologically and therefore critically upon the
church's concrete identity in order to help it boast in its Lord, and boast
only in its Lord. They attempt to assess the church's witness and pastoral
care in light of Scripture and in relation to a theological analysis of the
contemporary ecclesiological context. They propose changes in the
church's concrete identity that will conserve, reform or more radically
restructure it, in order to help it embody its witness more truthfully and
better demonstrate the superiority of its way of life. Contextual ecclesial
praxis informs ecclesiology, and ecclesiology informs contextual ecclesial
praxis, in a practical hermeneutical circle.[70]

Ecclesiology, in short, is a form of theological reflection that should be
explicitly practical and prophetic. Unfortunately, however, ecclesiology

70. See Juan Luis Segundo, S.J., *The Liberation of Theology*, trans. John Drury (Maryknoll, NY:
Orbis, 1982), ch. 2.

displays the problem inherent in all attempts at "prophecy." Apart from outrageously obvious mistakes, it can be remarkably difficult to say which prophetic interpretation is right or which practical proposal is suitable. Who could show to everyone's satisfaction which of the ecclesiologies just cited has the best grasp of the ecclesiological context and indicates the right ecclesial response to it? Such judgments are extremely difficult to make without the benefits of a hindsight that can see and assess their practical consequences. Who, in Eusebius' time, would not have been tempted to agree with his triumphalist reading of recent history as the providential merging of Rome and victorious Christianity?[71] If we had been in Germany in 1933, some of us would no doubt have found it all too easy to have found reasons for quietly dismissing Barth's and others' prophetic call and for joining the German Christians.[72] Nor would anyone claim, I would think, that a decision for or against the parties in the Reformation would have been easy for those *in medias res* or that it is straightforward for us today.

Judgments about the Christian thing, the concrete church and the ecclesiological context cannot be avoided; they are part of any ecclesiology, whether they are acknowledged or not. Clearly, such judgments are best made consciously and explicitly. The tendency of modern ecclesiology, though, is to include little explicit analysis of the church's concrete identity and its context. A given blueprint ecclesiology may indeed respond adequately to its context. But, again, the lack of such analysis increases the likelihood that it will not, even though it may be consonant with Scripture and tradition. In such a case the theologian would have misconstrued the historical movement of the church and its present shape, or misinterpreted the ecclesiological context, or both. As a result, the blueprint, although fine as a presentation of doctrine, would be unfruitful or impractical in the concrete in that, like most bad judgments, it would respond to what is peripheral rather than to what is central. And because the blueprint is developed without explicit consideration of the ecclesiological context, it may well take longer to recognize its inadequacy.

To make this clearer, let us look at two examples of ecclesiological misjudgment, one imaginary and one factual. If I lived in Europe in 1935 and published an ecclesiology based upon a communion model, I could reasonably be accused of misreading the context and the recent history of the

---

71. See Markus, *Saeculum*, p. 48.
72. See Robert P. Eriksen, *Theologians Under Hitler* (New Haven: Yale University Press, 1985).

church. In spite of its impeccable Scriptural and patristic warrants, my model would likely be wrong. To advocate a doctrine of the church that stresses unity and harmony would, in that context, be to act as a false prophet because it would privilege a perspective on the church that draws it too close to the prevailing fascist ideology. That such a misjudgment was all too easy can be seen from the case of Teilhard de Chardin, who in 1924 asserted that "There is *only one Evil* = disunity," and was able even in 1936 to say: "Fascism opens its arms to the future. Its ambition is to embrace vast wholes in its empire. . . . Fascism may possibly represent a fairly successful small-scale model of tomorrow's world."[73] If adopted in such a context, my model would likely contribute to the sinfulness of the church, for it would become correspondingly more difficult for Christians to discern the incoherence in saying *Christus est Dominus* while engaging in fascist practices that serve another lord. The ecclesiology would render the church's witness untruthful and idolatrous.

A second example of ecclesiological misjudgment can be drawn from William T. Cavanaugh's *Torture and Eucharist*.[74] Cavanaugh narrates the story of the church in Chile during the Pinochet regime. For a remarkably long time, the church failed to do anything significant to respond to the state's torture of its citizens and their subsequent disappearance. One major reason for this, according to Cavanaugh, was the church's self-understanding. The Chilean church had adopted a European ecclesiology, a Maritainian "distinction of planes" model that prescribed a fundamentally organic relation between the nation state and the church. The former is to deal with political matters while the latter looks after the "soul" of the nation and avoids any involvement in the political sphere.[75] This ecclesiology of harmony prevented the church from recognizing that its own central practice, the Eucharist, conflicted radically with the practice of torture that had become central to the Pinochet state. The two-tier model inhibited the church leadership from seeing the Eucharist as a political practice that challenged the politics of the regime. Although not unreasonable in the abstract, this ecclesiology proved in practice to be useless in preventing the distortion of the church's witness and pastoral care.

73. Pierre Teilhard de Chardin, "The Salvation of Mankind" in his *Science and Christ* (London: Collins/Harper and Row, 1968), p. 80. The quotation is taken from Nicholas Lash, *Believing Three Ways*, pp. 95f.
74. William T. Cavanaugh, *Torture and Eucharist: Theology, Politics, and the Body of Christ* (Oxford: Blackwell, 1998).
75. Cavanaugh discusses Maritain's ecclesiology and its role within Latin America in ibid., ch. 4.

These two examples indicate the need to set up another criterion by which to assess all ecclesiological proposals, namely, how well such proposals respond to the ecclesiological context for which and within which they are made. This practical, contextual criterion will require some expansion of the scope of ecclesiology. It is not enough simply to presuppose a shared construal of the realities of the concrete church and its context. Rather, theologically informed yet critically sophisticated descriptions of both are vital elements of any practical-prophetic proposal so that others may assess and, if need be, challenge them.

To avoid confusion, here it is appropriate to anticipate very briefly some later points. To incorporate contextual analyses into ecclesiological reflection is not to make a correlationist move, or at least not the usual kind. My proposal should not be confused with what is sometimes called "practical" or "contextual" theology, with which it does indeed share some elements. Even if one were to agree with Don S. Browning, an advocate of practical theology who argues that theology is "a practical discipline through and through," it does not follow that theology is best done by means of a "critical correlational approach."[76] The tendency of the correlation method to distort Christian theology by uncritically assimilating normative humanistic beliefs is exemplified by Browning's contention that the social sciences are "to articulate a normative vision of the human life cycle" as a kind of universal that can be "mediated" to particular individuals and groups.[77] Similarly, the ecclesiologist, Johannes A. van der Ven, insists on the principles of non-competition and equal status between theology and the social sciences. His ecclesiology suffers, as a consequence, from an account of the context (and the church, all too often) that is excessively dependent upon modernistic and explanatory sociological categories, with little or no critical contribution from theology.[78]

Practical-prophetic ecclesiology must indeed engage with all relevant non-theological disciplines. The following chapters will discuss how to

76. Don S. Browning, *A Fundamental Practical Theology: Descriptive and Strategy Proposals* (Minneapolis: Fortress, 1991), pp. ix and 44.
77. See Browning's "Pastoral Theology in a Pluralistic Age" in Don S. Browning (ed.), *Practical Theology: The Emerging Field in Theology, Church and World* (San Francisco: Harper and Row, 1983), p. 187. A somewhat similar move is advocated by pluralist theologians, whom I discuss critically and in some detail in chapter 4.
78. See Johannes van der Ven, *Ecclesiology in Context* (Grand Rapids: Eerdmans, 1996), pp. 39f., 94f. For a sympathetic account of this genre, see Gijsbert D. J. Dingemans, "Practical Theology in the Academy: A Contemporary Overview," *Journal of Religion* 76:1 (1996), 82–96. Dingemans's account suggests, to me at least, that in seeking to meet "modern university standards" (p. 96), its practitioners undermine the means of discerning how those standards might conflict with Christian witness and discipleship.

integrate both theological and non-theological contextual analyses into ecclesiology without turning away from ecclesiology's primary function. That function, we recall, is to aid the church in performing its task of truthful witness within a particular ecclesiological context. It is also to help the church in its pastoral task of fostering good discipleship so that its members may more truly embody their claims about Jesus Christ and about the life made possible in and through him. Accordingly, final judgments about such matters can only be theological. Practical-prophetic ecclesiology must deny – if it is to be truly prophetic – any proposal to change the concrete church made merely in order that it may better fit the norms of a non-Christian worldview or social context. Nor can it allow social science or any other non-theological discipline to have the final word on our understanding of the ecclesiological context. Both church and context must be critically analyzed using all available tools, but within a thoroughly theological horizon. The next chapter presents such a horizon; chapter 5 discusses how theology can engage with non-theological disciplines; and the appropriate critical tools are described in chapter 7.

The critical points made in this chapter have been the following. To the extent that modern ecclesiology is governed by an abstract, rationalistic and overly theoretical approach, it makes it difficult for theologians to acknowledge the realities of the church's concrete identity. Ecclesiology is misguided if it attempts to construct, on the basis of a single model or principle, a systematic blueprint for the church that applies normatively always and everywhere. Such a blueprint can be very powerful and replete with profound theological language. Yet it may well prove to be a harmful response to the ecclesiological context and thus practically and prophetically false. Ecclesiology is not a doctrinal theory that can be worked out without close attention to the concrete life of the church. Practical-prophetic ecclesiology is not well done by trying to find the best model of the church, nor need it always describe the church in terms of a particular model, since models function less as systematic principles than as summary principles for other, ultimately more significant proposals.

More constructively, this chapter has argued that ecclesiology is a practical-prophetic discipline that seeks, above all, to help the concrete church perform its main tasks ever more adequately. Ecclesiology should be expanded by incorporating critical analyses of the concrete church and its context into the arguments for its proposals, so that these can be analyzed, challenged and improved. It should also make as explicit as pos-

Blueprint Ecclesiologies tend to occlude the concrete lives of churches, L

sible the various elements of the imaginative judgments that govern its construals and analyses, again with a view to making them available for critical consideration. Ecclesiology, on this view, serves the church *in medias res*, as a contextually-applicable set of practical-prophetic proposals.

3

A theodramatic horizon

The previous chapter described and critically analyzed some of the methodological characteristics of modern ecclesiology. These characteristics make it significantly more difficult than it need be for theologians who focus upon the church to carry out one of their chief responsibilities, namely to reflect critically and practically upon the church's concrete identity. As a consequence, contemporary ecclesiology does not contribute as much as it could to the church's task of glorying in Jesus Christ alone and of aiding the church's disciples to embody their witness as truthfully as possible within particular ecclesiological contexts. Indeed, blueprint ecclesiologies sometimes obstruct the church's efforts. The chapter also began to note some of the elements of an alternative approach. The contextual criterion supports the principle that ecclesiology should be as explicit as possible about the many judgments it must make, including its construal of the ecclesiological context. Every theological proposal should be assessed not only with regard to its conformity to Scripture and the tradition of its interpretation, but also with regard to its fittingness for a particular ecclesiological context. All ecclesiological judgments are made within an ecclesiological context, and all should serve the church's work within that context.

Later chapters will present further analysis of modern ecclesiology in relation to the ecclesiological context. The concern of the present chapter is to consider one of the most significant of the background elements of ecclesiology, namely the horizon or metanarrative. This, we recall, provides the over-arching framework within which other judgments are made, judgments about how to interpret Scripture and tradition, and how to construe the mode of God's presence, the church's past and present identity, and the ecclesiological context. In order to bring more diverse analytic tools into ecclesiological reflection in a theologically appropriate way, we need to be able to situate them within a suitable horizon, and make that horizon explicit. The horizon described here draws heavily upon the theodramatic theory of Hans Urs von Balthasar.[1] My interest in Balthasar's work, however, is quite restricted. I appropriate only what is relevant for the purpose and make little use of Balthasar's ecclesiology as such or of his theology generally. Some of his proposals, indeed, seem less than helpful for the church's work within the present ecclesiological context.[2] The concern of this chapter, then, is not to delineate a horizon that is demonstrably consistent with Balthasar's theological *oeuvre*. Instead, it is to borrow Balthasar's splendidly imaginative conception in order to articulate a Christian metanarrative that is particularly suitable for practical-prophetic ecclesiology. While there may be other versions of the Christian metanarrative that conform just as well to Scripture and tradition, the theodramatic one outlined here encourages rather than hinders the development of an expanded ecclesiology. Moreover, it can foster active engagement between theological and non-theological discourses without having to resort to a humanist or an anti-humanist metanarrative.

Additionally, Balthasar's theodramatic theory is appropriate in that it provides a resource for clarifying some of the differences between the methodological traits of modern ecclesiology and the practical-prophetic approaches to be proposed here. It does so, furthermore, without having to rely upon historical periodization. Balthasar contends that theological discourse should reflect the true nature of revelation and Christian existence prior to the eschaton. The relations between God, world and church are best conceived, he believes, as something rather like a play. The play can be described in terms of one or other of two main types of Christian horizons and theological styles, the epic and the dramatic.[3] Dramatic theology, as we will see in some detail shortly, takes the perspective of a participant in the drama, of one who lives entirely within the movement

---

1. Hans Urs von Balthasar, *Theo-Drama: Theological Dramatic Theory*, vols. I–V, trans. Graham Harrison (San Francisco: Ignatius Press, 1988–1998), referred to in the text as (TD volume, page). For an overview of Balthasar's theology, see Edward T. Oakes, *Pattern of Redemption: The Theology of Hans Urs von Balthasar* (New York: Continuum, 1994).
2. One example, to my mind, is Balthasar's unfortunate way of making theological distinctions in terms of purported masculine and feminine attributes. For an uncritical account, see Oakes, *Pattern of Redemption*, pp. 254–259.
3. Balthasar has a third category, the lyric, which is not relevant for my purpose here. He draws the categories from Hegel's *Aesthetics: Lectures on Fine Art*, trans. T. M. Knox (Oxford: Clarendon Press, 1975), vol. II, pp. 1035–1237.

of the play. It displays the tensive and conflictual nature of Christian existence, reflecting in its very form the ongoing dramatic struggle that constitutes discipleship (TD I, 22).[4]

In contrast, epic theology steps out of the drama to take an external, spectator's perspective upon the completed play. The epic horizon can be seen especially in church documents, catechisms, and those large-scale systematic theologies in which the Christian life is laid out as a whole, as if nothing further needs to be done or known. By distancing itself from the confusions of the struggle, epic theology is able to develop a "tidy" account of Christian doctrine (cf. TD I, 20). It may assume, incorrectly, that the play runs along mechanically according to principles that can be known to us in advance of the action (TD II, 53f.). While such an approach can be very useful for certain purposes, it has evident drawbacks if it becomes the sole form of theological discourse. It may fail to recognize new developments in the drama. And in ignoring or dissolving the tensions inherent in our existence as Christians, epic theology may become so "static" or "essentialist" that it distorts its account (TD II, 12).

Whether or not Balthasar is right in his assertion that Christianity is best thought of in terms of a play, there are obvious parallels between epic theology and the methodological traits of modern ecclesiology. Neither is usually found in absolute form, of course. Nor are "epic" and "modern" identical concepts; some premodern theology is epic in form. But the epic style and the blueprint form of modern ecclesiology clearly share some characteristics. Both would describe the church in terms of its final perfection rather than its concrete and sinful existence. Both would treat the church's ideal being as normative, rather than presenting careful and critical descriptions of its activity within the confusions and complexities of a particular ecclesiological context. The epic horizon is also reflected in the rhetoric of modern ecclesiology to the extent that it implies that it presents the final and definitive account of the doctrine of the church, one that is adequate for all future contexts and developments within the play.[5]

The similarities between the epic and modern styles of ecclesiology suggest that premodern theological reflection upon the church may give evidence of rather more dramatic horizons and styles. We can get some

---

4. Robert W. Jenson also uses the metaphor of drama in his *Systematic Theology: Volume I: The Triune God* (New York: Oxford University Press, 1997), esp. pp. 75ff.

5. For a historical study of the turn towards essential definition in Roman Catholic ecclesiology, see G. Thils, *Les Notes de l'Église dans l'Apologétique Catholique depuis la Réforme* (Paris: Desclée, no date).

idea of the various approaches of premodern ecclesiology by very briefly looking at the work of three standard theologians: Augustine, Thomas Aquinas and John Calvin.

Augustine's rejection, noted earlier, of Eusebius' interpretation of history as the merging of Rome with Christianity into a final peace, can readily be seen as an anti-epic move. The rejection reflects a judgment about the ecclesiological context that is made explicit in the *City of God*.[6] The well-known metaphor[7] of the two cities divides humanity into two, according to whether their actions display a love of God or a love of domination (CoG 1.1). Augustine clearly affirms the ontological relation between the City of God and the church. The City is already present within the church, in that some members of the latter are predestined eventually to live in the former (CoG 8.24). But the City cannot function as a model for the church because their concrete identities are distinguished quite radically (CoG 20.9). Having abandoned his earlier "politics of perfection,"[8] Augustine contends that while the City of God is pure and spotless, the church is made up of members of both cities.[9] Against the Donatists, then, perfection is not a present possibility for the church. Moreover, the members of the two cities do not constitute the church simply as a bipartite body, as Tyconius held, such that one part could be described in terms of perfection. Rather, the church is a thoroughly mixed body (CoG 1.35). As such, its life is one of dramatic struggle (CoG 18.49, 16.25) until it attains the eschatological peace of the heavenly City (CoG 19.13).[10] "The Church proceeds on its pilgrim way in this world, in these evil days. Its troubled course began ... with Abel himself ... and the pilgrimage goes on from that time right up to the end of history" (CoG 18.51). The church is, indeed, "even now the kingdom of God," but, quite unlike the City of God, it is "a kingdom at war" (CoG 20.9). Its task is therefore to gather those who have already been chosen for "testing and training" so as to "raise them from the temporal and visible to an apprehension of the eternal and invisible" (CoG 10.14).

---

6. Augustine, *City of God*, trans. H. Bettenson (London: Penguin, 1984). Cited in the text as (CoG page.paragraph).
7. Jean Bethke Elshtain refers to CoG 15.1, where Augustine notes that he is "speaking allegorically." See Elshtain, *Augustine and the Limits of Politics* (Notre Dame: University of Notre Dame Press, 1995), p. 95.
8. Robert A. Markus, *Saeculum: History and Society in the Theology of St. Augustine*, rev. ed. (Cambridge: Cambridge University Press, 1970), p. 103. Elshtain takes the point a little further in her *Augustine*, p. 98.
9. See Robert A. Markus, *The End of Ancient Christianity* (Cambridge: Cambridge University Press, 1990), p. 176.   10. See ibid., p. 79.

Augustine's metaphor of the two cities thus inhibits any tendency to overlook the struggles and confusions of pre-eschatological Christian existence. Other images and metaphors can be read as having a similar function. For example, the phrase, "Body of Christ" occurs frequently in his work and is applied to both the pilgrim and the heavenly church.[11] But this is not because it is the systematic principle of his ecclesiology. It is used because it permits a distinction to be made between the pilgrim church and the heavenly church, yet it also joins them together in Christ. The phrase thereby maintains rather than overcomes the tensive character of ecclesial life. Augustine is not a system builder in anything like the modern or epic sense. His work is occasional, responding to the pastoral problems facing the church of his day.[12] Even his use of the word "church" shifts continually.[13] The structure of the *City of God* depends not upon an underlying definition of the church, but upon the narrative description of the dramatic patterns of church history.[14] Augustine presents his theology of the church by situating it within its ecclesiological context, which he calls the "saeculum" (CoG 19.17). His ecclesiology in the *City of God* takes the form of an open-ended narrative of the history of the two cities "in their interwoven, perplexed and only eschatologically separable reality."[15]

One might think that if ever there were a premodern epic theologian it would be Thomas Aquinas. Certainly, Thomas presents nothing like the explicitly dramatic narrative of the *City of God*. But as Balthasar and others have noted,[16] both his *Summae* are structured by an underlying narrative of creation's movement from God and its return to God, a narrative drawn from the neo-Platonic *exitus et reditus* schema. Recent studies have brought to the fore the more dramatic aspects of this narrative.[17] The

---

11. See, e.g., *Homilies on I John*, conveniently in *Augustine: Later Works*, trans. John Burnaby (Philadelphia: Westminster, 1955).

12. Herbert A. Deane, *The Political and Social Ideas of Saint Augustine* (New York: Columbia University Press, 1963), p. viii. See also Jaroslav Pelikan, *The Christian Tradition: 1 The Emergence of the Catholic Tradition* (Chicago: University of Chicago Press, 1971), p. 306; also C. Clifton Black, "Serving the Food of Full-Grown Adults: Augustine's Interpretation of Scripture and the Nurture of Christians," *Interpretation* 52:4 (1998), 341–353.

13. Stanislaus J. Grabowski notes that Augustine's concept of the church is "formed of several elements" so that his use of the word "church" and the city metaphor associated with it can "shift even within the same sentence." *The Church: An Introduction to the Theology of St. Augustine* (St. Louis, Herder, 1957), p. 493.

14. See Robert A. Markus, "Church History and Early Church Historians" in *From Augustine to Gregory the Great*, vol. II (London: Variorum Reprints, 1983), pp. 1–17.

15. Markus, *Saeculum*, p. 71.

16. Balthasar, TD V, 61–65; M.-D. Chenu, O. P., *Toward Understanding St. Thomas* (Chicago: Regnery, 1964), p. 310.

17. See esp. Thomas S. Hibbs, *Dialectic and Narrative in Aquinas: An Interpretation of the Summa Contra Gentiles* (Notre Dame: University of Notre Dame Press, 1995).

dialectical form of Thomas's theological inquiry reflects its location within the "drama of conversion, of sin and virtue, of rejection or acceptance of God's grace."[18] Rather than attempting to get the spectator's definitive perspective upon the whole, Thomas works within a tradition of Scriptural interpretation. Theological inquiry is historical, ongoing and open-ended.[19] It moves along by dealing with points of controversy as they arise in the course of the church's attempts to witness to its Lord.[20]

The open-endedness of Thomas's theological style is evident in those areas of the *Summa Theologiae* where he comes closest to talking directly about the doctrine of the church. There he refrains from defining the church or from saying more than is necessary to establish a contested point.[21] As George Sabra rightly notes in his study of Thomas's ecclesiology, he uses a number of different concepts and images to describe the church, chief among which are *corpus Christi mysticum* and *congregatio fidelium.*[22] These are not models, though, in the sense of modern ecclesiology, for Thomas's ecclesiology is governed by the principle of "saving" the text of Scripture.[23] That is, what Thomas says about the church is primarily intended to demonstrate the coherence and reasonableness of Scripture. His ecclesiology is structured by neither a model nor a narrative of the *saeculum*, but by the narrative of creation and redemption revealed in Scripture and explicated in the authoritative tradition of its interpretation.

If Scripture is construed as revealing the movement of all things from God and their return into God, then theology, which depends upon Scripture, must follow the same narrative pattern. Furthermore, Thomas argues, it must do so not only with a speculative interest but also with practical considerations in view; doctrine and morality continually bear upon one another.[24] Accordingly, the *Summa Theologiae* includes a long

18. Nicholas Lash, *The Beginning and the End of 'Religion'* (Cambridge: Cambridge University Press, 1996), p. 142.
19. This applies even to natural law. See Pamela M. Hall, *Narrative and the Natural Law: An Interpretation of Thomistic Ethics* (Notre Dame: University of Notre Dame Press, 1994).
20. See Avery Dulles, S. J., "The Church According to Thomas Aquinas" in his *A Church To Believe In: Discipleship and the Dynamics of Freedom* (New York: Crossroad, 1982/1987), p. 169; also Alasdair MacIntyre, *Whose Justice? Which Rationality?* (Notre Dame: University of Notre Dame Press, 1988), pp. 164–182.
21. E.g., *Summa Theologiae*, Ia 117.2 ad 1; Ia IIae 114.6; IIa IIae 183.2; IIIa 8.1,3,4 and 6; 48.2 ad 1; 70.1.
22. According to George Sabra, *Thomas Aquinas' Vision of the Church: Fundamentals of an Ecumenical Ecclesiology* (Mainz: Matthias Grünewald, 1987).
23. For this understanding of the way Thomas read Scripture, see Bruce Marshall, "Aquinas as a Post-liberal Theologian," *The Thomist* 53 (1989), 353–402; also Eugene F. Rogers, Jr. *Thomas Aquinas and Karl Barth: Sacred Doctrine and the Natural Knowledge of God* (Notre Dame: University of Notre Dame Press, 1995).
24. *Summa Theologiae*, Ia 1.4f. See Chenu, *Toward Understanding St. Thomas*, pp. 311f.

second part where Thomas discusses in great detail the shape of true discipleship, and the third part, where he discusses the *reditus* explicitly as the "way" of Jesus Christ.[25] The second part and much of the third part of the *Summa* together constitute a kind of practical ecclesiology, for it is there that Thomas gives an account of what he believed to be the best thinking of his time about the beliefs, practices and valuations that should be embodied in the concrete church. His work helped the church to perform its pastoral role of training and teaching its members how to acquire those dispositions that orient them properly to their final end and so enable them to be truthful disciples.

Calvin's theological treatment of the church is, as William Bouwsma says, "thoroughly practical."[26] The *Institutes of the Christian Religion*[27] are not a systematic theology in the sense of a view of the whole worked out in terms of one or two principles. Rather, as Serene Jones has argued, Calvin is concerned to explicate Scripture faithfully, and "to edify, uplift, and defend the particular community of faith to whom he speaks."[28] Consequently his ecclesiology serves the church's pastoral function of aiding its members to become more truthful disciples (ICR 4.1.1; 4.1.4). The church is a thoroughly mixed body in this world (ICR 4.1.17,20), so although Calvin avoids making right discipline (ICR 4.12) one of the marks of the church, it is clear that his concern is primarily with the church's pedagogical function, with its task of fostering the practices of true piety. He insists upon the third and "principal" use of the law for believers because they need "to learn more thoroughly each day the nature of the Lord's will" (ICR 2.7.12.). The visible mother church (ICR 4.1.4) helps Christians respond to their call to sanctification (ICR 3.19.2), teaching them how to mortify the flesh and vivify the spirit (ICR 3.3.5) through practices of fasting, prayer (ICR 3.20), communal worship, and the like.

Calvin is guided in his ecclesiology by his constant reference to Scripture and by his "insistence on the church as a functioning community."[29] The Christian community is found concretely in particular congregations and parishes, in those "individual churches, disposed in towns and villages according to human need, so that each rightly has the name and

25. *Summa Theologiae*, IIIa prologue; Ia. 2 proem. For the relation between Christ as "way" and the "five ways" of Ia 2.3, see Rogers, *Thomas Aquinas*, pp. 61ff.
26. William J. Bouwsma, *John Calvin: A Sixteenth Century Portrait* (Oxford: Oxford University Press, 1988), p. 214.
27. John Calvin, *Institutes of the Christian Religion*, ed. John T. McNeill (Philadelphia: Westminster, 1960). Cited in the text as (ICR book.chapter.paragraph).
28. Serene Jones, *Calvin and the Rhetoric of Piety* (Louisville, KY: Westminster/John Knox Press, 1995), p. 36.   29. Bouwsma, *John Calvin*, p. 216.

authority of the church" (ICR 4.1.9). To be sure, Calvin discusses the marks of the church (ICR 4.1.9), but these are developed with pastoral and ecumenical concerns in mind, to help the Christians of his day find a church that was truly such (ICR 4.1.10–18). Calvin also mentions, almost in passing, his twofold construal of the church (ICR 4.1.7). Here, too, the distinction serves to recall the confusions of pre-eschatological existence and our future hope rather than to establish an ideal invisible church as the basis for an epic ecclesiology. In sum, his focus is on the concrete or "visible" church as the "external means" by which God brings us into "the society of Christ" (ICR 4 title).

In all three of these premodern theologians doctrine and practical concerns are interwoven. Doctrines about the church are formulated to serve the tasks of the church rather than for theoretical purposes. As a consequence, ecclesiology is often hard to distinguish from what amounts to a form of Christian social ethics in which the society in question is the church. The primary focus is upon Scripture and upon how it throws light upon the issues that affect Christian discipleship and witness at this particular point in God's play.[30] In their various ways, all three theologians acknowledge the struggle and conflict inherent in the life of the church, and they all avoid idealistic descriptions of its present identity.

It is possible that these somewhat more dramatic aspects of premodern approaches to ecclesiology often go unremarked because premodern texts are read within a largely epic horizon. It may be, too, that they are placed within a modern narrative, as the early stages of the progress of ecclesiology towards its proper method or model. The result would be to emphasize those methodological elements that are similar to the modern and epic views, and revise or ignore those elements that do not fit such views.[31] This is not, to repeat, in itself necessarily wrong; indeed it can be very useful, provided it does not rule out alternatives.

One further reason, then, for appropriating Balthasar's theodramatic

30. For an Eastern example, see Amanda Berry Wylie, "The Exegesis of History in John Chrysostom's 'Homilies on Acts'" in Mark S. Burrows and Paul Rorem (eds.), *Biblical Hermeneutics in Historical Perspective: Studies in Honor of Karlfried Froelich on His Sixtieth Birthday* (Grand Rapids: Eerdmans, 1991), pp. 59–72.

31. This tendency is especially visible in the tradition of theology *ad mentem* of Thomas Aquinas, which arose after Leo XIII's *Aeterni Patris*. For references to such epic exercises in ecclesiology, see Sabra, *Thomas Aquinas' Vision*, p. 15. Even the subtle Yves Congar sought to establish Thomas's "definition" of the church. See Congar, *L'Église. De Saint Augustin à l'époque moderne* (Paris: Cerf, 1970), pp. 232f. Nor are Roman Catholics alone in this. To take only one example, Paul Avis's very helpful study of the Reformers' "concept of the church" searches for a "central principle" amid all its variety. See Paul D. L. Avis, *The Church in the Theology of the Reformers* (Atlanta: John Knox, 1981), pp. 1–8, 215.

Theodrama
v.
epic =
totalis
objectiue .

horizon is that it provides a strong counterweight to the epic tendencies of modern ecclesiology, and may on that account help us to retrieve traditional resources to overcome too heavy a reliance upon blueprints and the method of models. It is fair to say that Balthasar's construction, in spite of the evident influence of Hegel,[32] is an explication of something like a horizon that can frequently be found within premodern Christianity, especially during the patristic period, but which has been largely abandoned during the modern period. At the same time, his theory draws upon the insights of modernity so as to constitute a horizon that is suitable for practical-prophetic ecclesiology as our societies move into a late-modern or postmodern era. In order to retrieve a premodern horizon along the lines of Balthasar's theodrama for use within the contemporary, postcritical ecclesiological context, I will have to make a case that it is better, in terms of both function and truth, than its alternatives. The argument will build over the remainder of this book. For the rest of this chapter, I will first give an overview of Balthasar's theodramatic theory in so far as it forms a suitably Christian metanarrative. Then I will discuss a few of its implications for practical-prophetic ecclesiology. The task of this chapter is largely descriptive. In the coming chapters, I test the usefulness, coherence and truthfulness of this horizon.

Balthasar notes how it is rather ironic that throughout its history the church has so frequently condemned the stage. For revelation itself is "dramatic at its very core" (TD II, 51), and shows that Christian existence itself is "inherently dramatic." Indeed, Balthasar forthrightly denies the liberal thesis of the progressive integration of world and church. On the contrary, the dramatic struggle is intensifying (TD II, 96; V, 22). It is "the fundamental law of post-Christian world history" that the more the Kingdom of Christ is proclaimed in the world, the more determined will be the opposition to it, yet that which is for or against the Kingdom will be ever harder to tell apart (TD IV, 21). Scripture, too, is dramatic rather than epic.[33] It is not best to interpret it as if it were a story told by one who knows and reveals the entirety of the drama of salvation from the perspective of its conclusion. It may look like a "final, immovable word", but in

---

32. Balthasar has been accused of remaining within the Hegelian horizon, treating drama as the means by which the lyric mode (the self alone before God) and the epic modes can be unified into a greater totality. See J. B. Quash, "'Between the Brutally Given, and the Brutally, Banally Free': Von Balthasar's Theology of Drama in Dialogue with Hegel," *Modern Theology* 13:3 (1997), 293–318.

33. For an excellent account of Balthasar's hermeneutics, though restricted to the *Theological Aesthetics*, see William T. Dickens, "The Doctrine of Scripture in Hans Urs von Balthasar's *The Glory of the Lord: A Theological Aesthetics*," PhD Diss., Yale University (1997).

fact it "journeys along with history" (TD II, 105), functioning like a "vast net" within which "the attested and generative word of God can traverse unhindered" (TD II, 108). It is thus a "part of the drama itself, moving along with it" (TD II, 112). Under the direction of the Spirit, Scripture constantly mediates between "the drama beyond and the drama here" (TD I, 22). It reveals the whole as something rather like a play authored by the Father and directed by the Spirit, the chief actor of which is the Son. The dramatic character of Christian existence "here" is thus grounded in the primary drama "beyond", in the life of the immanent Trinity. It is Christ's work *pro nobis* that draws creation into the primary drama. And the play continues on after the Resurrection, as we join it by responding or failing to respond, as individuals and as the church, to God's work for us. Our existence (echoing *Hamlet*) is therefore a play that we play within the overarching divine play. So to understand our roles, as individuals and as the church, we must situate them within the primary drama, for "one cannot construct a theodrama from below" (TD II, 53; see V, 61–65).

We must begin our account of the drama, then, within the Trinity itself. God is absolutely free in God's self-possession. God can, therefore, freely choose to surrender Godself: "as Father, he can share his Godhead with the Son, and, as Father and Son, he can share the same Godhead with the Spirit." In so doing, God does not lose Godself in order to gain Godself through the mediation of the other, for "he is *always* himself by giving himself" in "absolute love" (TD II, 256). This explains God's free self-giving to the world as love without having to say that God "needed" the world process and the Cross in order to become Godself ("to mediate himself" in a Hegelian fashion) (TD IV, 323). The mission of the Son *pro nobis* is thus an entirely gratuitous extension of his procession into the economy of salvation. But "whereas in his *processio* he moves toward the Father in receptivity and gratitude, in his *missio* . . . he moves away from him and toward the world, into the latter's ultimate darkness" (TD IV, 356).

Balthasar insists that we should be quite realistic about suffering within creation. The dramatic tension of our existence must not be replaced by a "Stoicism with Christian trimmings" (TD IV, 76). Nor can suffering be domesticated by "a short-sighted, petit-bourgeois rationalism" that insists on its educative function (TD IV, 192; V, 498ff.). More than anything else it is the experience of suffering in its various forms that makes it difficult for people to approach God. We must acknowledge that there is no way to explain away the problem. Our only response can be that Jesus, who did not do away with suffering, suffered with us (TD IV, 195). It is he who experiences absolute suffering – utter God-forsakenness – for our sake, in order that the sinner's alienation from God may be taken "into the Godhead, into the 'economic' distance between Father and Son" (TD IV, 381). It is this freely obedient suffering on the part of the Son that makes him "the matrix of all possible dramas", for "he embodies the absolute drama in his own person" (TD III, 62). It is he who, in his work *pro nobis* (TD IV, 239), makes possible the "primal mystery," namely our communion (*communio*) with God in which "God, out of his freely bestowed love, allows that which is not God to participate in all the treasures of his love" (TD, II 127).

In becoming flesh, Jesus Christ creates a stage (TD III, 41), "an acting area for dramas of theological moment, involving other, created persons" (TD III, 162). He thus makes it possible for us, both as individuals and as the church, to play our respective parts within the "all-embracing drama" (TD II, 69). However – and this for us is one of the more significant points of Balthasar's theodramatic theory – if Christian existence is to be genuinely dramatic and not merely a puppet-play, our response must be really our own. We must be genuinely free to choose to play our parts well or badly, or even to refuse to play them at all. God's "loving respect" for us makes possible that freedom, for God becomes "latent," "accompanying" us rather than overwhelming us with God's presence (TD II, 276). Thus in a way analogous to (and dependent upon) the way the Father makes room for the Son within the Godhead, God gives us a place on the stage where we may make our own free response in gratitude. Our acting space is therefore not to be thought of as somehow located in a sphere separate from God. Rather it is located within God's sphere, within the one theo-drama. Our incorporation into the play is made possible by Christ, and thus our parts are to be played *en Christoi*. We are actively and freely involved in Christ's work, though not in a way that blurs "the distinction between Christ's preeminence and his followers and collaborators" (TD IV, 239). Our involvement takes the form of the "progressive incarnating of the word of thanks in our lives." Since it is indeed our own, free response, it is also the "progressive self-realization of finite freedom within the context of infinite freedom" (TD II, 291).

Our response takes the form of following Jesus Christ in gratitude.[34]

34. One may be reminded of Barth's notion of "correspondence" here. See John Webster, *Barth's Ethics of Reconciliation* (Cambridge: Cambridge University Press, 1995), esp. pp. 57f; also Webster, *Barth's Moral Theology: Human Action in Barth's Thought* (Edinburgh: T&T Clark, 1998), pp. 125ff.

We follow the historical Jesus as well as the Risen Christ, so our disciple-ship may well include suffering. Not that our suffering will add anything to Christ's all-sufficient redemptive suffering, but within his suffering "a place has been left for the disciples" (TD IV, 388). We must expect our roles to be difficult to play since, as we noted earlier, Christ's victory has ushered in "the most dramatic period of world history" (TD III, 37). While the Resurrection has indeed brought about our ultimate liberation from the powers of evil, it has increased our danger, for the devil "intensifies his enslavement of mankind more than ever" (TD IV, 369; see V, 203ff.) as part of the "eschatological intensification *within* the victory of Christ" (TD IV, 370). Our activity is thus a part of the larger "struggle between the divine and that which is hostile to the divine, a struggle *over* the world," not only *within* the world (TD III, 53).

God calls each one of us to respond to our own unique mission, one that "automatically" allots the one called to "a combat role in the task of world liberation" (TD III, 231). Each of us is called to "walk along a spe-cially designed personal path toward identity with the exemplary proto-type" (TD II, 292). Our role or mission or part (the terms are virtually synonymous for Balthasar) individuates and personalizes us to the extent that we actively respond to our call. Jesus, again, is the model. Jesus so completely accepted his mission that it became his personal identity; he *is* his mission. The Son's absolute, yet absolutely free, obedience rendered his person utterly unique and his work of universal significance (TD II, 32). For us, however, there is always a "tragic" division between our indi-vidual identity and the part we are called to play, between our "I" and our calling. But the more we respond to our call the more we become who we uniquely are, for "each conscious subject is created for the sake of his mission, a mission that makes him a person" (TD III, 208). Being a person is thus not a "natural" thing, nor something we construct through auto-nomously self-creative activity. It is, rather, a gift of grace:

> [I]f man freely affirms and accepts the election, vocation and mission
> which God, in sovereign freedom, offers him, he has the greatest
> possible chance of becoming a person, of laying hold of his own
> substance, of grasping that most intimate idea of his own self – which
> otherwise would remain undiscoverable. (TD III, 263)

The more we give ourselves up to discipleship, therefore, the more we become who we really are in Christ (TD III, 162). (This argument is, of course, Balthasar's explication of the conditions of discipleship stipu-lated in Matthew 16:24f. and par.)

It is important to note that the call to participate in the theodrama can by no means be limited to Christians, for no one is a pure spectator; "everyone has some part to play" even outside the church (TD III, 534). The Spirit of Christ is not bound to the church but is everywhere within the world. The church has much to learn from non-Christian traditions, for "Jesus can work, directly, outside the church" in both individuals and in groups (TD III, 528f.). Non-Christian elements of culture "can be an obstacle to grace" and contribute to a less than satisfactory "religious culture" within the church (TD IV, 209, note). But Balthasar also acknowledges how the early church borrowed many social practices from pagan culture, modifying them for their own use. Thus Paul borrows from pagan ethics (TD IV, 182f.), and Israel takes its religious forms partly from pagan origins. Such moves indicate that "the antecedent forms cannot be dismissed as simply negative" (TD IV, 211). Hence there is a "fluid" relation between the church and the "total human community" (TD I, 647).

For those whose vocation is to play an explicitly Christian role in God's play, the call is always also a summons to membership and activity within the church. What distinguishes the members of the church is their knowledge of the way things are. This gives them the opportunity "explicitly to adopt [Christ's] standpoint (Matt. 3:14) and to receive the fullness of his power so that they can continue his work in the world" (TD III, 279). Balthasar's understanding of the relation between the individual Christian and the church is complex and tensive. The Christian enters the community as part of her response to being addressed as an individual by God, for our personal mission not only individuates us, but has a "socializing" effect, too (TD III, 349). The call to play one's part in the drama thus precedes, even though it necessarily leads to, one's membership in the church. Hence communion with other Christians cannot be a condition for fellowship with God, since "it is through *personal* confession of Christ and relationship with him that the individual becomes a member of his Mystical Body" (TD III, 450, my emphasis). The goal of the church, then, cannot be to achieve community for its own sake. Nor should its liturgical celebrations or any other of its cultural activities be thought of as having as their primary goal the engendering of communal fellowship. Rather, the goal of all that the church does is communion with the Trinity (TD III, 452).

At the same time, though, the church is not merely the aggregate of its members; in some ways it does precede the individual. Like Jesus himself, we as individuals need the community, for "being-in-the-flesh always means receiving from others" (TD III, 177). Our individuating response to God's call is mediated to us by the church (TD III, 128). Our free response cannot be made without interaction with other free subjects (TD II, 202). Moreover, our individuating response to grace is progressive. We must discover, learn, and grow into our roles, and for this we must interact with the Christian community over time. A vital element of the church's work is thus to help us to discover what our particular role is and to help us play it better. Yet the community should not think that its function is to provide those roles for its members. Individual Christians do not select one of a range of character-types the church offers us, nor should we seek to become so molded into a particular kind of Christian character that we lose our individual mission and personality.

The relation between the Christian community and the individual is thus a dialectical one: our call is unmediated, yet it must be mediated through the church (TD II, 391). The relation is a "concrete metaphor" of the relations within the triune God (TD II, 415). Yet Balthasar emphasizes that the consequence of following Christ in discipleship will be solitude, both as the church and as an individual: "Christ is *the* individual among men; he is utterly lonely." The church, therefore, "will have to be 'solitary' in an environment that hates her." And the church must itself be a "Christologically fashioned community: though she is Christ's community of love, she consists of individuals who live their lives following the solitary Christ" (TD III, 448).

Balthasar places considerable emphasis upon the dramatic existence of the church as it responds and fails to respond to its call to play its part within the theodrama. The church *in via* lives a tensive existence, caught between the "already" and the "not yet," between time and eternity, between its traditions and the need for constant newness, between authority and inspiration (TD IV, 453f.), and so on. As a consequence the church's history is almost inevitably tragic (TD IV, 455). For the struggle for and against God's redemptive activity takes place not only between the world and the church, but within the latter itself. Until the eschaton, this cannot be avoided: as *corpus permixtum* the church has "to continue to endure the inner tension between her ideal and her fallen reality" (TD III, 443).

Yet the church must not be simply passive in its endurance. As the book of Revelation shows in its account of the seven churches of Asia,

> each church and all the individuals in it have to act on their own decision . . . . [Their] works consist not only in patient endurance or

martyrdom but equally in cleansing the community of diverse kinds of offence, in inner conversion and a return to the "former works" ... and also in the external successes that can be granted even to a community that has "but little power." (TD II, 61)

Balthasar's account of the relation between divine and human freedom enables him to recognize clearly that "the gospel does not replace human decision and arrangements" in constituting the concrete church (TD II, 86). In spite of our "frail finitude" we in the church must accomplish something of "ultimate value" (TD IV, 76). We are indeed saved only by Jesus Christ, but if everything came from God alone, there could be no drama; if all were passive, then "all Christology would dissolve in Monophysitism and the doctrine of grace dissolve in extreme Predestinarianism" (TD II, 184). Thus the church is "always two things at once: on the one hand, she is constituted by Christ's self-dedication, and, on the other hand, she must continually exercise and ratify this constitution in ways that are ever new" (TD III, 429). This is the church's mission, its role in the theodrama, which Balthasar sums up in dramatic form as the mystery of the church: "What the church does is Christ and his work; but he *lets* her do it" (TD III, 431).

Balthasar's theodramatic horizon and his conception of the place and action of the church within it are both compatible with the initial account of the church in chapter 1 above, though clearly he brings out the dramatic aspects of ecclesial existence rather more. Balthasar makes his own ecclesiological proposals within this horizon, but we will not follow him any further, for the concern here is to push ecclesiology in a more practical-prophetic direction than he does. It will take the remaining chapters to draw out the implications of this horizon for that ecclesiology, for it is best to do so by contrasting it with alternatives. For the remainder of this chapter, I note just a few salient points with regard to the relations between church and God, church and disciple, and church and world.

Within the theodramatic horizon, *everything* is located within the sphere of God's creative and redemptive activity. All human activity is dependent upon the prior activity of God, yet because of our location within the theodrama, we are truly free to play our own part in ways that are in some sense really independent of God. That is, we can and do choose to act in ways that are contrary to God's will, yet those decisions are made within and become part of the theodrama. Both divine and human agency, moreover, must be understood, as in premodern theology generally, without any kind of division of labor. It is not the case, as has sometimes been assumed in modern theology,[35] that God acts in certain areas while humans are left to act in other areas more or less alone. Human agency is *fully* constitutive of *all* human institutions and bodies, including the church. At the same time, divine agency is *fully* constitutive of all such bodies, including those that are non-ecclesial and non-religious. There is nowhere where God is not creatively and redemptively present.

This has a number of implications for ecclesiology. Most broadly, it raises theology to the position of metadiscourse, to that form of reflection that situates all other forms of reflection.[36] If God is active everywhere, then all human activity bears some relation to God, and to bracket out that relation can only be a temporary move. At the same time, this conception of the divine–human *concursus* relativizes in at least one significant way the status of the church and its theological discourse as they relate to other religious and non-religious bodies. It is indeed the case that the church is different from such bodies both in degree and in kind because the Spirit is active within it in a distinctive manner. And it is also the case that, as a consequence, our activity has possibilities – true discipleship and convincing witness in preaching and sacraments, for example – that are unavailable elsewhere. Yet the theodramatic horizon suggests that we consider *all* religious and non-religious bodies to be constituted concretely by both kinds of agency, divine and human. To deny this would be to deny the freedom and governance of the Spirit-director of the theodrama and place such bodies outside the play. The formal similarity between church and other religious or non-religious bodies does not, though, imply that they are merely diverse concrete expressions of some deep-spiritual or proleptically eschatological harmony. With a theodramatic horizon we have strong reasons for denying a final unity underlying all conflict and difference. What binds all things together is not an ontological ground, a shared subjectivity or a humanist goal, but the location of all action under the directorship of God. The unity of all things is to be found, then, not in the depths of our being, but in what must remain unknown to us prior to the eschaton, namely the script of the theodrama. As we will see later, this point has some significant implications for the use of the twofold construal.

35. See Kathryn Tanner, *God and Creation in Christian Theology: Tyranny or Empowerment?* (Oxford: Blackwell, 1988), esp. chapter four; William C. Placher, *The Domestication of Transcendence: How Modern Thinking about God Went Wrong* (Louisville, KY: Westminster/John Knox Press, 1996).
36. See John Milbank, *Theology and Social Theory: Beyond Secular Reason* (Oxford: Blackwell, 1990), p. 1.

Both within and outside the church, our agency is dependent upon the divine agency, but yet we work in our own thoroughly human way. Within the church, as within other groups and as individuals, human activity is sufficiently independent (through grace) that it does not simply make manifest, in a more or less distorted fashion, the underlying divine presence. Were that the case, the theodrama would be, for humanity at least, a mere puppet-play. Rather, our activity should be expected to run at times counter to the divine activity, manifesting our finitude and sin. When it does so, such activity still remains constitutive of the church's concrete identity, for if it did not, the church could not be said to play any role of its own in the theodrama. Its identity is thus thoroughly dramatic in form, for it is the embodiment of its struggle to follow, reject or ignore the movement of the Spirit in its midst. Something formally similar can be said about other religious and non-religious bodies, too: the Holy Spirit, human actions that display finitude and sin, as well as grace-enabled action in accordance with God's will – these are constitutive of all human institutions and groups, whether they make any attempt to follow God's will or not. It is within and by means of this confused mix that we make our contribution to the theodrama.

That both the church and other religious and non-religious bodies have not dissimilar agential constitutions has both positive and negative implications for the church's relations with what is not the church. Solely for purposes of clarification, let us make a very simple distinction between two common theological uses of the word "world." "World" can denote that part of creation that is actively working against Christ and his church. The church must reject this form of world wherever it can be discerned. We can call this form of world, "anti-Christ," though the phrase is perhaps too sharp, disguising the fact that what it labels is often very difficult to detect. (I would use "anti-Christian," but it is likely that on occasion some forms of anti-Christian or anti-church activity may be prompted by the Spirit.) But "world" may also signify that part of creation that does not work against its creator and redeemer. This world can include the communal embodiments of all religious and non-religious traditions and societies that do not intend to follow Christ. Such traditions and societies may or may not have been more or less influenced by Christian ideas and practices. We can call this world the "non-church." While it may well include elements of anti-Christ, where it does not, this non-church world consists simply of fallen humanity outside the concrete church.

Within a theodramatic perspective the non-church world becomes theologically laden, for it cannot be understood as independent of God's activity. And since the Holy Spirit is present and active not only within the church but in what is non-church, sometimes a fruitful relation – though one that must remain thoroughly tensive – can arise between the church and the non-church. The church can learn from what is non-church. Prophetic voices may arise there in, for example, non-theological intellectual disciplines, or in non-Christian religions. One might argue, to take a random example, that advances in science in the last hundred years or so have enabled the church to acknowledge that, in certain periods at least, it may have misunderstood the accounts of creation in Genesis 1 and 2. It may have been prompted by non-church challenges to discover (eventually on its own terms) that it had been thinking of God's creative activity in overly simple ways.

The non-church world is thus not only the place where the church is to witness to its Lord, it is also the place from which the church may learn about its Lord and about true discipleship. The tension that should always exist between church and non-church is thus not only something to be endured, but also something to be acknowledged as a gift. The church benefits from the non-church world, even as the world benefits (whether it thinks it does or not) from hearing and seeing the gospel of Christ truthfully embodied. Even the anti-church is part of the play, in spite of its theological absurdity. All human activities – response, neutrality and rejection – are made within the one overarching theodrama. And they can only be fully understood in so far as they are situated within the theodramatic framework.

Since the church can at times learn from the work of the Spirit working in what is non-church, it seems reasonable to propose that the church should make a habit of listening to the non-church, of trying to discern the Spirit's action in its challenges, of seeking out its wisdom in case Christ's word is spoken there. This, of course, is not an easy or straightforward thing to do. For one thing, to acknowledge the need to listen and learn is to deprive Christians of the comfort and security of knowing that they have, or have access to, all the answers. Moreover, it is often difficult, as we noted earlier, to make the "prophetic" decisions as to which non-church elements are suitable for modification and appropriation by the church, which should be ignored, and which are anti-Christ. Too many mistakes have been made in the past for anyone to feel confident about such decisions in the present. The church has blithely accepted into its concrete identity many anti-Christ elements, such as slavery and the oppression of women, that now strike many churchpeople as obvious candidates for rejection. Perhaps because of the church's past sinfulness, some Christians now seem to believe that modern society holds so much wisdom that the church should conform closely to it. But we should not be overquick to embrace what is non-church. Much of modern Western culture is more anti-Christ than merely non-church, in spite of its rhetoric to the contrary. The non-church is penetrated through and through with anti-Christ elements and the discernment of spirits is a perilous undertaking.

But things are yet more complicated and perilous, for the church itself is penetrated throughout its concrete form by both non-church and anti-Christ elements.[37] The church is not separated from the rest of humanity by easily discerned boundaries.[38] While it does indeed have a unique place within the theodrama, and thus a unique concrete identity, for much of their time its members live in the world, their actions informed as much by their place there as by their life in the church. World and church are therefore mixed and mutually constitutive in the concrete. Conflict is to be expected, then, not only between the church and the world, but within the church, too. The church is a body that must struggle to understand its role, in part because Christianity is an essentially contested concept, and in part because it must continually purge itself of anti-Christ elements and appropriate, modify or reject non-church elements as its seeks to witness faithfully to the gospel. Such intraecclesial conflict should not be avoided by enforcing unity, for it may frequently be fruitful. Indeed, as I will suggest in a later chapter, the church can be understood within a theodramatic horizon as the *locus* and embodiment of a set of ongoing arguments about how best to witness to Jesus Christ and to follow him in true discipleship.

The dramatic horizon has significant implications for Christian discipleship. The Christian is called to a life of courageous struggle in the midst of conflict and disharmony. The struggle may tear into one's very identity as a person. Not that Christians move melodramatically from one

---

37. For an incisive account of how some non- or anti-Christian elements penetrate into the church's own activities, see Philip D. Kenneson and James L. Street, *Selling Out the Church: The Dangers of Church Marketing* (Nashville: Abingdon Press, 1997). A more general argument is found in Stanley Hauerwas and William H. Willimon, *Resident Aliens: Life in the Christian Colony* (Nashville: Abingdon Press, 1989).

38. See Kathryn Tanner, *Theories of Culture: A New Agenda for Theology* (Minneapolis: Fortress, 1997), esp. chapter five.

crisis to another as if one lived in a soap-opera. The drama moves not at our pace, but at the tempo set by God. Most of one's discipleship may well be rather humdrum and ordinary, as we strive to learn and interiorize the beliefs and practices that foster our Christian personhood. Giving ourselves over to the regularities of Christian institutions is itself often part of the challenge. However, the theodramatic horizon does suggest that if one's discipleship becomes too easy or actually dull, one should wonder whether it is lacking in some way. The horizon indicates the inadequacy, furthermore, of a view of Christianity common among both its adherents and its critics, that it is essentially a crutch for helping the weak or the weak-minded get through life. It is true, of course, that the gospel is our support and comfort in times of suffering. But not all of us are especially afflicted by life's misfortunes at all times. We need to learn practices that challenge us, pushing us to become courageous and vital disciples who can make our contribution to the upbuilding of a courageous and vital church.

The courage displayed by any good disciple is a contributing factor in the tensive relation between the individual and the church. The theodramatic horizon emphasizes the point that the church is not the kind of collective that demands the individual give herself over to the group; rather, we each are to give ourselves over to Christ in discipleship. It may well happen that for some disciples, participation in the church will involve much more than, say, simply joining in the Sunday service with an attitude of enthusiastic but unreflective conformity. It is true that every disciple must learn in humble obedience from the church those practices, beliefs and valuations that enable her to become a better disciple. Yet it may be on occasion that an individual's contribution to the church's witness will require her to be a prophetic thorn in its flesh. She may find herself having to challenge certain ecclesial cultural patterns as embodying either hitherto unnoticed anti-Christ or presently unsuitable non-church elements. Her challenge may arise under the influence of non-church or anti-Christ traditions of inquiry, or it may be a prophetic response directly to some aspect of the tradition, or, most likely, it will be a combination of both. Failure to respond to such a call, if it is indeed truly such, would be a failure of discipleship. It would, furthermore, hinder the church's task of witness by tacitly supporting a falsifying embodiment of it. Naturally, to mount such a challenge is difficult, since it may be misdirected or its motivation misunderstood. But it should not be made more difficult than it need be by an ecclesiastical culture that brooks no dissent or discussion. Such internal challenges are a part of the dramatic struggle that constitutes Christian ecclesial existence, and should not be countered by overly epic and idolatrous claims to mastery of the theodrama. As Balthasar remarks, it is the saints who are the best interpreters of theodrama, for what they know is "lived out in dramatic existence" (TI II, 14).[39] One task for ecclesiology is to find a place among the church's practices for such solitary or minority forms of prophetic discipleship.

The theodramatic horizon removes the possibility of any closure for Christian existence to the other side of the eschaton. On the contrary, it brings to the fore the tensiveness inherent in all aspects of Christian existence. The church is situated *in medias res*, dealing confusedly and sometimes sinfully with events somewhere in the middle of the story; or is it nearer the end or the beginning? We do not know. We do know, to our joy and comfort, that the outcome of the theodrama is (already) successful. But, with the Augustine of the *City of God*, we ourselves possess no resting place here, be it a secure theological system, a normative pattern of social or political life, or a determinate method of interpreting Scripture.[40] For we do not have the epic view; we cannot know the twists and turns of the plot yet to come. The church and both forms of the world are all altered by changes in time and place. Conflict and confusion, as well as comfort and trust, are our lot.

The open-endedness and tensive character of Christian ecclesial existence can be illustrated with reference to H. Richard Niebuhr's well-known typology of the relationship between "Christ" and "culture."[41] Niebuhr proposed a range of five typical ways the gospel could be related to its cultural environment, ranging from simple rejection of that envi-

39. Who the saints are, though, may be an increasingly difficult question to answer. See Radner, *The End of the Church: A Pneumatology of Christian Division in the West* (Grand Rapids: Eerdmans, 1998), pp. 131–137.

40. The label "determinate" is drawn from Stephen E. Fowl, *Engaging Scripture: A Model for Theological Interpretation* (Oxford: Blackwell, 1998), pp. 33ff. See also George A. Lindbeck's "Atonement and the Hermeneutics of Social Embodiment," *Pro Ecclesia* 5:2 (1996), 144–160. The theodramatic horizon is generally compatible, I believe, with both Fowl's work and with the kind of realistic-narrative reading of Scripture proposed by Hans Frei and developed ecclesiologically by George A. Lindbeck. See Hans W. Frei, *The Eclipse of Biblical Narrative* (New Haven: Yale University Press, 1975); George A. Lindbeck, "The Story-Shaped Church: Critical Exegesis and Theological Interpretation" in G. Green (ed.), *Scriptural Authority and Narrative Interpretation* (Philadelphia: Fortress Press, 1987), pp. 161–178. For an excellent account and development of Frei's and Lindbeck's interpretive practices, see Gerard Loughlin, *Telling God's Story: Bible, Church and Narrative Theology* (Cambridge: Cambridge University Press, 1996).

41. H. Richard Niebuhr, *Christ and Culture* (New York: Harper and Row, 1951).

ronment by the church, through its transformation by the message of the gospel, to an accommodationist type in which the gospel and its ecclesial embodiment simply constitute the religious aspect of the all-embracing culture. Niebuhr's typology can be interpreted in a dramatic or epic way.[42] He seems, on the epic reading, to advocate the transformationist relation as the best approach because he considers it to be suitable for all circumstances. Within a theodramatic horizon, though, his typology could be used only if it is understood to lay out a range of possible responses on the part of the church to its context, responses that must be decided upon in an ad hoc manner. At one time and place it may be appropriate for the church to try to transform society in its direction; at another it may be better for the church to go its own way in solitude. Since such decisions are never obvious, intraecclesial conflict over them can be expected.

In any event, even if it is interpreted in a dramatic way, Niebuhr's typology has only limited usefulness. It trades on the Troeltschian assumption – one clearly not shared by the premodern theologians examined above – that Christianity is a pure religion, in the sense that it lacks a social ethic of its own and so needs to be embodied in cultures.[43] It thus assumes that Christianity is somehow separable from culture, as if there are two more or less clearly describable entities that can be correlated in different ways. Whether or not one works within a theodramatic horizon, this does not really seem to be the case. The distinctions between Christ and culture, like those between church, non-church and anti-Christ, are very rough-and-ready, for they are abstractions that can only exceptionally be clearly discerned in the concrete. The church and its witness always contains elements of the other two and has done so from the beginning. And within the Western world, at least, the other two contain elements of the church and the gospel. Such abstract distinctions may sometimes be heuristically useful for ecclesiological reflection, but not if they are used as if one can indeed divide up human realities into neat conceptual packages.[44]

42. For a dramatic appropriation of Niebuhr's typology that is thoroughly informed by Scripture, see Walter Brueggemann, "Rethinking Church Models Through Scripture," *Theology Today* 48:2 (1991), 128–138. See also his "'In the Image of God' . . . . Pluralism," *Modern Theology* 11:4 (1995), 455–469.
43. See Stanley Hauerwas, *A Community of Character: Toward a Constructive Christian Social Ethic* (Notre Dame: University of Notre Dame Press, 1981), pp. 36–39; also Arne Rasmusson, *The Church as Polis: From Political Theology to Theological Politics as Exemplified by Jürgen Moltmann and Stanley Hauerwas* (Notre Dame: University of Notre Dame Press, 1995), pp. 234–245.
44. This is a central thesis of Tanner's *Theories of Culture*. The topic is discussed below in some detail in chapter 7.

The primary benefit of the theodramatic horizon is that it enables ecclesiology to aid the church in the performance of two main tasks within the contemporary ecclesiological context. These tasks, we recall, are to witness to its Lord in the world and to help the individual Christian in her task of discipleship. The previous chapter argued that ecclesiology better supports these tasks if it explicitly analyzes the ecclesiological context and the present state of the concrete church, rather than relying on theoretical constructs alone. In bringing the contextualism of practical-prophetic ecclesiology into a theodramatic horizon, the present chapter gives further support to the earlier contention that ecclesiology cannot be done adequately by developing a blueprint or normative ideal. We cannot claim to be able to map out the answers to all major ecclesiological questions in a form that is universally applicable. We cannot imagine what kind of concrete church could respond perfectly to all those future contexts we cannot presently anticipate. Nor can we discern, more than as in a glass darkly, the shape of the eschatological church at the end of the play.

More positively, the theodramatic horizon indicates where ecclesiology may be expanded and modified in order to perform its function better. These modifications will be discussed in some detail later, but a summary of them can be given here. Theological analysis is fundamental and remains the dominant form of discourse, for the church cannot be understood apart from its setting within a trinitarian-structured theology. But since the theodramatic horizon brings all human activity, both religious and non-religious, into the sphere of God's play, all such activity, insofar as it bears in any way upon the church, is patient of ecclesiological reflection. Creation and redemption can hardly be restricted to the sphere of the concrete church. Ecclesiology should therefore extend the parameters of its inquiry into the actions of the Spirit among those outside the church, too, and assess its significance for the concrete identity of the church. For example, ecclesiology may undertake its own theological study of world religions. Some suggestions for approaching such a study are discussed in chapter 5.

Ecclesiology can also be expanded to make greater and more explicit use of diverse critical-analytic tools. Our activity takes place within God's sphere, but it is free and thoroughly human, and should be analyzed as such. The two agencies that constitute human activity within the theodrama cannot be separated, and so cannot be analyzed adequately if treated independently of the other. But neither can human activity be effectively analyzed if it is construed as the more or less distorted human expression of divine will. Both theological reductivism as well as any form of non-theological (e.g., sociological) reductionism are ever-present dangers for ecclesiological reflection. However, the theodramatic horizon suggests the possibility of a expanded form of theological reflection that avoids, on the one hand, splitting the divine and the human into two separate orders (ecclesiological Nestorianism), or, on the other hand, so confusing them that the human is overwhelmed by the divine (ecclesiological Monophysitism). If it works within this horizon, ecclesiology can appropriate those analyses of human behavior developed apart from, and often in conflict with, the church. The church has throughout its history found it necessary to respond to the challenges of philosophical inquiry, even when that philosophy has been thoroughly antagonistic to Christianity. Ecclesiology can do something similar with historical, sociological and cultural inquiry as well, bringing them within the theodramatic horizon. However, this is not at all to suggest that the results of such non-theological, and often anti-theological, analyses be brought into theological inquiry as if they were neutral and normative. An account of how diverse forms of inquiry can engage with one another in the search for truth is the topic of chapter 5 below, and chapter 7 suggests some ways whereby ecclesiology can make fruitful use of history, sociology and cultural analysis.

Ecclesial life takes the form of a grand, never-ending experiment. If we are to play our evolving roles as we should, we should engage in ongoing and self-critical evaluation of our ecclesial thought and action, i.e., practical-prophetic ecclesiology. As a consequence, ecclesiology will find it useful to develop its *own* forms of cultural, social and historical analysis. It may follow Augustine and develop a theologically informed history of our ecclesial response within its various socio-cultural contexts, discerning where it was sinful in the past and where reform is presently necessary. No historical view is final within a theodramatic horizon, of course. Even the narrative descriptions of Israel in the Old Testament required reinterpretation as the church grappled with shifts and reversals in the theodrama and looked back on its past with different concerns in view. Or ecclesiology may follow Thomas Aquinas and develop – in a more postcritical manner, no doubt – careful and detailed analyses of the kind of social practices, beliefs and valuations through which the church presently seeks to witness truthfully to its Lord. Or ecclesiology may follow Calvin, and bring together both the diachronic approach of Augustine and the more synchronic approach of Thomas to focus attention on "individual churches" with their distinctive needs. In every case it will need to modify the premodern approaches to make them suitable for use within the present ecclesiological context, and it will make its construal of that context explicit. These possibilities are explored in chapter 7.

In sum, this chapter has argued that the criteria for assessing an ecclesiological proposal within a theodramatic perspective are different, or better, differently ranked, from those used in modern and epic ecclesiology. All forms of ecclesiology share a concern for coherence with abiding Christian principles. But theodramatic ecclesiology is not governed by the blueprint criteria of completeness, normativity, universal application and systematic coherence. Rather, it is judged by how well it promotes the church's practical coherence with the principle laid down by Paul, that the church boast in the Cross of Jesus Christ, and only in the Cross of Jesus Christ. Its assessment is therefore in terms of how well it fosters the church's truthful witness and its members' discipleship within this particular context, as well as its practical-prophetic force and application within a particular scene of the theodrama. Naturally, its proposals are to be as clear and coherent as possible. So the scope and tools of ecclesiological inquiry should be expanded to include both theological and non-theological analyses of the historical and socio-cultural factors that bear upon the life of the church.

The remainder of the book develops these suggestions from the theodramatic horizon into a set of constructive methodological proposals. At the same time, I make a cumulative argument to the effect that something like a theodramatic horizon is the most fruitful horizon within which to reflect upon the church's concrete identity within ever-shifting ecclesiological contexts. The next two chapters turn to examine and respond to an ecclesiology developed within an alternative horizon, the pluralist. Doing so will require us to formulate some ideas on the question of how the church may make truth claims – essential to its witness and discipleship – within the contemporary ecclesiological context.

4

Pluralist ecclesiology

The previous chapter outlined a theodramatic horizon and noted some of its ecclesiological implications. One task of this and the next two chapters will be to confront the theodramatic horizon with two other horizons within which much modern ecclesiology is currently done, horizons that are more epic than dramatic. There are three main reasons for doing so. The first is to show that the alternatives are comparatively unsuitable for situating practical-prophetic ecclesiological reflection. One of them is internally incoherent and difficult to make consistent with Scripture and the tradition of its interpretation. Both of them foster an epic style that can result in major problems for ecclesiology within the present context. The second reason is to test the theodramatic horizon by showing that it responds as well or better to the challenges and concerns – both theological and non-theological – that have prompted theologians to work within the alternative horizons. The final reason for the confrontation is more constructive, namely to use the challenges and the theodramatic framework together to formulate some of the principles and procedures by which the scope of ecclesiology can be expanded into the concrete.

The following chapters are thus devoted in part to examining the relation between ecclesiology and various ways of understanding the relations between God, the church and the world. It is expedient to divide the various horizons within which most contemporary ecclesiology is done into two main groups. These groups parallel to some extent the ways of construing the relation between Christianity and other religions in contemporary theories of religion and salvation, and so I will use the same labels, which are pluralism and inclusivism. In such discussions a third view, the exclusivist, is usually mentioned, although it is infrequently met with these days. Each label reflects a set of beliefs about the nature and function of religion, especially with regard to truth and salvation.[1] Both of the latter issues, we recall, need to be addressed by any form of practical-prophetic ecclesiology. Some account of the possibility and rationality of religious truth claims is essential to maintaining the church's witness to its Lord who, the church claims, is the way, the truth and the life of all creation. The issue of truth also bears upon the question of salvation and upon the relationship between the church and non-Christian religious bodies.

I will be discussing both pluralism and inclusivism in some detail in due course, but we need a preliminary description of the three positions before we look into their ecclesiological implications. The first position, that of pluralism, is the topic of this and the next chapter. In general, pluralists believe that all the world religions aim at salvation, though each religion describes salvation in such a way that it is incommensurable with any other religion. The pluralist is usually a perspectivalist (following Alasdair MacIntyre's use of the term), in that she believes that it is not possible to make truth claims from within any particular religious system.[2] Religions are non-rational (though not necessarily *ir*rational) perspectives within which the categories of truth and falsity do not function. Consequently one cannot claim that one's own religious system is more truthful or a better way to achieve salvation than any other. Most pluralists couple their perspectivalism with a relativist understanding of religions (again following MacIntyre's use of the term "relativist"). According to the relativist, each religious perspective has its own principles and standards of rationality. Since there is no universal rationality applicable to all religions, each religious perspective is equally incapable of demonstrating the superiority of its truth claims over any other perspective. It therefore becomes largely pointless to argue about their conflicting claims. All religions should be understood as making equally reasonable claims about how to achieve salvation.

Exclusivism is sometimes taken as the contrast position to pluralism, though it has largely died out in its traditional form in the mainline churches. The exclusivist insists that membership in the visible church is necessary for salvation because the church has exclusive access to truth

---

1. The threefold typology is developed in some detail by Gavin D'Costa, *Theology and Religious Pluralism: The Challenge of Other Religions* (Oxford: Blackwell, 1986).
2. For both perspectivalism and rationalism, see Alasdair MacIntyre, *Whose Justice? Which Rationality?* (Notre Dame: University of Notre Dame Press, 1988), p. 352.

and salvation. Other religious bodies lack any (significant) religious knowledge and without it they lack the means to salvation. Exclusivism is therefore not at all perspectivalist with regard to Christianity (or which-ever religion is favored by the exclusivist), though it may well be perspec-tivalist with regard to non-Christian religions. We might say that it is relativistic, in that Christianity and non-Christian religions cannot rationally engage in debate with one another, since only Christianity is (religiously) rational. On such grounds the exclusivist can disregard the claims of other religious bodies.

The third position, that of inclusivism, could be understood as an attempt to mediate between the two previous positions. Inclusivists believe that most religions aim at salvation and that they have some access to religious truth. But they also believe that the Christian description of salvation in and through Jesus Christ surpasses all others and, as a conse-quence, members of other religions achieve salvation in a way that is implicitly Christian. Christianity is superior to all other religions since it has unique access to knowledge of the unique source of truth and salva-tion, Jesus Christ. The doctrines and practices of other religions can there-fore be assessed in the light of Christian claims. Inclusivists thus generally reject both relativist and perspectivalist conceptions of relig-ious beliefs. (I discuss inclusivist ecclesiology in chapter 6.)

These three labels are rather too broad and unclear and so have been subject to some criticism recently.[3] Proponents of any specific type often do not fit the ideal description exactly. My own proposals embrace and reject elements of all three. But whether or not they are adequate as a typology for discussing soteriology or theories or religion, they will do for the purpose here. They provide a convenient set of categories by which to examine the ecclesiological implications of typical horizons within which the relations between God, world and church are considered. We begin in this chapter with a critical analysis and assessment of the plural-ist horizon and then turn to consider the kind of ecclesiological proposals it supports. In the next chapter I will construct a theodramatic ecclesio-logical response to its challenges.

Pluralist theories of religion are themselves somewhat diverse.[4]

3. See S. Mark Heim, *Salvations: Truth and Difference in Religion* (New York: Orbis, 1995), pp. 4f.
4. Heim, *Salvations*, discusses the work of three important pluralists: John Hick, Wilfred C. Smith and Paul Knitter, pp. 13–98. Some idea of the range of views possible within the pluralist horizon can be seen in a collection of essays, edited by John Hick and Paul F. Knitter, *The Myth of Christian Uniqueness: Toward a Pluralistic Theology of Religions* (Maryknoll, NY: Orbis, 1987).

However, to introduce the pluralist horizon prior to examining its ecclesiological implications, we need only look at a representative sample. My account centers on the work of John Hick, referring when appropriate to other pluralists. Hick sets out his position in a number of works, perhaps the best known of which is the expansion of his Gifford Lectures, published as *An Interpretation of Religion*.[5] Hick takes the stance of an external observer, one who stands back from adherence to or bias towards any single tradition. A significant example of this is the way he calls the transcendent "object" of all religions, the "Real," so as to avoid privileging a theistic perspective (IR 9ff.). He believes that the Real is too transcendent and ineffable to be known by us as it is in itself (IR 236ff., 249), and cites passages from the documents of many religions that suggest that they would agree with this contention. The attempts of religions to image the Real are its manifestations within different "streams of human thought-and-experience" (IR 248f.). Because the Real is ineffable, the stories and doctrines of any one religious body must be considered to be mythological rather than reflecting some objective correspondence with the Real as it is in itself.[6] As a consequence, our personal experience of the Real and our thinking about it are always structured by the beliefs and concepts of a particular community (IR 236). That does not mean that our experience cannot be a genuine one, as if it were *merely* a human construct. Hick explicitly rejects non-realist religious views (IR chapter 12). However, he believes that the descriptions of the Real that inform the doctrines of each religious community are relative to that community. Since they are only relative, those of one religious body cannot logically be compared with, or conflict with, those of another. Religions are perspectival in that they are imaginative and mythological constructs by which their adherents seek meaning and organize their lives within what is finally an incomprehensible reality.[7]

Hick does, however, introduce a criterion by which to assess the truthfulness of religious beliefs. The truth of religious claims is of a purely practical kind. They are true insofar as they evoke an "appropriate

5. John Hick, *An Interpretation of Religion: Human Responses to the Transcendent* (New Haven: Yale University Press, 1989). Cited as (IR page). For a detailed analysis of earlier versions of Hick's theory, see Gavin D'Costa, *John Hick's Theology of Religions: A Critical Evaluation* (Lanham, MD: University Press of America, 1987); also Peter B. Clarke and Peter Byrne, *Religion Defined and Explained* (New York: St. Martin's Press, 1993), pp. 79–97.
6. See also Gordon D. Kaufman, *An Essay on Theological Method* (Atlanta: Scholars Press, 1990), p. 44.
7. See Hick, *The Metaphor of God Incarnate: Christology in a Pluralistic Age* (Louisville, KY: Westminster/John Knox Press, 1993), pp. 16off.; also Gordon D. Kaufman, *God, Mystery, Diversity* (Minneapolis: Augsburg Fortress, 1996), pp. 194ff.

dispositional attitude" that orients the individual and her community toward to the Real (IR 248). Their function is thus to promote the "transition of human existence from self-centeredness to Reality-centeredness" (IR 367). Hick calls this function "soteriological," for he believes that there is a common concern for salvation in all the world religions (IR chapter 2). This soteriological criterion serves to distinguish the world religions, which all seek a "transformation of our present existence" by the Real (IR 21f.), from the non-soteriological religions of more "archaic" or "pre-axial" times (IR 32f.). The introduction of a criterion by which to assess the practical effect of religious beliefs is common in pluralist theories. Most reflect a humanist horizon (whether Christian-humanist or not) and are formal enough that they can be applied to all religions and function as the basis for dialogue among them. Paul Knitter, for example, proposes the criterion of "eco-human well-being,"[8] while Gordon Kaufman uses humanization and modernization as practical criteria, fleshed out by a normative anthropology.[9] All insist that the beliefs and practices of particular religions should be revised so as to accord with their norm.[10]

Before examining an ecclesiology worked out within this horizon, it is worth noting just two of the more significant differences between Hick's theory and the theodramatic horizon. First, in marked contrast to Balthasar's horizon, Hick's pluralism is a theoretical formulation of a horizon within which many people live today. We noted in chapter 1 how prevalent is the perspectivalist and relativistic view of religious truth. So it is likely that many would find Hick's philosophy of religion quite congenial and his theory can be understood as an attempt to respond to significant cultural aspects of the contemporary ecclesiological context. Questions then arise as to whether or not his particular kind of response is appropriate, whether it provides a convincing account of religious bodies, and whether it is suitable for a Christian theologian, especially one who uses it to ground his reflection upon the church.

Second, Hick's clearly post-Kantian horizon is rather more epic than dramatic. Dramatic or conflictual interaction between religions is undermined by his denial of the possibility of the Real revealing itself in

---

8. Paul F. Knitter, *One Earth, Many Religions: Multifaith Dialogue and Global Responsibility* (Maryknoll, NY: Orbis, 1995), pp. 118ff.

9. Kaufman's normative account of what it is to be human is developed in chs. 10–13 of his *In Face of Mystery: A Constructive Theology* (Cambridge, MA: Harvard University Press, 1993), pp. 125–193. See also Knitter, *One Earth*, pp. 107f.

10. See Kaufman, *God, Mystery, Diversity*, pp. 24ff. Kaufman attacks a Buddhist theology on the same grounds on pp. 157–182.

any way that could ground genuine conflict between objective truth claims. Instead, the Real discloses itself in a thoroughly immanent way, through the imaginative constructs of the human quest for meaning. There can be no claim about the Real, then, that could provide critical leverage against any particular human mediation of the Real by standing over against that mediation. There appear to be some significant historical judgments lying behind these assertions about religious language, in Hick's work and in that of other pluralists. He rightly notes the wars and oppressions that have usually accompanied assertions of one religious body's beliefs over against those of another, or over against a minority within itself. Both violent and more subtle confrontations have been exacerbated, moreover, by the connection usually made between salvation and claims to knowledge of *the* truth about the Real (IR 371f.).[11] The connection has been used to warrant coercion, in part because knowing the truth that leads to salvation can be considered as something of ultimate significance, more so than freedom or life itself. The connection has also supported claims made by religious bodies like the Christian church that it is superior in some salvifically significant way to all other religious bodies, again leading to violence or ideologically supported oppression. These historical issues are weighty, indeed, for they bear directly upon the sinfulness of the church and the truthfulness of its witness. Any attempt to recover a theodramatic horizon for ecclesiology will have to respond adequately to such concerns. Clearly, one part of that response must be to find ways by which the religions can engage in peaceful co-existence and dialogue.

How, then, does a pluralist horizon bear upon ecclesiology? As yet there are few explicitly pluralist ecclesiologies; though many pluralists make some remarks about the church, most of these do not go beyond a dozen pages or so. One of the most well-developed pluralist ecclesiologies is Peter Hodgson's *Revisioning The Church: Ecclesial Freedom in the New Paradigm,* a book we looked very briefly at in chapter 2 above.[12] We will take this as our example, although Hodgson makes little or no explicit reference to Hick's theory and it may be that he would disagree with some aspects of it. Nevertheless, his book reflects a sufficiently similar horizon for use here as an instance of pluralist ecclesiology.[13]

11. See also Kaufman, *In Face of Mystery*, pp. 378–381.
12. Peter C. Hodgson, *Revisioning the Church: Ecclesial Freedom in the New Paradigm* (Philadelphia: Fortress, 1988). Cited in the text as (RC page).
13. Hodgson's pluralism seems to be somewhat less Kantian than Hick's, and more Hegelian. I will omit consideration of those few passages in which Hodgson writes more like an inclusivist.

Hodgson is explicitly committed to pluralism, contending that the inclusivist position on truth claims and salvation is an untenable "halfway house" (RC 94). The problem with inclusivism is that it is "parochial" (RC 102), for it makes claims about the cognitive and soteriological superiority of one religion, i.e., Christianity, over all others. This, he believes, is wrong. Hodgson justifies his criticism within the terms of his revisionist-correlationist view of the relation between church and world. On this view, the correct response to an ecclesiological context is for the Christian community to revise its doctrines to accord with cultural beliefs. He finds pluralism to be "intellectually honest" (RC 94) because it is the only one that can be correlated with the "new cultural paradigm." Within this paradigm, the "only consistent and intellectually defensible position" is "that the great world religions have equally valid claims and that each is culturally relative" (RC 94). Religious truth claims are therefore not of universal import, but apply only intrasystemically: "what is true for us is not truth for all" (RC 95). Hence there can be no genuine disagreement between religions since a particular religion's claims have no objective force outside that religion. Incommensurable and of equal worth, they cannot falsify one another nor can one set be reasonably considered as superior to another.

Hodgson believes that the new cultural paradigm, and the pluralist view to which it gives rise, together require "a new theological paradigm, a revisioning of the entire theological agenda" (RC 18). His aim in the book under discussion is to provide an ecclesial self-understanding appropriate for the new paradigm. The church must recognize that it is a historical as well as a spiritual entity. Because it is situated within the world, it is necessary to reject the New Testament notion of salvation history and apocalypticism in which the church plays a special role (RC 35). At the same time, though, other parts of the New Testament reveal a way of being church that is both part of the original Christian self-understanding as well as more congenial to the new paradigm. Here Hodgson makes use of an erstwhile common liberal-Protestant narrative interpretation of the early church. According to his version, "originally" the church was an "ecclesia of freedom", i.e., a "nonprovincial, nonexclusionary, nonhierarchical, noncultic community" engaged in "world-transforming praxis" (RC 23f.). Soon however, the community deviated from this, its true form, to develop a concrete identity that displayed the characteristics Hodgson rejects: cult, hierarchy, provincialism, exclusiveness and sacerdotalism, and so it became more like "religious communities in general" (RC 24).

How should we conceive of the relation between the church-as-it-should-be and non-Christian religious bodies? Hodgson revises ecclesiology so as to accord with the new criterion or paradigm by means of a twofold construal of the church's ontological structure. His version, however, has two stages. In the first, the visible church is the more or less distorted expression of its essence, the ecclesia of freedom. The ecclesia was formed by a combination of historical factors and the disciples' experience of Jesus (RC 22f.) and can be described by means of images and concepts such as Body of Christ and koinonia (RC 28ff.). It is best defined as "a transfigured mode of human community, an image of the realm and rule of God embodied in a diversity of historical churches" (RC 103). These essential features set the ecclesia "apart from other religious communities as a unique form of redemptive existence" (RC 27).

What might have been an inclusivist assertion becomes pluralist by means of a second use of the twofold construal. The ecclesia is itself a manifestation of a prior, universal salvific reality which is its source and essence.[14] The true form of the church (ecclesia), that which governs its distinctive features, is a "spiritual-historical sign, sacrament, and fore-taste of a transcendent, divinely given transfigurative ideal", namely the Kingdom of God, the "basileia of freedom" (RC 23). The basileia is expressed or imaged in ways other than ecclesia by the distinctive forms of the world religions (RC 60, 63). Hence the basileia can be said to take a plurality of "religiocultural shapes" (RC 106). The church is thus a unique form of the basileia, insofar as it is a manifestation of ecclesia, which is unique. But it is not superior to other forms, since basileia can be imaged as well in other religious bodies, their "*equally* valid claims" (RC 94, my emphasis) arising out of the *same* source. The major religious bodies are thus all on a par as distinctive yet partial and inadequate productions and images of the same reality, the basileia. The Christian church, as the expression of ecclesia, is only one version of that universally accessible salvific reality. Hodgson notes one obvious implication: all missionary work directed at members of other religions should be abandoned (RC 102).

The first question to be posed to Hodgson's ecclesiology is whether or not it is an adequate response to the present ecclesiological context. Clearly Hodgson means to situate his theology of the church within the context of modern culture. Like Hick's, Hodgson's own account of

14. See also Hick, *The Metaphor*, p. 140.

salvation and religious truth conforms to what many in our society are thinking, and in a way that would be difficult to surpass. By his double use of the twofold construal he can postulate a reality prior to the church that unifies all major religions. Thereby Hodgson solves the problem of salvation and truth outside the church with considerable ease and aplomb. The difficulties over rival religions' truth claims and the distinctive ways of life they warrant are resolved by adopting a version of religious relativism and perspectivalism that conforms to many contemporary cultural presuppositions. Moreover, his emphasis upon the anti-ideological and practical consequences of his view of the church is arguably in line with some of the contemporary theological developments. And those who might fear the entry of the church into the public sphere will be relieved to find that the values Hodgson believes the church to enshrine are very similar to those of American culture anyway, and appear to run directly counter to any past form of ideological misuse of Christianity. Thus his ecclesiology provides us with a view of the church that many in our culture would find acceptable.

Yet the price of conformity to the new paradigm for the church's self-understanding will strike some Christians as being too high. Hodgson advocates far-reaching institutional, liturgical and pastoral changes in the church's concrete identity. His arguments for these changes could be challenged on a number of fronts. Biblical scholars now think of the history of the early church as being far more complex and variegated than is suggested by the liberal-Protestant narrative of the early church's decline into institutionalism.[15] And while the Roman tradition, for example, has at times erred quite egregiously in overemphasizing the hierarchical structure of the church, there are more nuanced versions of hierarchy that may well be acceptable, especially for those in the Roman tradition for whom some kind of hierarchy is a requirement of dogma. The cult, too, has indeed been the subject of abuses, yet there are ways of understanding eucharistic practice that might well be more convincing to Orthodox, Roman and many Protestant Christians than those Hodgson proposes.

We can leave these issues aside, though, to focus on what is perhaps Hodgson's most fundamental pluralist-ecclesiological move, namely his unifying and epic version of the twofold construal. It is this which makes possible his relativization of the church to the same status as that of other

---

15. See, e.g., N. T. Wright, *The New Testament and the People of God* (Minneapolis: Fortress Press, 1992), pp. 452f.

religious communities with regard to truth and salvation. The church is certainly unique concretely, but at its deepest core, at that spiritual place which matters ultimately, it is identical to the world-religious bodies. For the latter are also concretely unique expressions of the same thing, namely the basileia of freedom. Furthermore, they are as capable of fostering the cardinal values of the basileia as is the church. The distinctiveness of the church's concrete identity is thus finally of little real significance. It is "but one of several religiocultural shapes assumed by what Christians call the kingdom of God but what other religions give other names" (RC 106).

This central thesis of pluralist ecclesiology requires a revision of Christology. The particular person, Jesus, is indeed responsible for the unique shape of the religious body, the ecclesia of freedom, that follows him (RC 22f.). But according to Hodgson, Jesus' significance for that body lies less in what is distinctive about his person and work than in the way he made possible for his disciples the experience of the basileia of freedom. Jesus is a symbol whose function is to prompt us to work for the goods of the basileia of freedom, namely "liberation, justice and truth" (RC 95). Something like that same experience – albeit mediated in a plurality of ways – is available to members of other religious bodies founded by other religious leaders (RC 95). Presumably it prompts them, too, to work for the same goods. In consequence, it is difficult not to think that, for Hodgson, Jesus' significance has become only relative, lying primarily in bringing to expression what can be known and is available elsewhere, perhaps especially in modern liberal societies influenced by the new paradigm.[16]

Hodgson's correlation of ecclesiology with pervasive cultural assumptions about religious claims and bodies has led him, on my reading, to deny some key elements of the church's traditional self-understanding. That self-understanding, we recall, includes the conviction that in and through the Holy Spirit, the Christian community has been given the task of proclaiming and following Jesus Christ. The church does so because it believes that Jesus is the true and good news about the world and its relation to the Father. He is the good news because God has redeemed us and all his creation through his Cross and Resurrection. He is ultimately the sole way to the Father, for it is through him and the

16. Similar Christological revisionism can be found, e.g., in Knitter, *Jesus and the Other Names: Christian Mission and Global Responsibility* (Maryknoll, NY: Orbis, 1996), pp. 97f.; Knitter, *One Earth*, p. 35; Kaufman, *God, Mystery, Diversity*, pp. 116ff.; Hick, *The Metaphor*, pp. 112ff.

activity of the Spirit that we may come to live in communion with the Father. We recall that these beliefs do not involve the claim that the church *possesses* the truth; one cannot possess a person. The claim to ecclesial superiority is only derivatively a claim about itself. While penultimate truths are to be found in all kinds of places, the ultimate truth about the Real is *there*, in the person and work of Jesus Christ; it is nowhere else, not even in the (pilgrim) church. The church is superior only when and insofar as it acknowledges and follows Jesus as the center of all truth. This is something it rather frequently and variously fails to do, thereby becoming markedly *inferior* to other bodies. But if, through the Spirit, we do acknowledge this in true discipleship we are given, so the Christian claims, the basis for a way of life that is preferable to all others.

It must be confessed that this self-understanding has often been recast in a direction that has come close to, indeed at times has fallen over into, hubris and idolatry. Too often the church has seen itself as possessing the truth, as knowing about God in ways that are not always dependent upon God's self-gift. Often, too, these claims have been made to serve ideologically in order to support brutal and oppressive regimes, both ecclesiastical and secular. So Hodgson is quite right to try to do something about their misuse. But his rejection of the distinctive, Christological basis for the beliefs and practices of the Christian church seems to be throwing out the baby with the bathwater. His move makes it difficult to respond to urgent pastoral questions arising within the present ecclesiological context, such as: What is the point of belonging to the church? Why should I give myself over unconditionally to Christian discipleship? Why should I glory solely in the Cross of Jesus Christ? To such questions, Hodgson says that it is enough to "maintain a fundamental loyalty to a relative religion, knowing that what is truth for us is not truth for all" (RC 95). The implication seems to be that, after all, we all agree about what *really* matters, namely the basileia of freedom.

But this response is unconvincing. It is not a religious worldview or even the church that is finally what is at stake for Christians. Christians are faithful to the triune God whose faithfulness is revealed in Jesus Christ through the Holy Spirit. Jesus' revelatory significance is *nonpareil* as a consequence of what he has done and what has been done through him. It is because of his Cross and Resurrection that Christians believe him to be the revelation of the source and summit of all values, so that putting anything else before him, such a worldview or a religious body, would be idolatry. We must indeed acknowledge that non-Christians do not think of Jesus in anything like this way and, furthermore, that Christians have often misused their religious beliefs in horrific ways. Yet neither fact has traditionally been understood as requiring the church either to relativize Jesus' ultimate revelatory and salvific status, nor to downgrade the force of its claims about him. The question then arises as to whether the pluralist case is strong enough to make such revisionist moves obligatory.

Before I address that question, however, let us take a step back from the pluralist challenge for a moment and describe religious bodies and their interrelations from another, less theory-laden angle that situates them within a more dramatic horizon, although one that is not specifically Christian.[17] From the point of view of one who lives within a religious body, it is not unreasonable to hold that religious bodies are different from one another to the extent that, concretely at least, each is unique. Certainly they share many things, but the common elements are positioned within different complexes, different webs of belief and practice which are themselves structured according to principles and beliefs that include significant elements they do *not* share.[18] Consequently, any common elements may be more diverse than may first appear. Accepting this account of religious bodies – an account rather more radically pluralist than the pluralist theory itself – does not depend upon any particular set of religious beliefs or a theory of religion. It only requires that one acknowledge that the various religions' doctrines and practices – not all of them, perhaps, but at least the organizing and normative ones – are really distinct from one another, rather than variegated expressions of what is fundamentally identical. And this is, after all, usually what members of diverse religious bodies have claimed. They act as if the differences matter, so much so that they have been willing to suffer to preserve those claims against those who deny them. Unfortunately, too, they have sometimes inflicted suffering upon others for the same reason.

The diversity to be found in the concrete identities of the various religious bodies has to do with the goals and tasks each counts as ultimate. The Buddhist community, for example, is distinctive in its concern to help its

17. For this alternative angle I rely upon J. A. DiNoia, O.P., *The Diversity of Religions: A Christian Perspective* (Washington: Catholic University of America Press, 1992); and Heim, *Salvations*; also William A. Christian, Sr., *Doctrines of Religious Communities: A Philosophical Study* (New Haven: Yale University Press, 1987). The stance taken here might be termed an "agnostic" one; see Peter B. Clarke and Peter Byrne, *Religion Defined*, esp. pp. viii and 204ff.; the category is discussed below in chapter 7.
18. See also Kaufman, *In Face of Mystery*, p. 436.

members achieve Nirvana, the goal unique to the Buddhist. This goal is formulated according to its own particular set of beliefs about the Real, knowledge gained by Buddha's Enlightenment. And similar things can be said of Islam and Judaism as well as Christianity and other religions. These religious bodies may or may not be wrong in what they claim to know about the Real, partially or even *in toto*, but whether they are right or wrong, they do seem to be unique and do seem to consider themselves to be engaged in quite distinctive ways of life and goals. They do not, that is, seem to be aiming at the same goal or, to use the Christian term (which is part of the problem), they do not have the same concept of salvation.

Furthermore, the goal of each religion, and the doctrines and institutions and practices that are developed in conformity with that goal, depend in large part upon belief in the reality of what they claim. It would be a little strange, for example, for a Buddhist to devote her whole life to the pursuit of Nirvana if she does not believe that such an experience or state can really be attained. Similarly, it would be odd for an Orthodox Jew to devote his life to Torah-observance while believing that the Torah is not in some real way a gift from God, or for a Muslim to submit to the will of Allah if she thought the Qur'ān was simply a human construct. While many religious people would acknowledge the mystery and incomprehensibility of whatever they consider to be the Real, they also would want to maintain that what they believe is a true way of describing things, more or less; or better perhaps, that it reflects more adequately than any other such descriptions the way things really are between ourselves and the Real.

If such a belief is indeed a genuine truth claim, then it seems reasonable to include as part of the claim a belief in its universal applicability, that it is not merely "true for us." This does not necessarily mean that every religious body believes everyone else should be aiming for the same goals or adopting the same way of life as it does. Orthodox Jews, for example, might not think it appropriate for non-Jews to live the way they do, but they do believe they know why it is inappropriate. They may also believe that those who do not live in a similar way, or who cannot do so because of their Gentile status, are less fortunate in that respect than they are. Thus many religious people would be likely to say, if pushed, that their beliefs, and the practices and institutions which embody and foster them, are in some genuine way superior to all others. This would apply even to adherents of Hinduism, a way of life that is arguably tolerant of greater diversity than Christianity and which, therefore, might find the Christian emphasis upon right belief misguided. Such toleration, however, might reasonably issue in a claim for the superiority of Hinduism in that its thinking about tolerance is better – more truthful – than that of Christianity because it corresponds more closely with the way the Real really is.

The beliefs, practices and valuations of each particular religious body are orientated to whatever it takes to be of ultimate significance. Buddhists, for example, have traditionally believed that achieving Nirvana is the supreme goal in life. Their claim applies to all people, since it would be odd for a Buddhist to say, for example, that Nirvana is a goal only for people who live within certain cultures. Earlier missionary activity by Buddhists under King Ashoka seems to argue against merely relative claims, too.[19] Buddhists seem to contend that if everyone understood reality well enough they would all see that Nirvana should be their goal too, rather than, for example, participation in the life of the triune God.[20] Many Buddhists, including Buddha himself according to traditional sources, have also contended that the Eightfold Way discovered by Buddha, and enshrined particularly in the Buddhadharma, is the only way to achieve Nirvana.[21] Although Buddhism has nothing like an ecclesiology, a functionally equivalent doctrine about the superiority of the Buddhist community, especially the Sangha,[22] could reasonably be extrapolated from these claims, as long as it is not pushed in a Christian direction. Thus one could say that the communal tradition that grew up in response to Buddha's teaching is the best means to achieve Nirvana. Hence the Buddhist communities are superior to all others in that the best thing (Nirvana) can be achieved best (and perhaps only) through them.

Similar observations can be made with regard to the communities of Muslims and Jews and members of other world religions, perhaps of all religious bodies. Each seems to believe and to act (though they, of course, must speak for themselves) in ways that suggest that they make it possible for their members to learn something vitally important about the Real, something that members of other religious bodies cannot know, or

19. See Heinz Bechert, "The Buddhist Community and Its Earlier History" in Hans Küng, et al., *Christianity and the World Religions: Paths of Dialogue with Islam, Hinduism and Buddhism* (New York: Doubleday, 1986), p. 335.
20. See the discussion of Zen Buddhist writers in Hendrik M. Vroom, *No Other Gods: Christian Belief in Dialogue with Buddhism, Hinduism, and Islam*, trans. Lucy Jansen (Grand Rapids: Eerdmans, 1996), pp. 13–42.
21. See the quotation from the Dalai Lama in Heim, *Salvations*, p. 151. Also DiNoia, *Diversity of Religions*, p. 5.   22. Bechert, "Buddhist Community," pp. 329–331.

cannot know as well. Furthermore, even though what they know is available only through a particular tradition, it is not relative to a particular cultural situation but has universal significance. That knowledge consists not only of right beliefs but of right behavior, too; *agenda* as well as *credenda*.[23] These are embodied concretely in the life of the religious body, thereby determining its present identity and what it seeks to become. In light of its particular set of beliefs about the Real each religious body develops distinctive practices and institutions that render it, so it may reasonably claim, the best, most truthful, communal response to the Real.

Distinctiveness and disagreement among religious bodies regarding their ultimate goals does not mean that they must disagree over everything. It is possible for members of one religion to accept the idea that members of other religions are making objective truth claims, and that they have distinct goals. And this acceptance of their status does not necessarily require the denial of the claims of the value of the goal. Thus a Christian can easily accept that there may indeed be an experience of something that can be called Nirvana, and that the only way to achieve this is through giving oneself over to the Buddhadharma and learning the practices taught in Buddhist communities. Moreover, the Christian can admit that, when it comes to achieving Nirvana, the Buddhist religious body is superior in its way of life to the church, since the latter, of course, does not have the same goal and has not developed suitable practices toward it. The Christian may also think that some of the practices of Buddhism that lead towards Nirvana could be usefully adopted within Christianity. That is, she may judge that some of the Buddhist practices are superior to their equivalents within Christianity. Similarly, the Buddhist might think that the Christian church offers superior ways to follow Jesus Christ than do its own religious practices. Moreover, a Buddhist might conceivably think that there are some aspects of Christianity that would be worth further investigation.

Yet although each religious body may share many penultimate goals and convictions with other bodies, its ultimate goal is distinctive and normative. To postulate a common goal or a deep-spiritual identity among all such bodies runs counter to what seems to be the genuine diversity of their concrete identities as each aids its members in achieving its goal. Every religious body's beliefs and practices differ and conflict in

23. Christian, *Doctrines of Religious Communities*, p. 6.

significant areas (though no doubt not in all) with those of other bodies.
And membership of any one body will likely involve, however implicitly
held, the belief that it is superior to all other religious bodies, because it is
orientated towards ultimate truth.

This non-theological and low-level account of religious bodies is compatible, at least, with a Christian theodramatic horizon. It is also considerably more pluralist than Hodgson's account. His double use of the
twofold construal undermines genuine plurality even though, like other
pluralists, he affirms the diversity of religious bodies.[24] The key difference between the pluralist view and the more dramatic one just outlined
is that the former rules out the diversity of ultimate religious goals. As a
consequence, the significance of the diversity of religious bodies' concrete
identities is considerably reduced. It may be that someone advocating
something like Hodgson's or Hick's position would accept, in spite of its
dangerous wording, the notion that the Buddhist community is indeed
generally superior to all others in helping its members to achieve Nirvana,
or the Jewish community in helping its members follow the Torah. But
such superiority could be only of a relatively insignificant kind. The particularities of the way of life that foster the achievement of Nirvana, like
those which foster the attainment of Christian salvation, are of value for
pluralists insofar as they enable Buddhists and Christians to achieve the
transformation of their existence towards some *universal* goal that lies
beyond (or deep within) the particularities and goals of each body. We recall
that for Hodgson the church shares with other religious bodies the goal of
bringing about the community of freedom and equality. For Hick, the
goal of all religious bodies is, or should be, Reality-centeredness. For
Gordon Kaufman the goal is humanization; for Knitter, eco-human well-
being. These laudable aims function as criteria by which to assess the concrete identities of all religious bodies, all of which are to serve the same
ultimate goal.[25] The ecclesiological consequence of imposing such external and universal criteria upon religious bodies is that their concrete identities are reduced to secondary and dispensable status. Any particular
belief or practice that conflicts with the universal norm, or which
obstructs the movement towards the universal goal, must be forfeited.

Thus, as they themselves acknowledge, the pluralist view of the
religions is incompatible with the more radically pluralist self-

24. Gordon Kaufman's affirmation of genuine diversity is expressed in his rejection of
Hick's "utterly monolithic" account of religion; see *God, Mystery, Diversity*, p. 225. Knitter
responds to criticisms on this issue in, e.g., *One Earth*, pp. 38ff.
25. See Hick, IR Part Five, esp. pp. 368ff.

considered or the positivist reading.

understandings of the religious bodies themselves. It is also incompatible with the traditional understanding of the church's task, which I have described as witnessing to Jesus Christ and of helping its members follow him in discipleship, in such a way that we boast only in him and what he has done for us all. For the concrete church, the issue turns upon the revisionist Christology. We have seen how Hodgson revises Christology and the traditional self-understanding of the church. And Kaufman, who is comparatively more open to plurality than Hick, is equally forthright in requiring religious bodies to reconstruct their symbol systems so that they accord with the criteria of pluralism.[26] To be sure, they retain the central significance of the symbol of Jesus Christ for Christianity. However, Jesus' significance is no longer understood primarily in terms of the Scriptural witness to him and the church's tradition of interpretation of that witness. Rather, it is now understood in terms of the universal norm which, in turn, is developed according to a liberal anthropology or humanist vision worked out more or less in isolation from Scripture. Discipleship must be embodied differently, for it is no longer the person and work of Jesus Christ that governs the concrete identity of the church, but Jesus as the symbol of the ultimate norm.

The consequent modifications of the church's concrete identity would be severe; its worship, for instance. Christians offer worship to the Son because it is in and through his person and work that the Spirit draws us to the Father. We give praise and thanksgiving to God because Jesus Christ saves the world which cannot save itself. But such practices do not accord with the pluralist criterion, for Jesus cannot be the sole savior. Rather, there are many such saviors who, moreover, save the world not by their actions but by providing humanity with the visions and symbols necessary for the humanizing and ecological activity by which *we* save the world.[27] The church's praise and thanksgiving cannot be offered to God, then, in response to the Good News of salvation in Jesus Christ. Instead, worship becomes part of our effort to save ourselves, where "save" means to preserve our planet and our species in freedom and harmony. The Eucharist becomes something other than a participation in, or remembrance of, the redemptive suffering of the Son of God. Like prayer more generally, it becomes a form of self-motivation.[28]

---

26. Kaufman, *God, Mystery, Diversity,* pp. 39, 214. See also Knitter, *One Earth,* pp. 124ff.
27. See Hodgson, RC 95; Knitter, *Jesus,* p. 74; Hick, *The Metaphor,* pp. 27, 36; Kaufman, *God, Mystery, Diversity,* p. 111, *In Face of Mystery,* p. 84, 92.
28. See Paul D. Molnar, "Myth and Reality: Analysis and Critique of Gordon Kaufman and Sallie McFague on God, Christ, and Salvation," unpub. manuscript.

In view of the drastic consequences for the church (as well, presumably, for other religious bodies), the question arises as to whether pluralist theories of religion and religious bodies are in fact correct. This is a legitimate question, for there is no mere perspectivalism here; pluralists make it quite clear that views contrary to their own in these matters are wrong. The strongest reason for accepting a pluralist theory would be if it were the only rational one, if indeed the church's traditional self-understanding, as well as the self-understanding of other religious bodies, are all so plainly irrational that they must change if they are not to be naively and dangerously "parochial." To continue to maintain the religions' traditional self-understanding in such a case would be to fall into a rigid and defensive traditionalism; it would be both logically and morally wrong. The remainder of this chapter makes the case that the pluralist view is, in fact, far too weakly supported to require such a revision. It is incoherent and, despite the excellent intentions of its proponents, it is at least as much of a threat to human relations as the more usual and more genuinely pluralist way of viewing the religions. And to the extent that an ecclesiology adopts such a horizon it too will be incoherent and will render the church's concrete identity susceptible to ideological distortion.

We can approach the question from a consideration of Hick's theory. We saw how his version of pluralism makes a number of universally applicable claims of its own, including some about religious language. He shares the broadly agnostic view of pluralism, and warrants it by asserting that the Real is too ineffable for our concepts to describe it. The backing for that warrant in turn is that the ineffable nature of the Real is something about which all the religions agree. But do they? Premodern Christian theology does not exactly disagree, and Hick is able to cite passages from the Fathers, Augustine, Thomas and some of the mystics that support his contention (IR 238). William Placher, too, has recently discussed in some detail the ways in which Thomas Aquinas, John Calvin and Martin Luther each rule out linguistic hubris.[29] But Placher also shows that although these theologians insist on the incomprehensibility and mysteriousness of God, they also insist that genuine opposition among doctrines about the Real is possible such that one view may be true while another may be wrong or grossly inadequate. Furthermore, opposition among doctrines is possible not only within a particular religion, but

---

29. William C. Placher, *The Domestication of Transcendence: How Modern Thinking about God Went Wrong* (Louisville, KY: Westminster/John Knox Press, 1996), pp. 21–68.

between different religions.[30] Thomas and Luther would consider a doctrine of another religious community to be wrong that involved the belief that God is nonexistent (as Theravada Buddhism and Marxism seem to claim),[31] or that there are many gods (as Hinduism), or that God is simply an impersonal force with whom one could not communicate (as some forms of Deism). These Christian theologians would also agree that what is revealed in Jesus Christ is unique and unsurpassable, and that as a consequence all other purported revelations of the Real are drastically relativized. In this they would find themselves in some disagreement with the Islamic community over the revelatory status of the Qur'ān, and with Judaism over the status of the Torah. It is likely, too, that representative theologians from these other religions would make similarly conflicting claims.

This suggests that Hick's beliefs about religious language are supported less by an induction from religious bodies' own views than by an *a priori* theory of religion. Hick, like other pluralists, relies upon beliefs that function axiomatically within a post-Kantian philosophical tradition often called liberalism.[32] Among the tenets of liberalism are the following: Tradition-free knowledge is preferred to that which is accessible only from within a tradition. The former is rational because it is universally applicable, the latter is distorted by parochial prejudices and is thus irrational and, to the extent that it disagrees with tradition-free knowledge, wrong or irrelevant. The practical and humanizing consequences of religious beliefs for society and morality are valued over their doctrinal and community-forming aspects. Religious beliefs are true only insofar as they lead to appropriate practical consequences. And it is assumed that diverse ways of life can be adequately comprehended and assessed in terms of a universal humanistic norm.

Most of those who concern themselves about such matters, including many liberals, now acknowledge that all inquiry is guided by sets of assumptions and beliefs peculiar to a given tradition of inquiry.[33] Moreover, it is generally acknowledged that such traditions are not grounded

30. William A. Christian, Sr., *Doctrines of Religious Communities*; and Paul J. Griffiths, *An Apology for Apologetics: A Study in the Logic of Interreligious Dialogue* (Maryknoll, NY: Orbis, 1991).
31. Marxism is seen by Hick as a post-axial, soteriological quasi-religion; see IR 5, 306.
32. See, e.g., chapter one of Kaufman, *God, Mystery, Diversity.*
33. See, e.g., Alasdair MacIntyre, *Three Rival Versions of Moral Enquiry: Encyclopedia, Genealogy, and Tradition* (Notre Dame: University of Notre Dame Press, 1990); Jeffrey Stout, *Ethics After Babel: The Languages of Morals and Their Discontents* (Boston: Beacon Press, 1988); Richard Rorty, *Contingency, Irony, and Solidarity* (Cambridge: Cambridge University Press, 1989), esp. pp. 44ff.

upon a foundation that is common to them all, or that is independent of them, or normative for all of them. Rather each is grounded in a particular group of people who have been socialized more or less effectively into adopting that tradition as the means by which to live and argue about how to live. The traditioned nature of inquiry, it is sometimes said, goes all the way down. While there may be many common elements among the way people live, each tradition organizes these into a particular configuration in terms of which its adherents organize their lives and situate themselves vis-à-vis members of other traditions.

The pluralists' claims regarding the truth status of religious language reflect neither a generalization from the religions themselves nor a tradition-free perspective, but are formulated from within a particular tradition. The community of those who adhere to this tradition are perhaps to be found within the modern, Western university.[34] One of the axiomatic beliefs of pluralism, however, is that the particular doctrines of religious communities cannot have universal application and, as a consequence, they cannot make a claim for superiority. The problem is that they are insufficiently "impartial" (Hick, IR 2) or too "parochial" (Hodgson) because they are made according to the principles and convictions of a particular tradition. In making this restriction, the theory evidently claims to know something about the nature of religion – the status of its language, the shared goals – that is true for all religions. Thus it claims in effect to have an understanding of the religions that is superior to that which is possible from within a particular religious tradition.[35] This claim would likely appear to be irrational to many members of religious bodies. A Muslim, for example, might well be baffled by the idea that one can come to a superior knowledge of how to submit to the will of Allah apart from the Qur'ān. Yet that seems to be the pluralist claim.

The greater difficulty is that the pluralist claims are universal and religious, yet made on the basis of beliefs found within a particular tradition. It is therefore hard not to understand the pluralists to be doing something identical to what they rule out when done by others. That is, they look very much as though they are making universal, non-relativistic *religious* claims from within a particular tradition. To do this is not wrong in itself; it is what traditional religious people do all the time. The problem, of course, is that the pluralist theory denies the rationality of making such claims. As Kaufman contends: "There is no room for

34. See Kaufman, *God, Mystery, Diversity*, pp. 204ff.; MacIntyre, *Three Rival Versions*, pp. 216ff.
35. See Hick, IR 6.

parochial preference for one's own tradition or community or one's own familiar values and ways of thinking."[36] According to their own arguments, their claims about, say, the metaphorical status of religious language and the goal of all religions, are parochial. For they want to assert such views over against other views on these matters as non-perspectival and non-relativist claims, and they seem to assume (naively, on their own view) that they can rationally do so.

As a *religious* perspective that asserts that all other religious perspectives that disagree with its central beliefs are simply relativistic, the pluralist theory moves away from genuine pluralism toward an almost exclusivist position. They rightly stress the need to replace violent confrontation among the religions with peaceful dialogue. They take the moral high ground, advocating tolerance and humanity, eager to listen to others. There is no reason at all to doubt the sincerity of such rhetoric. But the terms of dialogue are set by them, according to liberal humanist beliefs, and not by religious bodies themselves. Any challenge from more traditional religious bodies on such matters is ruled out not only as wrong, but as irrational. Anyone who does not accept the liberal conditions for dialogue cannot be taken seriously. And all such dialogue is to serve the universal goal of all religions, rather than the diverse goals of each religious body.[37] Their rhetoric thus sets up a falsely exclusive alternative: one can either adopt their beliefs about religion, or one maintains a rigid, parochial and primitive fundamentalism. Any disagreement from more traditional religious bodies on these matters is ruled out not only as wrong, but as irrational: anyone who does not think as they do about these matters cannot be taken seriously. As such, the pluralist horizon destroys rather than affirms difference and otherness. Rather than fostering religious bodies with diverse concrete identities, it subsumes them into its Procrustean bed, ruling out of consideration any beliefs and practices that conflict with its own.[38]

But perhaps pluralists are correct in asserting that this is indeed the way it must be. To fail to adopt their position would be to threaten what is now a global society with the likelihood of violence consequent upon religious conflict. Theirs is evidently a speculative assertion, but one that is not entirely unreasonable, given the history of religions. We can,

36. Kaufman, *God, Mystery, Diversity*, p. 10.   37. See Knitter, *One Earth*, p. 133; *Jesus*, p. 62.
38. A narrative of the movement from diversity to unity as humanity overcomes "ignorance" and "doctrinal obstructions" can be found in Wilfred Cantwell Smith, *Towards a World Theology: Faith and the Comparative History of Religion* (Philadelphia: Westminster, 1981), pp. 3–20.

however, take a turn at speculating for a moment on what might happen if the pluralist view were to become generally accepted by society. The loss of significant distinctiveness and of the possibility of superiority would make it more difficult for any religious body to make a reasonable case that one should join it rather than another body. Some might then ask: Would it not be better for people like us Christians to abandon our membership in the church altogether and opt instead for a religious body that was clearer upon humanity's common goal? After all, Christianity has been historically quite confused on the matter, with its insistent yet mistaken emphasis upon Jesus as the ultimate ground of all value, not as illustrative of other, more universally accessible values.

The reduction of religious beliefs to metaphors and stories that promote the universal goal would, I think, make it difficult for many to see much point in religious bodies at all. Surely, one might say, we now know the appropriate principles for achieving freedom, so why not grow up a little bit and drop the religious business altogether? If we need symbolic mediations of such values, would not music, art and poetry do as well? Such a proposal might appear especially reasonable to those whose reading of history indicates that religious bodies in fact work for the most part in the opposite direction to freedom and equality. It would not be enough, for those sufficiently familiar with societies outside the USA at any rate, to say (with Hodgson and others) that *some* kind of religious commitment is necessary for society if it is not to self-destruct (RC 94). One might argue that Canada, Japan and many parts of Europe seem to have considerably more social cohesion than the USA, without anywhere near the religiosity of the last. Would it not be better, then, to dispense with the religious aspect and simply witness to those values, and build non-religious communities that embody them in appropriate practices?[39]

Should we keep on with religious activity anyway, it could only be on something like aesthetic, psychological or sociological grounds. The effect would be to leave the field clear for the kind of do-it-yourself religiosity already prevalent in our societies. A private religion – and a relativistic and perspectivalist religious view is logically private even if held by a number of people – may well prove to be unsupportive of one's concern for humanization or freedom and equality, or for anything or anyone outside of one's own interests. But even if all agreed that the goal

---

39. Perhaps Richard Rorty would agree with this suggestion. See his *Achieving Our Country: Leftist Thought in Twentieth-Century America* (Cambridge, MA: Harvard University Press, 1998).

of humanity should be some such universal, the loss of genuine truth claims for religions would mean that the religions themselves could provide no concrete help in working towards that goal. Nor could they contribute to the debate about the means to that goal. If I introduce my religious perspective into the public square to argue for specific activities to promote some concrete answer to such questions, I will have a goal in mind that is formed by my religious view, perhaps a society that fosters Nirvana, or the beatific vision, or the American way, or the triumph of the proletariat. But my appeal to my own religious doctrines can now have little or no practical or critical function. At most, they can provide some motivation for those who happen to share them.[40]

If the pluralist horizon were to became pervasive – and we are still merely speculating, of course – it seems unreasonable to think that as a consequence disagreement and division would disappear. While they would be ruled out from religious discourse, they would still exist, surfacing in areas other than the religious. For the key questions that any society must attempt to answer would remain: What are the goals we, as individuals or as a society, should aim for? How should they be ranked? Who does the ranking and on what grounds? What does humanization mean, concretely? These key words require some kind of warrant, and if that warrant is no longer embodied in a religious tradition, it must be had from non-theological traditions and communities, or theoretical constructions. Postulating a set of abstract values as common to all world religions does nothing of itself to unite society. It simply shifts the burden of debate into other, equally contentious and divisive areas where truth claims are permitted.

Some of the dogmas of modernity that support the pluralist horizon have come under substantive criticism recently. Pluralist theory relies upon a modern liberal metanarrative according to which humanity has achieved progress towards enlightenment and freedom as it has broken through the shackles of traditional patterns of thought and behavior to learn to think for itself. Some have asserted that Western cultures have become increasingly incredulous of such humanist, emancipatory, yet ultimately self-congratulatory metanarratives.[41] The very notion of

40. In her *Politics of God* (Minneapolis: Fortress Press, 1992), pp. 255ff., Kathryn Tanner argues that revisionist talk about God or the Real can merely reflect what is already believed on other grounds. Merely dressing up prior commitments in theological garb deprives the theologian of any critical leverage for discerning the limitations of a particular agenda, social or otherwise.

41. Such "incredulity toward metanarratives" is noted in Jean-François Lyotard, *The Postmodern Condition: A Report on Knowledge*, trans. G. Bennington and B. Massumi (Minneapolis: University of Minnesota Press, 1984), p. xxiv.

universal goals or "primary goods" has been attacked,[42] while others have noted how the liberal metanarrative betrays an underlying will-to-power. Power is exerted through programs that do not repress and coerce so much as channel our activity into ways that are determined, quite arbitrarily, to be "normal."[43] The pluralist metanarrative encompasses everything, drawing it into a totalizing discourse that makes it difficult to acknowledge, let alone to promote, the genuine diversity of those communities that do not fit into its structures or meet its standards of what counts as normal religion.[44]

It is true, of course, that religious bodies rely upon metanarratives, too. They view everything, including other religions, from their own perspective, and pass judgments upon everything according to their norms.[45] And while a religion like Christianity may accept the independence of scientific discourse, for example, it locates scientific inquiry as a subset of its own overarching narrative. However, as I will argue in the next chapter, a religious metanarrative need not be a totalizing discourse, and the church's task of witness, properly understood, should mitigate any temptation to construct one. Already we can note that, unlike pluralism, the church can coherently acknowledge the rationality and integrity of other religions and other forms of inquiry, even while it disagrees with them. Religions have always recognized that other religions make claims that conflict with their own. They take these seriously (at times violently so, to their shame), for they know that other religions are centered upon beliefs that have the same logical status as their own. Each religion is explicitly centered upon a particular tradition and the distinct community that embodies it, rather than based upon a single, universal foundation. Unless the pluralist theory of religion likewise acknowledges its own traditional grounding, which it cannot do without radical modification, its discourse must remain hegemonic and oppressive.

There are significant political issues involved here. One of the strongest criticisms of the church is to bring up those times when it fostered

---

42. The phrase "primary goods" is that of John Rawls, developed in his *A Theory of Justice* (Cambridge, MA: Harvard University Press, 1971), p. 62 and §15. For a critique of the notion, see Michael Walzer, *Spheres of Justice* (New York: Basic Books, 1983).

43. See Michel Foucault, *Discipline and Punish: The Birth of the Prison*, trans. Alan Sheridan (New York: Vintage Books, 1977).

44. For a careful argument along these lines, see John V. Apczynski, "John Hick's Theocentricism: Revolutionary or Implicitly Exclusivist?," *Modern Theology* 8:1 (1992), 39–52.

45. For a brief example, see the discussion of the Resurrection from within a Buddhist tradition by Rupert Gethin, "The Resurrection and Buddhism" in Gavin D'Costa (ed.), *Resurrection Reconsidered* (Oxford: One World, 1996), pp. 201–216.

practices and beliefs among its membership that benefited the dominant members of society and held in check those whom they oppressed. The church's leadership thereby gained secular enforcement of its religious monopoly, and the secular power gained the church's ideological support. Although it is possible to be too melodramatic about such matters, something not too dissimilar may be at work in pluralism, in spite of good intentions. Modern liberalism has its social base in the powerful societies of the West and its intellectual base in their academic institutions. Those who dominate these societies and finance such institutions have an interest in ruling out challenges to their power. Religious bodies have historically functioned not only to support the powerful, but also in the contrary direction, as the base for reformist or revolutionary challenges. If religious bodies can be domesticated by undercutting their critical force, they not only present less of a challenge, they can also be used to support the status quo. And if, furthermore, the essence of all religious goals can be shown to be identical to the essential liberal values of the strongest Western nations, then religious bodies can do nothing other than promote and preserve the practices and valuations of liberal capitalist democracies. Those religions that embody their disagreement with such values cannot counter them. For their concrete identities can be easily dismissed by the dominant society as abnormal ("fundamentalist"), immoral or even irreligious.[46] If the church reconstructed its concrete identity so as to embody pluralist-humanist beliefs, it could become an agent for Western values, much as it was at times during the colonial era. But this time its own voice would be silenced more effectively, since any challenge it might offer would be ruled out as irrational.

In sum, the pluralist challenge to the church's traditional self-understanding fails on a number of fronts. The church has a number of reasons for rejecting an ecclesiology constructed within a pluralist horizon. Within ecclesiological discourse, the double use of the twofold construal relativizes the concrete church and radically undermines the church's task of witness to the Good News of Jesus Christ. The church loses its ability to engage with and learn from genuinely different religious bodies on its and their own terms. The church can no longer contribute to the ongoing public debate over the concrete shape of society, for it has no

---

46. As MacIntyre says, "[O]nly by the circumvention or the subversion of liberal modes of debate can the rationality specific to traditions of inquiry reestablish itself sufficiently to challenge the cultural and political hegemony of liberalism effectively." *Whose Justice?* p. 410.

reason to develop a concrete identity that is significantly distinctive. The pluralist horizon supports an ecclesiology that fails, in short, to meet the criterion of practical-prophetic adequacy. A pluralist ecclesiology is not suitable for the church within the present ecclesiological context.

Pluralist ecclesiology is a strong version of the modern ecclesiological method described in chapter 2, and with the epic kind of theology noted briefly in chapter 3. It approaches the concrete with a set of *a priori* commitments derived abstractly according to a normative model of the essential aspects of religion. As a result, it finds it difficult to acknowledge the irreducible diversity of the concrete, and even harder to respond to it. The possibility of a receptive moment, of humbly listening to others, is undermined, in spite of a manifest concern to foster dialogue. All is made to fit within a epic system worked out apart from any context and community, according to beliefs that "we" moderns all accept as axiomatic without adequate justification.

I suggest that one appropriate response to both theoretical and popular forms of pluralism is for the church to become an agent for particularity and for the genuine debate that particularity makes possible. The church should educate its members to acknowledge that they, and members of other religious and non-religious bodies, make and embody claims that may logically conflict with others. To be an agent for particularity is a necessary part of the church's prophetic role in the present context. Given its traditional concern for the oppressed and marginalized in society (a concern admittedly often lost sight of), the church should attempt to counter the pluralistic horizon. It should do so not only to be able to perform its own tasks, but also to help other, less powerful religious and non-religious bodies to flourish.

This chapter has for the most part engaged in negative apologetics. In the next chapter I make a constructive case for the proposition that religious bodies can be quite distinctive, and that each may logically make truth claims which conflict with claims made by other bodies. And this in turn makes it reasonable for one religious body to engage in debate with other religious bodies and to argue that, in spite of its sinfulness and failures, it makes possible the best way of life.

5

A theodramatic response to pluralism

The previous chapter argued that pluralism furnishes an unsatisfactory horizon within which to reflect theologically upon the church, especially in the present ecclesiological context. It requires the concrete identities of all religious bodies to conform to a pluralist-humanist ultimate goal, and imposes upon them an alien notion of normal religion. Its epic move is warranted by appeals to its supposed universalism, while in fact it depends upon the beliefs of a particular tradition. The pluralist revision of Christology would lead to an ecclesiological relativism that would undermine the church's witness and pastoral activity, and leave its membership with little reason to devote their lives to Christian discipleship. Pluralist ecclesiology would require the church to reject Paul's rule and to modify its concrete identity so that it fostered only those practices which conform to the religious beliefs and goals of Western liberalism.

The discussion of pluralism was fruitful in that it brought to light notable issues to which any practical-prophetic ecclesiology needs to respond. Pluralists rightly stress the necessity of dialogue among the religions. One important reason why they seek to modify the church's traditional Christological convictions and their ecclesiological corollaries is that they believe that such convictions rule out genuine dialogue. The present chapter responds to this challenge by arguing that an ecclesiology done within a theodramatic horizon must consider genuine dialogue an essential part of the church's witness and discipleship, for reasons, moreover, that depend upon traditional Christological and trinitarian doctrines. The horizon fosters a far more pluralistic theory of religion and religious bodies, one that permits arguments over truth and superiority while acknowledging sinfulness and confusion. Moreover, within a theodramatic rather than epic horizon, it becomes theologically appropriate for the church to encourage a genuine plurality of religious and non-religious bodies, both for the sake of the truthfulness of its own witness as well as to support those bodies which are threatened by the more powerful.

The following discussion moves initially within a Christian framework, and amounts to something like a partial sketch of a theodramatic theology of religions. Later in the chapter the argument broadens to become an exercise in constructive, ad hoc Christian apologetics. There I draw upon the work of Alasdair MacIntyre to present an argument which responds to another challenge to the theodramatic horizon, that of postmodernism. Throughout, the discussion is concerned with the possibility of truth within religious bodies. I begin by noting some elements of a theodramatic notion of truth, restricting my remarks to what is useful for the primary concern, namely the concrete identity of the church and practical-prophetic reflection upon it. The question here is: What kind of ecclesial life follows from a theodramatic concept of truth?

The logical possibility of making religious truth claims is essential for the task of the church as traditionally conceived, since that task includes, as we have said, witnessing to Jesus Christ as the truth.[1] Within theological discourse, both the notion of truth as well as the conception of how one attains it are governed by our understanding of Jesus Christ. A theological understanding of truth is thus not one of those things, like the principles of logic, say, that theology can take over from other disciplines without further ado. We recall, too, that thinking of ourselves as grace-enabled players in God's play denies us the possibility of establishing any resting place prior to the eschaton. Our own resources provide no trustworthy basis for constructing epic systems of belief and practice. This does not mean, though, that there is no religious truth or that we could not know it if there were. It suggests, rather, that truth is not something we can *possess*, as if it could belong to us. This is not only because truth is ultimately a person rather than, say, a set of statements. It is also because we must always *receive* the truth, and receive it in a personal and trinitarian way, through our trust in the faithfulness of the Director. We receive the truth in the gift of the self-presence of God in the Spirit, by which we are led in Christ to the Father.

To stress the receptive moment is not to say that we should simply sit

---

1. Bruce D. Marshall makes this point well in two articles: "What Is Truth?" *Pro Ecclesia* 4:4 (1995), 404–430; and "'We Shall Bear the Image of the Man of Heaven:' On the Concept of Truth," *Modern Theology* 11:1 (1995), 93–118.

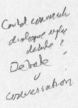

back and wait for some revelation or religious experience (though to be sure, prayerful preparation is always appropriate). Our roles within the play are truly our own, and they require us to struggle towards the truth. We do so by searching the Scriptures and the tradition of their interpretation, using them as normative guides for our inquiries as to how best to witness to Jesus Christ and embody his way truthfully. But Scripture and tradition do not contain truth, as if it were bits of information that lie embedded directly in the text. If that were the case, truth would be in our possession independently of the Spirit's gift. We could then piece the bits together into a set of doctrines and precepts and call the epic product, say, "The Definitive Ecclesiology" or "The Definitive Christian Morality." But to attempt to do this would be mistaken, in part because, as I noted earlier, the Scriptural witness to the truth is too rich and multifaceted to be mapped out into a single internally coherent and complete system, and in part because it is always situated by the Spirit within a particular ecclesiological context. Certainly we can discern abiding principles and doctrines, but other factors enter in that condition our understanding and use of them. A theodramatic horizon reminds us that using Scripture and tradition to receive the truth involves the same kind of struggle that is inherent in all aspects of Christian existence. Scripture and tradition are not themselves the truth, but are normative witnesses to it. They represent, we might say, earlier encounters with Christ and the Spirit and as such they are now the primary means by which we are led to receive the truth, for the Spirit is faithful and true. While they remain the normative means through which truth is received, they also journey along with the theodrama, guiding us in different ways as we enter new episodes of the play.

A theodramatic horizon, with its strong conception of the *concursus* of divine and human action, indicates that we receive truth by two means, both of which are necessary: by the activity of the Spirit, and through our active engagement with views different from our own. The latter is surely an uncontroversial assertion. Many would agree that one of the best ways of gaining greater knowledge and awareness is to engage in debate with those whose views challenge our own. Indeed, one way to conceive of the function of Scripture and tradition is that it provides us with debating partners who have responded to their call to discipleship and have furthered the witness of the church. We can engage with them and learn from them as we attempt to make our way to the same goal in our different contexts. As our ecclesiological context continues to shift, we must respond appropriately to change, something often very difficult to do. Both as individuals and as a religious body, we need help. Our sinfulness and finitude blind us and our leaders to our misreadings of Scripture and their consequences for our concrete identity. For example, we tend to focus on certain principles and beliefs to the neglect of others, perhaps because we are misguided by our own interests to the neglect of others' or because we desire the security and control of an epic view. By engaging with other readings of Scripture and tradition, as well as with other views of the Real and of reality, even if these are equally or more sinful or erroneous, we are challenged to reconsider entrenched misreadings and overcome some of the obstacles we place in the way of the Spirit of truth.

The struggle towards truth therefore takes the form of ongoing debates between the church and diverse religious and non-religious bodies and their adherents. Such debates occur not only at the level of ideas, but in their communal embodiment, within and between religious and non-religious bodies whose concrete identities conflict internally and with one another. One of the tasks of the church, then, is to search out those who do not live as it does. To do so is not at all an act of aggression, as if we sought to stop them from being different; quite the contrary. The reason we engage with others is twofold. First, we need to hear what they have to say so that we may learn from them, from their insights into the truth and from their assessment of our own understanding of it. Second, we witness to them about our Lord in truthful discipleship so that they may learn from us and we may learn more about him to whom we witness. We believe that the Holy Spirit is active in their midst, and so we believe that we may be led by the same Spirit to learn something from them. And it may be that, as a consequence, we find it necessary to acknowledge contritely and explicitly that one or other of our beliefs or practices is sinful or erroneous, and needs either to be abandoned or modified in some way.

Pluralists also insist upon engagement with others. There are, however, significant differences between theodramatic debate and pluralist dialogue. We have seen that dialogue in modern-liberal circles generally has consensus as its goal. Consensus is the result of the willingness of the participants to question all beliefs and practices in order to bring to the surface an underlying, presently unseen harmony. Presupposing this epic harmony, dialogue involves revising convictions so as to produce a more complete and truthful view than any participants could have separately. The dialogue partners can display a rational and moderate attitude, for they assume that they already agree about the fundamental goal of the dialogue. Any remaining disparity is either inconsequential, or will be overcome in due course, if not in this debate, in future years as the area under discussion becomes better mapped.

The relation between debate and truth within a theodramatic horizon cannot be understood along such epic or modern lines. We must engage with others in debate, but not on the assumption that we will achieve consensus, or even should try to do so. The point of debate is primarily to help one another to receive the truth. Rather than an underlying harmony or shared goal, basic disagreement is more likely. Nor can there be any compromise with the truth for the sake of agreement, since truth rather than agreement is the primary goal. The church usually learns from its interlocutors, and may well find it necessary to reconsider some of its beliefs and practices. But if it is indeed devoted to an ultimate goal that is distinct from other religious bodies, then some conflict must persist, for that goal must be maintained. Certainly, the Christian who seeks to play her role in the theodrama must display humility in debating with her critics, for she seeks but does not possess the Spirit of truth. Having no interest superior to that of the truth, she is bold and tenacious in her witness to it when she sees it, to the extent of giving offence if need be by maintaining her beliefs at the cost of confrontation. She expects and encourages similar tenacity and boldness in her interlocutor, and responds to it with courage, imagination and good humor. Such confrontations can never become violent or coercive, since that would be to oppose the Spirit of truth. But, to repeat, neither can she accept any compromise for the sake of a greater good than truth, for she believes that there is no greater good than the triune God.

The theodramatic kind of debate is appropriate, with suitable modifications, at all levels: between individuals, Christian and non-Christian, between individuals and the church, and between the church and other religious and non-religious bodies and their individual members. It is a commonplace of ecclesiology that one cannot be a member of the church without engaging with other Christians and with the church as a religious body, for it is in them and through these others that the Spirit is present. I noted earlier that a theodramatic horizon indicates that this engagement must remain tensive. The individual disciple may be called to challenge the religious body, including its authorities, as well as being challenged by them. And it is likely that she will also be called, as an individual disciple, to engage in debate with non-Christians.

Within this theodramatic horizon, the church cannot be thought of

*Suddenly
humility language =
scarcely the
premises for
debating a
position.*

simply as the repository of truth. Rather, it is the communal embodiment of the search for truthful witness and discipleship within the theodrama. It is a religious body which knows that truth cannot be possessed, but must be continually received, and with due humility in face of its sinfulness and finitude. It is a religious body that knows that the gift of truth is essentially dependent upon genuine engagement with both the divine Other and human others. There may well be other religious bodies that hold similar beliefs.

The implications of this proposal for understanding the two central tasks of the church are significant. Witness is sometimes described rather simplistically as the church telling the world what it knows about the gospel. While that way of putting the matter is true in some sense, it gives the misleading impression that the church possesses a body of facts and precepts that it simply passes out to others. Its job then is seen, to exaggerate a little, to be something akin to that of an unimaginative school teacher who writes on the chalkboard the day's chemistry facts for the students to write down and memorize. Proclamation is limited to instruction, as if there were no real need to move beyond simple telling to engagement and debate.

A somewhat better notion, though still inadequate, is that the church witnesses to the gospel by living it. All the world has to do is simply look at the church and it will see the gospel embodied there. This notion is inadequate not only because of the church's sinfulness, which often occludes rather than manifests the gospel, but because it makes an assumption about how the church witnesses which itself obscures the gospel. If, as I have suggested, the gospel includes the claim that no one can receive the truth apart from the Holy Spirit who is active within other religious and non-religious bodies, then the very form of the church's witness must display that claim. Witness does not only involve continually pointing away from the church to Jesus Christ as the *locus* of truth. The church must also build into its concrete identity practices that display its conviction about the *way* to truth, practices that embody its need for other religious and non-religious bodies with which to engage in spirited debate.

This theodramatic understanding of witness suggests some of the ingredients for making an initial response to one of the main concerns of the pluralists. We recall that the pluralists were rightly concerned about the coercive and destructive activity of the church in the past against those with whom it disagreed. That activity was seen to rest on two claims: that there is a necessary connection between truth and salvation, and that the church is the sole possessor of truth. But on the view that I have developed, such activity would appear to be inconsistent with the gospel, not only because it would be hard to reconcile with any form of discipleship, but more specifically because the two claims from which it arises cannot be maintained in such a lumpishly untensive way. The church does not possess the truth, it receives it. It often turns away from truth in sinfulness and error. Non-Christian bodies also receive truth through the same Spirit, and are thereby enabled to challenge the church, prompting it to renew itself. Genuine plurality among religious and non-religious bodies is therefore vital to the performance of the church's tasks. The members of other bodies are not simply passive, merely empty soil that must await the planting of the gospel before they can bear any fruit at all. On the contrary, they are participants in the one theodrama who actively respond to their own distinctive call. Furthermore, we believe that God is loving and merciful as well as just, and that our salvation is not our achievement. It would be counter to such beliefs to claim that those who respond to the Spirit's presence, and who are an integral part of the church's reception of truth, should not participate in some salvific way in the final outcome of the theodrama.[2] The church has no grounds whatsoever, within a theodramatic horizon, for thinking of itself as self-sufficient or superior in this way. It should continue to perform its tasks boldly, while humbly acknowledging that other religious and non-religious bodies also have access through the Spirit to truth, and may also be playing their respective parts within the overarching theodrama.

The contributions of non-Christians have clearly been essential to the formation of the concrete identity of the church. As the church engages with others it sifts through their resources. Christians argue among themselves over whether to reject certain practices, say, as anti-Christ, or whether to modify, privilege or ignore them as the products of the Spirit working within the non-church world. They may find it appropriate to take over in this way material from competing bodies as part of their response to new ecclesiological contexts. We can call this activity, "ecclesial bricolage," adopting a term from Jeffrey Stout.[3] A classic example of ecclesial bricolage is the struggle of the early church which, in order to develop a well-rounded concrete identity, had to borrow from the

---

2. I deliberately avoid saying the "same" salvation for it may be possible to talk of there being different salvations. I discuss this possibility briefly in the next chapter. It is explored in some detail by S. Mark Heim in his *Salvations: Truth and Difference in Religion* (Maryknoll, NY: Orbis, 1995).

3. Jeffrey Stout, *Ethics After Babel: The Languages of Morals and Their Discontents* (Boston: Beacon Press, 1988), pp. 74ff. Stout himself appropriates the term from Claude Lévi-Strauss.

Greco-Roman culture. As Wayne Meeks describes it, the early Christians mixed their own social practices with many other, non-Christian, cultural patterns, making them their own by embedding them within the Christian metanarrative.[4] Meeks notes how a similar activity can be detected within many self-aware religious traditions, even when they attempt to isolate themselves from external influence. The early church evidently felt the "[t]ension between the sense of sharing the culture around them and the sense of standing opposed to it," resulting in what Meeks nicely calls an "amphibian life."[5] In addition to non-Christian resources, the later church has its past identity to draw upon, by a similar process of retrieval, modification, or reform.

The practices and institutions, and the beliefs and valuations that together constitute the church's present concrete identity are the product of past ecclesial bricolage. That identity reflects the church's earlier struggles to hear and respond to the Spirit of truth through engagement with those, internal and external, who challenged its witness and the discipleship of its members. The function of a practical-prophetic ecclesiology is therefore to engage in external and internal debate over that identity, with the aim of improving the church's witness and pastoral care. A theologian who reflects upon the church will endeavor, for example, actively to seek out an overlooked challenge that suggests a needed reform, or to act as a *bricoleur* by imaginatively modifying a useful practice from another religious body so that it may be incorporated into the life of the church. Some account of the ways in which practical-prophetic ecclesiology should carry out these tasks is given in chapter 7.

In sum, a theodramatic notion of truth and ecclesiological reflection acknowledges, with pluralism, the pressing need for the church to engage with other religious bodies. It differs from pluralism in eschewing relativist and perspectivalist views of religious bodies and in rejecting a unifying goal or an underlying harmony among them. Instead theodramatic ecclesiology affirms their genuine otherness. It welcomes the challenges and opportunities they present, not as nuisances to be endured or overcome, nor as mere passive receptacles of the gospel, but as active players in the theodrama who, as gifts of the Spirit of truth, help the church more adequately conform to its Lord.

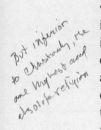

4. Wayne Meeks, *The Origins of Christian Morality: The First Two Centuries* (New Haven: Yale University Press, 1993), p. 109. Henri de Lubac, in his *The Motherhood of the Church* (San Francisco: Ignatius Press, 1982), p. 198, has also noted how each local church develops "more or less its own physiognomy composed of traits in which the worldly and the religious mingle."   5. Meeks, *Origins of Christian Morality*, pp. 10, 109.

Up to this point the discussion has taken the form of a theodramatic response to the challenges of the pluralist religious theory. Both theodrama and pluralism agree upon the possibility of some kind of truth, though they differ sharply, as we have seen, as to where and how it may be found. A recent development in philosophical and literary-critical circles presents a more radical challenge to the theodramatic horizon, for it denies both the modern and the theodramatic notions of truth. The challenge comes especially from those postmodern thinkers who have been influenced in one way or another by Nietzsche, such as Michel Foucault, Jean-François Lyotard and Jacques Derrida.[6] Each man has somewhat different concerns, and they are by no means in full agreement with one another.[7] Derrida and Foucault, too, present considerable difficulties in interpretation. Yet taken together, they may fairly be said to reflect a particular form of the postmodern horizon, one that constitutes a distinct alternative to theodrama and the modern horizon of pluralism. For convenience we can label that form, the neo-Nietzschean.[8] It is only as representatives of the postmodern challenge to theodrama that the neo-Nietzscheans are discussed here; not for their particular concerns and insights.

Within a postmodern horizon, the idea of a universal, tradition-free rationality by means of which one might progress towards timeless truths is unsustainable. Metaphysical structures and metanarratives arise out of contingent historical contexts, which cannot ground universally applicable humanist norms.[9] Thus far, of course, there is agreement with the theodramatic horizon. The church joyfully confesses it depends upon

6. See Foucault's essay "Nietzsche, Genealogy, History" in Paul Rabinow (ed.), *The Foucault Reader* (New York: Pantheon, 1984), pp. 76–100. Derrida's use of Nietzsche is via a critical reading of Heidegger, as Richard Rorty notes in his "From Ironist Theory to Private Allusions: Derrida" in *Contingency, Irony, and Solidarity* (Cambridge: Cambridge University Press, 1989), pp. 122–137.

7. E.g., Derrida critiques Foucault's *Madness and Civilization* (New York: Pantheon, 1965) in his essay, "Cogito and the History of Madness" in *Writing and Difference* (London: Routledge and Kegan Paul, 1978), pp. 31–63.

8. The term "postmodern" is too broad to specify the neo-Nietzschean concerns I address here. The broader concept of postmodernism as a cultural phenomenon is described in Frederic Jameson, *Postmodernism, or the Cultural Logic of Late Capitalism* (Durham: Duke University Press, 1991); also Paul Lakeland, *Postmodernity: Christian Identity in a Fragmented Age* (Minneapolis: Augsburg Fortress, 1997); and more critically, Pauline Marie Rosenau, *Post-Modernism and the Social Sciences: Insights, Inroads, and Intrusions* (Princeton: Princeton University Press, 1992). I discuss the bearing of postmodern cultural analysis upon ecclesiology in chapter 7. One who uses the label "postmodern" to refer largely to neo-Nietzscheans is Terry Eagleton, *The Illusions of Postmodernism* (Oxford: Blackwell, 1996); another is John Milbank, who also uses the label "neo-Nietzschean" in a similar way in his *Theology and Social Theory: Beyond Secular Reason* (Oxford: Blackwell, 1990), pp. 278f.

9. John Milbank cites this as a key element of postmodernity in his *Theology and Social Theory*, p. 2. It is a point, though, that was known well by premodern Christians and members of other religious bodies.

the particular historical person, the first-century Jew, Jesus of Nazareth. It is through his person and work that God has revealed and effected the good and true news of the expansion of the covenant with Israel so as to offer salvation to all people. And I have stressed in the above account how the truth about God, the church and the world *remains* historical and contextual, always contingent upon the movement of the Spirit. The postmodern view, though, is in certain respects more radical. Both theodrama and pluralism situate their claims within metanarratives or grand theories which make general sense of reality and our relation to it. The writings of the neo-Nietzscheans, by contrast, strive to show that all such metanarratives and systematic constructions betray evidence of arbitrary decisions made in confusion or in the interest of power and domination.[10] Genealogical analysis denies the assumption of humanist historiography that the past reveals to us our humanity. Humanisms are diverse and constructed; they should not be confused with progress towards enlightenment.[11] Humanist norms and goals rely upon anthropologies that in turn rely upon a set of false metaphysical assumptions inherent in the Western philosophical tradition.[12] Systems and theories can be shown to rely upon binary oppositions between normal and abnormal, author and reader, rational and poetic discourse, male and female, and the like. In every case, it seems, the one side usurps the other, so that the other is occluded or hidden from view, and what is different, unusual or marginal is lost.[13]

According to the neo-Nietzscheans, then, it would seem unlikely that any single system or institution could be true, or truer than others. True knowledge is a concept to be associated more often than not with power and domination rather than freedom. We recall that the pluralists were concerned to analyze religions as part of their work towards greater

10. For Foucault's description of his method in relation to a particular use of it, see *Discipline and Punish: The Birth of the Prison*, trans. Alan Sheridan (New York: Vintage Books, 1977), pp. 23–31.
11. See Foucault's article, "What Is Enlightenment?," trans. Catherine Porter, in Rabinow (ed.), *The Foucault Reader*, pp. 32–50.
12. Derrida takes this criticism all the way back to Plato in his essay, "Plato's Pharmacy" in *Dissemination*, trans. Barbara Johnson (Chicago: University of Chicago Press, 1981), pp. 63–171. Catherine Pickstock has offered a forceful argument against Derrida's reading of Plato's *Phaedrus* in her *After Writing: On the Liturgical Consummation of Philosophy* (Oxford: Blackwell, 1998), pp. 3–46.
13. For two examples of the ways Derrida pursues this insight, see, e.g., *Limited Inc.* (Evanston, IL: Northwestern University Press, 1988), and "Geschlecht: Sexual Difference, Ontological Difference," trans. Ruben Berezdivin, from the collection *Psyché: Inventions de l'autre* (Paris: Galilée, 1987), conveniently found in a slightly abridged version in Peggy Kamuf (ed.), *A Derrida Reader: Between the Blinds* (New York: Columbia University Press, 1991), pp. 378–402. See also Christopher Norris, *Derrida* (Cambridge, MA: Harvard University Press, 1987), pp. 134–138.

freedom and human well-being. They sought to penetrate below the confused self-understandings of religious bodies, to help them move towards
goals that would benefit all of humankind. This move is not possible for
the postmoderns, or not in the same way. For if the humanist constructs
that express our quest for meaning can be shown to rest upon arbitrary
and power-laden decisions, it would be irrational and, in some significant
sense, immoral to postulate a universal substrate among diverse systems,
or to situate all systems within a single system that is, supposedly, the
most enlightened. Instead, the correct way to act is to reveal, by deconstruction or genealogy, how these fictions are constructed. As a consequence, debate between competing systems, whether they are religions,
political systems, theories of language or anthropologies, is largely beside
the point. Debate ends as soon as the false construction is revealed and
dissolved; there is nothing further to talk about.

The neo-Nietzschean account is thus rather more epic than dramatic,
for there can be no real conflict between rival claimants to the most truthful way of life.[14] Despite its epic quality, though, it may be that neo-Nietzschean nihilism can be of some use for the church. Not only does it offer
a significant counter-challenge to the axiomatic beliefs of pluralism, it
brings to the fore some of the cognitive consequences of sin. Sin, as will-
to-power, as the love of domination, can be discerned in the knowledge
systems of all cultures and societies. This insight, although hardly new to
Christians, may prompt the church to acknowledge more explicitly and
readily that the human search for truth, even when it is undertaken
within the church, will always go astray without the active presence of the
Spirit of truth. The neo-Nietzscheans' ability to demonstrate the irrational aspects of all systems may enable the church and other religious
bodies to avoid relying too heavily upon such systems. Some theologians
have made use of their methods to mitigate the perennial tendency
towards epic discourse within theology.[15]

14. It may be that Foucault was moving towards a greater concern for enlightening debate.
See Christopher Norris, "'What Is Enlightenment?': Kant According to Foucault," in Gary
Gutting (ed.), *The Cambridge Companion to Foucault* (Cambridge: Cambridge University Press,
1994), pp. 159–196; also David Couzens Hoy, "Power, Repression, Progress; Foucault, Lukes,
and the Frankfurt School," and Jürgen Habermas, "Taking Aim at the Heart of the
Present," both in David Couzens Hoy (ed.), *Foucault: A Critical Reader* (Oxford: Blackwell,
1986), pp. 123–147 and 103–108 respectively.
15. See e.g., Mark C. Taylor, *Erring: A Postmodern A/Theology* (Chicago: University of Chicago
Press, 1984). For critical views of Taylor and other postmodern theologians that are
consonant with the anti-epic concern of the present study, see Gillian Rose, *The Broken
Middle: Out of Our Ancient Society* (Oxford: Blackwell, 1992), pp. 277–296; and Gerard
Loughlin, *Telling God's Story: Bible, Church and Narrative Theology* (Cambridge: Cambridge
University Press, 1996), pp. 10–17, 24–26.

Nevertheless, neo-Nietzschean postmodernity has come under heavy criticism from a wide range of viewpoints.[16] Here we need focus on only one major point of contention. If we were to bring a theodramatic horizon to bear strategically upon the neo-Nietzschean proposals, as if it were a new, deconstructing fiction, we could point out that those proposals are insufficiently subtle with regard to sin and the will to domination. The power of sin is active everywhere, not only in systems, but in those who seek to dissolve them. Moreover, the Spirit of truth may make use of fictive systems and be active within those who inhabit such systems. Something like this criticism has been made from within other horizons, too. Stephen White, a political philosopher who is not unsympathetic to the postmodern view, has noted how, "after the effect wears off, one is left with a rather simple bipolar world: deconstructionists and other postmoderns who struggle for justice, and traditional ethical and political theorists who are the ideologues of unjust order".[17] White notes that the postmoderns are very helpful in developing what he calls "responsibility to otherness" by their critiques that disclose alternative worlds.[18] But, he argues, they are less successful in developing the correlative "responsibility to act" in justified ways in the world. The postmoderns' "perpetual withholding action" inhibits any such constructive response.[19] As Gillian Rose has pointed out, this can be construed as an irresponsible unwillingness to engage with the difficulties of reality.[20] Deconstruction and similar skeptical moves can thus appear to be the playful practices of a dominant class which has plenty of free leisure time. White remarks:

> [O]veremphasis on disruption and impertinence creates for postmodern thinking a momentum that threatens to enervate the sense of responsibility to otherness, subtly substituting for it an implicit celebration of the impertinent subject who shows his or her virtuosity in deconstructing whatever unity comes along.[21]

White and Rose agree in arguing that, in spite of the ever-present possibility of an exercise of will-to-mastery, consistent and justifiable

---

16. Notably within theology from John Milbank, *Theology and Social Theory*, pp. 278ff.
17. Stephen K. White, *Political Theory and Postmodernism* (Cambridge: Cambridge University Press, 1991), p. 116.   18. Ibid., pp. 20ff.
19. Ibid., p. 16. White borrows the phrase from Allan Megill, *Prophets of Extremity: Nietzsche, Heidegger, Foucault, Derrida* (Berkeley: University of California Press, 1985), p. 271.
20. See Rose's Introduction and her essay on Derrida in her *Judaism and Modernity: Philosophical Essays* (Oxford: Blackwell, 1993), pp. 1–10, 65–87. For a theological appropriation of Rose, see Rowan D. Williams, "Between Politics and Metaphysics: Reflections in the Wake of Gillian Rose," *Modern Theology* 11:1 (1995), 3–22.
21. White, *Political Theory*, p. 72.

decisions have to be made that require some closing off of otherness, some homogenization.[22] Without sufficient attention to *both* responsibilities, postmodern virtues turn into their opposing vices. Similar criticisms have been made by others.[23]

Whether or not such criticisms are fair, the issues raised by the neo-Nietzschean critique are very significant for the church and need to be addressed. Making an external apologetic case for the reasonableness of a Christian understanding of truth and religious bodies must go beyond showing how religious truth can be more than merely perspectival and relative. It must also give some account of how religious bodies such as the church may reasonably maintain their truth claims and debate with other bodies, without thereby becoming repressive and irrational exercises of power. It must show how religious and non-religious bodies can maintain and develop their concrete identities in accordance with their convictions, and how they can pursue their responsibility to act in accordance with their respective metanarratives, but without these actions necessarily occluding the other. Simply put, for the church to continue to witness to Jesus Christ, it must be possible to show that one can speak the truth and live truthfully; that one can do so without hurting anyone; and that the more truthful one is, the more likely it is that one will acknowledge and support those who are different.

I cannot, of course, present anything like a knock-down argument for such proposals here, even if it were possible to do so. The best argument would be for the church to embody its convictions perfectly; but it has never yet done so. It may be that the decision as to whether or not to adopt the neo-Nietzschean form of the postmodern horizon cannot be made on purely rational grounds.[24] If so, then the best approach is to try to present a more convincing account of the issues from within other forms of the postmodern horizon. Some idea of a theodramatic response has already been given, but needless to say, it trades upon church-grounded beliefs in the logical possibility of truth claims and true communities. In the remainder of the chapter, I broaden the discussion to present a philosophical postmodern theory drawn from the work of Alasdair MacIntyre (filtered in part through the work of Jeffrey Stout and Charles Taylor).[25]

---

22. Ibid., p. 21.
23. See Richard Rorty, *Contingency, Irony, and Solidarity*, pp. 63f., 83; also Terry Eagleton, *Illusions of Postmodernism*, pp. 24ff. and *passim*.
24. See Nicholas Wolterstorff, *Divine Discourse: Philosophical Reflections on the Claim that God Speaks* (Cambridge: Cambridge University Press, 1995), pp. 164f.
25. Especially Stout, *Ethics After Babel*, and Taylor, *Sources of the Self: The Making of the Modern Identity* (Cambridge, MA: Harvard University Press, 1989).

The theory is meant to show, minimally, that we need not give way before such challenges without further ado, and that it is possible to formulate a more genuinely pluralistic view of religious bodies.

All three of those just mentioned agree with the postmodern contention that truth arises out of historically contingent constructs. But for them, this does not mean that the concept of truth is to be abandoned, for they respond to what MacIntyre calls the failure of the liberal project in a way that diverges from the neo-Nietzschean postmoderns. The liberal project, we recall, sought to discover standards of rationality that would be independent of authorities and traditions, relying instead upon universal reason. Rather than beginning with tradition-specific principles, the aim was to find principles that any intelligent individual could know and accept simply by the exercise of her or his own reason. Only by this kind of rationality, they believed, could genuine, timeless truth claims be made. But, as MacIntyre and the postmoderns agree, the project has proven to be too difficult. MacIntyre notes how in moral reflection we have not been able to find enough solid common ground to provide a starting point for rational debate. The debates over abortion, over whether a war might be justly fought, over the role of government in society – these have become interminable, degenerating into "the assertion and counterassertion of alternative and incompatible sets of premises."[26]

Although most theorists now acknowledge that all truth claims are made within one tradition or another, some, according to MacIntyre, continue to hold on to something like the liberal view of truth, at least with regard to certain fields of inquiry such as religion. Among these are arguably the neo-Nietzscheans, as well as the pluralists discussed in the previous chapter. Their belief that all truth claims are merely relative to a particular traditional perspective seems to be an inference from the absence of a universal basis for debate. They see that all forms of inquiry are governed by sets of commitments and working assumptions, and none of these satisfies the criterion of a universalist rationality. Because truth arises within a particular tradition, its force appears to be limited to that tradition, since its notion of rationality is incommensurable with any other. Traditions, then, might seem as though they cannot engage in rational debate with one another, let alone make a rational case for their being superior to the others. Since truth claims are assumed to be

26. Alasdair MacIntyre, *After Virtue: A Study in Moral Theory*, 2nd ed. (Notre Dame: University of Notre Dame Press, 1984), p. 6.

justifiable only upon non-traditioned, universalist grounds, "no claim to truth made in the name of any one competing tradition could defeat the claims to truth made in the name of its rivals."[27] Rational debate can only be intratraditional (WJWR 366). And so we are left with a collection of "very different, complementary perspectives for envisaging the realities about which they speak to us" (WJWR 352).

MacIntyre's response is to question some of the key presuppositions of this position. He notes how liberalism is itself a tradition (WJWR 345), one of the central principles of which is to inquire, seemingly interminably, into the principles for a "tradition-independent, rational universality" (WJWR 335). As a tradition of inquiry among others, however, and especially as a tradition that seems, for the moment at least, to have failed in its aim, it cannot claim on its own principles to have more hold upon our understanding of traditions of inquiry than others. Its normative theories of truth and rationality seem to have got it nowhere. Thus a way out of the liberal impasse that looks more promising than neo-Nietzschean skepticism is to examine the kinds of assumptions about truth and rationality and the conditions of their possibility that are operative in those traditions that accept their traditioned nature rather than seek to overcome it.

What, then, does it mean to reason within a tradition of inquiry? Here we can expand the scope of MacIntyre's theory explicitly to include religious traditions and their embodiments in religious communities. For some of the ethical traditions MacIntyre discusses are located within the church, such as the Augustinian and Thomistic, while others, such as the anti-religious traditions of the postmoderns, are located within bodies such as the secular university. Within a theodramatic horizon, moreover, it is reasonable to think of Christianity generally as a tradition of inquiry into how best to respond to Jesus Christ, and of the church as the communal embodiment of that inquiry.

Traditions and their embodiments vary a great deal, of course, but minimally and necessarily they are distinguished from one another by their members' commitment to a particular set of principles. In religious and ethical traditions such principles are usually embodied in privileged texts that "function as the authoritative point of departure" for inquiry (WJWR 383). They provide a normative account of the tradition's key aspects: its conception of the good, of the goal of human activity, of the

---

27. Alasdair MacIntyre, *Whose Justice? Which Rationality?* (Notre Dame: University of Notre Dame Press, 1988), p. 367. Cited as (WJWR page).

means to get there, and the like. Such texts must not only have a definable meaning, but be open to critical re-reading as the inquiry progresses. Hence, "every tradition becomes to some degree a tradition of critical reinterpretation in which one and the same body of texts, with of course some addition and subtraction, is put to the question, and to successively different sets of questions, as a tradition unfolds" (WJWR 383). A tradition's commitments and texts are embodied in a community of interpretation. Over the course of its history of interpreting its originating principles and texts the community develops sets of practices and institutions, rules and dispositions, by which its members live out their commitments. That is, they develop what I have been calling with regard to the church, a concrete identity. This identity provides the kind of normal everydayness, the taken-for-granted set of ways of thinking and acting that those who are new to the tradition must learn in order to be competent members of its community (WJWR 24).

Such everyday normality, however, is not usually present in all areas of the tradition, nor for any length of time, because traditions are inherently conflictual. They do not simply pass on information from one generation to another; they continue to pursue their inquiry. Hence they are historical rather than static in form:

> A tradition is an argument extended through time in which certain
> fundamental agreements are defined and redefined in terms of two
> kinds of conflict: those with critics and enemies external to the
> tradition who reject all or at least key parts of those fundamental
> agreements, and those internal, interpretative debates through which
> the meaning and rationale of the fundamental agreements come to be
> expressed and by whose progress a tradition is constituted. (WJWR 12)

Let us discuss how internal conflict arises first. When reflecting upon some aspect of reality within a tradition – and this would apply to all such, whether religious, scientific, literary, artistic, ethical, and so on – one usually does so, initially at least, by engaging in debate with those who inhabit the same tradition. The mode of argumentation will have something of a narrative quality about it, even if the narrative remains more or less implicit. For to make a case for a proposal within a tradition is not (and cannot be, on this view) to find ahistorical, universal principles on which to ground it. But neither is it simply to turn to a clear set of principles that govern the tradition and argue deductively from them. The principles of a tradition cannot be found without interpretation of the normative sources, and these have been subject to a history of interpretation, including a history of their social embodiment. As a result, those principles may have been reordered, some abandoned or others added during its history, with consequences for their present meaning and significance. Furthermore, no living tradition is monolithic or unanimous. Some who pursue their inquiries within a given tradition may well be critical of some aspects of its main trajectory. Their rejection of part of the tradition – a certain set of practices, say, that places them arbitrarily in an inferior position – may extend as far as constituting a separate strand of the tradition embodied in a more or less distinct community.[28]

Thus for me to make a case for a proposal within a tradition, I will have to give an account of how the inquiry about the matter under discussion has gone thus far. My account can then be extended in the direction I hope to take the tradition as a further stage of its development. My proposal may be highly critical of the present state of the tradition, perhaps invoking some forgotten principle or interpretation from its past; or it may be conservative, trying to maintain the status quo against what I regard as unwarranted criticism; or it may be something in between.[29] If my proposal is presented successfully, other members of the tradition may come to understand the tradition's principles and texts in a new way, thus developing the tradition to a new stage. This development may at times be so massive that the tradition of inquiry and the community embodying it splits into two, with a new set of principles emerging to constitute a new tradition as a rival to the old one. This is arguably the case with some of the traditions of inquiry into the nature of justice that MacIntyre discusses in *Whose Justice? Which Rationality?* It seems evident, for example, that some of the principles of modern liberalism have historical connections with parts of the Christian tradition.

What, then, of the charge of relativism and perspectivalism, with its corollary rejection of the logical possibility of making superiority claims by one tradition and its embodiment, religious or otherwise, over another? Internal conflict may eventually become so great that the tradition reveals its inability to maintain its coherence. Or perhaps it does quite the opposite, becoming sterile and rigid, so that members desert it

28. MacIntyre has been accused of presuming too much unanimity within the Christian traditions he discusses in WJWR. See the criticisms of Jean Porter, in her *Moral Action and Christian Ethics* (Cambridge: Cambridge University Press, 1993), pp. 16–18.
29. For an argument that the use of the imagination enables one to be highly critical of one's tradition without necessary recourse to others, see Sabina Lovibond, *Realism and Imagination in Ethics* (Minneapolis: University of Minnesota Press, 1983).

for other, more lively traditions. In such cases, the tradition has shown its inferiority vis-à-vis other surviving traditions. More usually, however, it is through external conflict that a tradition of inquiry may rationally justify its truth claims and way of life. The commitments which we embody as members of traditioned communities are admittedly contingent and positive in origin. We cannot, as we have seen, justify these commitments by appeal to putatively universal axioms. But we can show that our commitments do indeed correspond to reality by defending them successfully against all challenges to that correspondence. To justify the commitments of a particular tradition is thus to summon up and reply to as many questions as possible that challenge them, both internal and external. Evidently, many of the strongest challenges will come from other traditions. If we wish to maintain that our commitments are indeed true, then, we must listen to those traditions and engage in debate with them. To say that our claim is true is to say, in effect, that any attempt to falsify it can be rebutted successfully.

To deny the possibility of such conflict over truth on the basis of a normative theory would be, as we have seen, to "foist on the defenders of traditions some conception of truth other than that which is theirs" (WJWR 367). In spite of the incommensurability of the overall pattern of their commitments and their ultimate goals, adherents of most traditions have usually assumed that they share some standards and commitments with other traditions; to a basic logic, for example, and often to more substantive beliefs. These shared beliefs are sufficient for members of one tradition to recognize that their commitments and practices may logically conflict with members of another tradition. After engaging in debate, one party may come to understand that its belief or practice was mistaken. And if that belief or practice functions as a key principle within their tradition, the tradition has been shown to be inferior, at least by comparison to the first tradition and with regard to the issue in question.

The vindication of a tradition's truth claims can be described schematically as a dialectic (WJWR 354ff.). At the first stage, commitments are held without much reflection. The tradition develops and is embodied in a community, but with little or no self-awareness of its distinctiveness. (Examples of traditions at this stage are by no means limited to isolated tribal cultures; consider the heyday of the Enlightenment, or certain forms of twentieth-century scientism.) In a second stage difficulties arise enabling members to recognize that they belong to a tradition of inquiry that is one among a number of such traditions. Internal developments may have led some members to have noticed inconsistencies or inadequacies within the tradition, perhaps in its social embodiment or in authoritative interpretations of its normative texts. Contact with another tradition may have prompted such observations, perhaps by posing hitherto unthought-of questions, or by the application of new criteria of adequacy. The third stage determines the success or failure of the tradition. It may be that its members succeed in showing that it can respond to the internal and/or external challenges. It may do so by drawing upon its own resources, or by drawing upon the resources of another tradition, suitably modified so that they cohere with its own commitments, or both. Some reinterpretation of its principles may be required but, to the extent that those principles remain intact and are embodied in a coherent way of life, the tradition has vindicated its commitments and has reached a stage of maturity.

The ways in which one tradition can challenge the commitments of another are numerous. They all, however, involve grappling with the complexities of the history of inquiry that constitute that tradition's present form. Furthermore, the challenger cannot appeal solely to the commitments of her own tradition. As we saw with regard to pluralism, that would indeed be to apply one's own norms and criteria upon another without justification. Rather, the challenger must so engage with the commitments of the rival tradition that her argument satisfies, at least in part, the challenged tradition's criteria of rationality. Thus it is not enough, as almost everyone knows, for science to appeal to its own working assumptions about reality in order simply to rule out religious beliefs. Nor can religious traditions appeal to their own principles without further ado to assert the limited significance of scientific claims.

This is not to suggest that two traditions might share enough to establish a third area of easily-agreed-upon common ground, so that they could then step outside of their own traditions to judge more neutrally between their rival claims. To step outside one or other of the competing traditions would be to deprive oneself of sufficient standards for their rational assessment. So any judgment as to the truth of claims to which members of a tradition are committed can be made only according to the principles of one tradition or another, or to principles they share. A genuine challenge could take the form of trying to show how one of the doctrines or practices of the rival tradition is inconsistent with its key commitments. An example: one could appeal to scientific data to support the idea that homosexuality is an innate disposition or, as one could say, "natural," in a significant percentage of the population. One could then appeal to Roman Catholicism's apparent commitment to natural law to argue that its beliefs in that area are incoherent. A somewhat similar kind of challenge would be to appeal to evidence that two rival traditions accept and which indicates that a doctrine or practice of one of them cannot be justified. An obvious example here is the challenge by Western science to the practice of reading Genesis as a scientific document. Another challenge might try to show that, although a community pays lip-service to a doctrine, in fact it consistently teaches and practices patterns of life that contradict the doctrine. This is, of course, a particularly important challenge for ecclesiology. It has also been made to non-religious traditions, for example Gunnar Myrdal's classic analysis of the relation between liberal values and actual social practices in America.[30]

More radically, a challenge might try to show how a tradition has insufficient resources, theoretical and practical, to explain or assimilate certain significant aspects of reality. It may then go on to argue that its own tradition is better able to deal with any commitments from the other tradition that should be retained, and so provides a more comprehensive and coherent explanation of reality and thus a more truthful way of life. Classic examples of such radical challenges developed against religious bodies, especially the church, can be found in the work of those hermeneuts of suspicion, Marx, Nietzsche and Freud.

If the tradition, religious or otherwise, that is challenged in these and other ways cannot respond successfully to such criticisms (and there is of course a broad range of ways to do so), the tradition has failed. Its commitments and their embodiment are shown to be untrue. And if the challenging tradition can show that it can deal, not only with the criticisms it addressed to its rival, but also with all the challenges that the challenged tradition can mount against the challenger's own commitments, then it has shown itself to be a superior tradition. The challenger has shown that it was justified in asserting that its own commitments are true and that it is more worthy of adherence than the failed tradition. Those commitments from the defeated tradition that survive its demise may then be found to be better understood if reset within the norms and principles of the challenging tradition. In this way the first tradition is subsumed into its rival. When this happens, or when members of a tradition desert a sterile tradition for another, the rival tradition has been shown to be more truthful and thus superior.

30. Gunnar Myrdal, *An American Dilemma* (New York: Harper, 1944).

Of course, two or more traditions may often exist for some time before the superiority of one of them is demonstrated. Some traditions, indeed, have little explanatory power or are more obviously incoherent, and so die off relatively quickly. (Consider the various New Age religions, or, some might say, Marxist-Leninism and Enlightenment liberalism.) But many religious and non- or anti-religious traditions have proven themselves to be rich and flexible enough to persist for many centuries without obviously demonstrating either their superiority or inferiority. Two incompatible traditions may inhabit largely unrelated societies so that their adherents do not come into contact with one another frequently enough to make comparison possible or worthwhile, such as Christianity and Confucianism in the Middle Ages. Alternatively, some traditions may recognize that their commitments do not at this point really conflict with one another if they are properly understood, as has been argued is the case with Western science and some religious traditions.[31] Yet other traditions may simply have given up trying to engage with one another, perhaps because the debate became too violent (as frequently among religious traditions, or between capitalist and socialist economic traditions), or because the debate became sterile and interminable, or because another tradition engendered apathy or despair about issues of truth. On the view proposed here, however, a tradition's refusal to engage in debate, whether on skeptical grounds or not, throws doubt on whether its adherents may logically claim that their convictions are true.

According to this account, then, it is logically possible to argue for the truth or falsity of traditionally warranted beliefs, and thus for the superiority or inferiority of particular traditions and their concrete identities, without trying to find tradition-free principles by which to adjudicate among them. A tradition is true insofar as it can respond satisfactorily to internal and external challenges to its claims. Traditions are incommensurable in a sufficiently radical way that their commitments – in the case of religions, to their conception of ultimate truth – cannot be translated into another tradition without distortion or remainder. Yet they are by no means absolutely incommensurable; the commitments of one tradition may conflict with those of a rival tradition, and in such a way that one tradition can be shown to be false (or less true) to members of both traditions.

31. See, e.g., John Polkinghorne's 1993–1994 Gifford Lectures, published as *The Faith of a Physicist: Reflections of a Bottom-Up Thinker* (Minneapolis: Fortress Press, 1996); and Stanley Jaki, *Cosmos and Creator* (Edinburgh: Scottish Academic Press, 1980); also Thomas F. Torrance, e.g., *Divine and Contingent Order* (Oxford: Oxford University Press, 1981). For a forceful argument against improper ways of understanding science, see Mary Midgley, *Science As Salvation* (London: Routledge, 1992).

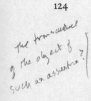

the transcultural of the object of such an assertion?

However, while there is no *a priori* reason to think that truthfulness and superiority cannot be demonstrated, concretely it may take the rest of time to do so. Nor is there any reason to think that superiority will always be demonstrated to everyone's satisfaction. This seems especially to be the case with religious traditions. Thus the superiority of a tradition is not necessarily demonstrated by the mass conversion to it by the members of another tradition. Many factors other than truthfulness are involved in making a tradition popular. It seems unlikely, for example, that the success of Christianity over paganism at the time of Constantine rested entirely upon the cogency of the arguments put forward by the Church Fathers or the truthfulness or rightness of the Christian way of life. A tradition may be popular, or at least keep going, for all the wrong reasons, including blatant incoherence. Its adherents may be willing to admit, if pushed, that their commitments provide them with a consoling yet ultimately unreal view of things, one that is convenient for them because it makes few demands upon their time and freedom of choice. In contrast, a tradition may be true, yet have few adherents. This may be explainable on the tradition's own terms, perhaps by a doctrine about the demanding nature of its way of life, or by a doctrine about election or grace.

criteria of truth

① Internal coherence, across history

Truth and superiority should not, then, be measured primarily by the number of a tradition's adherents, nor by its growth or decline, but primarily by two quite different criteria. First, a religious or non-religious tradition can be judged by its ability to demonstrate satisfactorily the internal consistency among its originating events, its normative texts and the history of their interpretation, and its concrete identity. The criterion of internal coherence need not be demonstrated by means of an epic system. The Christian tradition, for one, has reasons coherent with its central beliefs as to why it cannot be adequately mapped out in terms of a single systematic principle. Second, a tradition can be judged by its explanatory power, by its ability to respond to all challenges to its conception of reality and its concrete response to it. If any tradition, religious or not, can do both these things satisfactorily, then it can reasonably claim to be true. And if it can do so demonstrably better than rival traditions, then it can reasonably claim to be superior to them.

② Explanatory power = resistance to challenges

reasonable claim ≠ demonstration

MacIntyre's traditioned notion of truth and argument just outlined may be somewhat disappointing to some. We have been taught by modernity to associate truth with epic qualities such as certainty, knock-down proofs, and timelessness. He offers a much more conflictual, historical and contextual view of how we inquire into and arrive at truth and how we decide between rival claims and the traditions within which they arise. I have tried to show that his view is more coherent and reasonable than the modern view of truth, while it evidently coheres well with a theodramatic horizon.

The theory of traditioned inquiry suggests a way of moving beyond the difficulties of the postmodern horizon with regard to our responsibility to act. Unlike both the modern and the postmodern views, this theory encourages, indeed requires, our debating partners to be truly other, really different from ourselves, for without such difference our debate cannot be genuine and truth cannot be pursued. Debate and the pursuit of true knowledge and truthful practice are dependent upon the premise that it is logically possible for the other – whether a member of one's own tradition or of another tradition – to embody a relation to reality that reflects convictions that are genuinely different from our own without being radically incommensurate with them. We must engage with these convictions and their embodiment when they conflict with ours, because they may be superior. Difference and truth are thus mutually dependent; one cannot have one without the other. If we say with the humanist-pluralists that the other is not truly different, because her convictions must give way to mine or because they merely mask an underlying identity or shared goal, then we cannot truly debate. As a consequence, we cannot demonstrate the truthfulness of our tradition and its embodiment. If, however, we say with the postmoderns that all traditions and systems are necessarily untrue or mere exercises in domination, then we all are the same in our futility. We cannot be really different from others; our rejection of all constructions occludes the otherness of those who are in fact different from us. As a consequence, our activity cannot be responsive to their differences, for we do not permit them any means to challenge our convictions about who they are.

Certainly MacIntyre's theory does not prevent the collapse of the quest for truth into a quest for domination. The theory does not deny the reality of sin; nor is it proposed as a methodology by which all inquiry would become liberating and just. I have proposed it here as a suitable means by which the church can make sense of itself and its tasks (and its failures) to others within the present ecclesiological context. Many people believe that the Christian tradition and its central commitments have not as yet been falsified by any rival tradition. Christians have no compelling reason for not continuing to think that their tradition of inquiry and its embodiment in the church still offers the best way of drawing closer to the truth. For Christians to abandon their commitments and their tasks of witness and discipleship would be irrational. To give up their orientation to Jesus Christ as the ultimate truth and goal would be a false humility.[32] Furthermore, it would be a failure of its responsibility both to act, and to act for the other, within society. On the view I have outlined, it would follow that any society that aims towards truth and right must encourage debate among the plurality of traditions within and outside it, and then reform, abandon or develop beliefs, social practices and institutions that embody the results of that debate. MacIntyre's theory indicates that there is a logical parity among all as-yet-unfalsified traditions such that all of them qualify as participants in the debate. Religions are among such traditions. So it would be irresponsible of Christians not to bring their commitments with them as they debate with others about issues, such as morality, economics and politics, that affect society's shape and direction. And it would be irrational for others not to listen to the church's proposals and challenges, just as the church should listen to theirs.

It is doubtful that there is any sphere of social life where religious traditions do not have something to say. At the very least a Christian economist, for example, will want to ensure that his proposals conform to Christian norms and criteria, and do not inhibit Christians in their witness and discipleship. The non-Christian economist will likely have goals and norms that may well be somewhat distinct from Christian ones. It may be, then, that the proposals of the two economists may conflict. It would be irrational and irresponsible for the non-Christian economist to deny any role to Christian considerations in the thinking of his interlocutor, as it would be for the Christian economist to deny any role to, say, liberal or socialist considerations in the other. Christian elements in one's theory are not private options; they reflect one's commitment to a tradition of inquiry that is as public as the liberal or socialist traditions are. No one can ignore or dismiss any rival tradition's claims without undermining the truthfulness of her own. The more she does so, the more her own convictions become merely private, irrelevant opinions.

It needs to be said that the proposals I have made here are part of a Christian response to a set of specific challenges arising from within a particular context. Moreover, I have appropriated a philosophical argument

32. A point made by Jeffrey Stout, *Ethics After Babel*, p. 25.

that is itself more than likely developed within a Christian perspective, or certainly within a culture influenced by Christianity. The proposal is therefore not meant as an epic account, as if it were adequate for all times and places. Its formulation here is driven by my agenda, namely to aid practical-prophetic ecclesiology in its task of reflecting upon the witness and pastoral care of the church as this is embodied in its concrete identity. It may well be, then, that members of other religious bodies, especially those located more in non-Western cultures, may find it better to develop their own, rather different understanding of these issues. No matter; I am not attempting a normative, cross-traditional account here. The theory is meant as a first step in getting debate going among these religious bodies. (But even in this concern I may prove to be too agenda-bound. For members of one particular religious body may have reasons why they should not, in fact, engage in debate with other religious bodies. They may have a different view of truth, one as yet unfalsified, that does not require debate. This does seem unlikely though.)

MacIntyre's focus on moral traditions enables him to talk rather more easily than theologians can or should about superiority claims, given the church's history. His theory places the church's witness on the same logical level with the claims of all other unfalsified traditions, religious and non-religious, and their respective embodiments. Of the church and of them we can say, for non-theological as well as for theological reasons: All unfalsified traditions can reasonably claim to have access to truth of some kind; their goals will determine what kind. Many traditions, both religious and non- or anti-religious, believe that they are uniquely oriented towards humanity's ultimate goal and norm. Again, until such a tradition is falsified or subsumed within another, such beliefs are reasonable. Their orientation is embodied in their concrete identities, in the beliefs, practices and valuations which, they believe, reflect their goal more truthfully than any other body. It follows, then, that no single tradition or religion can possess the truth in epic form, for none has as yet subsumed all others into itself and so must still engage with them and learn from them. And to make that assertion is already to claim a view on the matter that is superior to those traditions or religions that think they do possess the epic view, and so initiates debate with them.

The church's concrete identity is, so Christians believe, closer to the truth than any other. Integral to the church's claim is its acknowledgment of sinfulness and failure in all areas of human endeavor. The church cannot say that its members are morally superior, nor perhaps do they have a greater chance to achieve salvation than others. Nor are they loved any more by God than the members of any other religious or non-religious group. They are, of course, loved by God, and in a special way, too, since they are called to be Christians. But one can say that God loves the atheist or the Hindu in a special, though different way, too. The church is indeed different from all other religious bodies, as any embodied tradition is from another. It believes it is a chosen people, a holy (concretely, in the sense of "set apart") nation, with a special relationship with God – all because it is called to follow and witness explicitly to the ultimate revealed truth, Jesus Christ. Because of its call, it can call itself the People of God, the people who are devoted to the trinitarian God. It can also say of itself that it is concretely the Body of Christ, for it is his Spirit which makes possible any success in displaying Christ's presence on earth through its witness and discipleship.

MacIntyre sums up the traditioned nature of moral inquiry in an epigram: "[T]he good life for man is the life spent in seeking for the good life for man, and the virtues necessary for the seeking are those which will enable us to understand what more and what else the good life for man is."[33] Such a view is clearly congenial to the theodramatic idea of a life on the way, a struggle with no clear conception of the goal. The Christian version of that epigram could be: *The life of discipleship is the life spent in seeking for what constitutes good discipleship, and the virtues and graces necessary for the seeking are those which will enable us to understand what more and what else the life of discipleship is.* One central task of the church is to be the *locus* and product of that search. So we can define it in terms of its vocation as *that religious body whose concrete identity is structured by its quest to discern how its response to its Lord should structure its concrete identity*. The function of practical-prophetic ecclesiology is to aid the church in that quest.[34]

Some of the ways ecclesiology can perform this function are discussed in chapter 7 below. But first, the next chapter must consider how another Christian horizon, the inclusivist, bears upon modern ecclesiology.

33. MacIntyre, *After Virtue*, p. 219. See also Eagleton, *Postmodernism*, p. 77.
34. The notion of a "quest" is from MacIntyre, *After Virtue*, p. 218. See also Stanley Hauerwas, *Sanctify Them In the Truth: Holiness Exemplified* (Nashville: Abingdon/T&T Clark, 1998), p. 128, and Kathryn Tanner, *Theories of Culture: A New Agenda for Theology* (Minneapolis: Fortress Press, 1997), p. 155.

6

Inclusivist ecclesiology

The previous two chapters were devoted, first, to a critical analysis of ecclesiological proposals generated within a pluralist horizon, and then to a constructive response to issues raised by pluralists and postmoderns regarding debate between traditions, truth, and the responsibility for the other. The present chapter discusses the same issues with regard to the inclusivist horizon and its bearing upon ecclesiology. Towards the end of the chapter, I conclude and summarize my case against the adequacy of the modern ecclesiological method. The guiding questions here are those that have accumulated over the course of the discussion as a whole: Does an inclusivist horizon enable ecclesiology to help the church's witness and its pastoral care within the present ecclesiological context? Specifically, can it help the church perform what I have argued is one of its more significant tasks within the present context, namely to promote genuine particularity among traditions of inquiry and their embodiments? Can an inclusivist ecclesiology help the church act responsibly for the other, for those who are different, even as it embodies its quest for truth?

"Inclusivism" is a term that encompasses a fairly wide range of positions, as J. A. DiNoia notes in his book, *The Diversity of Religions*.[1] DiNoia's definition is broad enough to encompass both a minimal and a maximal form of inclusivism. The maximal form is asserted by those who believe that "all religious communities implicitly aim at the salvation that the Christian community most adequately commends." Non-Christian

---

1. J. A. DiNoia, O.P., *The Diversity of Religions: A Christian Perspective* (Washington: Catholic University Press, 1992). S. Mark Heim points out how some seemingly inclusivist statements are actually pluralistic. See his *Salvations: Truth and Difference in Religion* (Maryknoll, NY: Orbis, 1995), e.g., pp. 66ff.

religious bodies may think and act as if their ultimate goals are distinctively different from the church's. However, their goals in fact orient them to some degree towards Jesus Christ, and to the extent that they do, their concrete identities may be truthful and their way of life lead to salvation. A minimal version of inclusivism says little or nothing about the salvific significance of non-Christian religions as such, but asserts "at least that salvation is a present possibility for the members of other religious communities."[2] It is evident that the Christological and philosophical presuppositions of both forms of the inclusivist position enable its adherents to maintain the traditional claims for the church far more easily than within pluralism. All inclusivists, as we noted earlier, believe that Jesus Christ alone is the savior of the world, that it is his grace which penetrates all religions and cultures, whether or not they are aware of him. Inclusivists would deny, furthermore, that this is simply a relative perspective. Rather, their claims reflect the actual state of affairs, namely, that all truth and all goodness come through Christ and his Spirit.

Of the two forms of inclusivism, it is the maximal kind that is of interest here, for it generates a distinctive horizon within which to reflect upon the church. Maximal inclusivism asserts that all that has been touched by the truth and goodness of Christ is in some way embraced within the church's reality. There is therefore a connection at the ontological level between the church and all that lies outside its visible boundaries, both religious and non-religious. Henri de Lubac displays a Roman Catholic version of this belief when he writes:[3]

> Nothing authentically human, whatever its origin, can be alien to her [i.e., the church catholic] .... To see in Catholicism one religion among others, one system among others, even if it be added that it is the only true religion, the only system that works, is to mistake its very nature, or at least to stop at the threshold. Catholicism is religion itself. It is the form that humanity must put on in order finally to be itself.

This maximal version of inclusivism thus becomes an epic framework for understanding all aspects of the relations between God, world and church. In identifying Christianity or, more narrowly, Roman Catholicism, with authentic humanity, the horizon pushes theological reflection in the direction of a Christian humanism. We can call this set of beliefs, "ecclesiological inclusivism." It is distinct from minimal inclusivism, which need have little bearing upon ecclesiology. Those who maintain

2. DiNoia, *Diversity of Religions*, p. ix.
3. Henri de Lubac S.J., *Catholicism: A Study of Dogma in Relation to the Corporate Destiny of Mankind*, trans. Lancelot C. Sheppard (New York: Sheed and Ward, 1958), p. 153.

the latter – as I think Karl Barth did in his *Church Dogmatics* period[4] – may be optimistic about the universality of salvation and may acknowledge the relation between Jesus Christ and all truth and goodness outside the church in much the same way as within a theodramatic horizon. But they do not attempt systematically to draw out the implications of these beliefs as they discuss the church, which may be treated as more or less a separate issue. Thus a theologian may be rather more inclusivist than exclusivist or pluralist about salvation and truth, but if her inclusivism is of a sufficiently minimal kind, it may be part of a theodramatic horizon and ecclesiology, since her inclusivism has no determinative bearing upon her understanding of the nature and function of the church.[5]

The discussion of inclusivism here is therefore confined to the maximalist, ecclesiological form. Perhaps the most influential exponent of ecclesiological inclusivism, and certainly one of the most profound, is Karl Rahner. So I will take him as my primary interlocutor, looking also at a couple of more recent theologians, Jean-Marie Tillard and Leonardo Boff, when appropriate.[6] Rahner's theology can be viewed anywhere between two extremes. At one end, his work can be read as a highly systematic theology grounded upon a philosophical-theological ontology and anthropology. At the other end, one can read his work as a series of occasional reflections upon diverse topics that cannot without distortion be forced into a system. There is some evidence that Rahner's own way of thinking, especially perhaps in his ecclesiology, moved from somewhere near the first reading to a position much closer to the second, as he moved from a systematic, sacramental approach to a greater concern for the concrete church and its task of witness.[7] Indeed, he comes at times quite close to the kind of occasionalist practical-prophetic ecclesiology I

4. Karl Barth could be understood as an exclusivist on the basis of the way he opposes "religion" to Christianity in his early work. I would say that by his *Church Dogmatics* period he had more of an inclusivist position, though one that had little bearing upon his ecclesiology. See *Church Dogmatics*, trans. G. W. Bromiley, II/2 (Edinburgh: T&T Clark, 1957), pp. 417f.

5. Non-ecclesiological inclusivist texts include Gavin D'Costa, *Theology and Religious Pluralism: The Challenge of Other Religions* (Oxford: Blackwell, 1986), and, more minimalist, S. Mark Heim, *Salvations*. My criticisms of ecclesiological inclusivism do not apply to these theorists of religion.

6. I regret that my examples must be Roman Catholic. Protestant inclusivists tend either to be of a minimalist kind, such as Wolfhart Pannenberg, or else to slip over towards pluralism.

7. See Michael Fahey's contribution to "A Changing Ecclesiology in a Changing Church: A Symposium on Development in the Ecclesiology of Karl Rahner," ed. Leo O'Donovan, S.J., *Theological Studies* 38 (1977), 736–762, esp. pp. 760f. See also E. Vacek, S.J., "Development within Rahner's Theology," *Irish Theological Quarterly* 42 (1975), 36–49. For an excellent book-length discussion of Rahner's evolving ecclesiology, see Richard Lennan, *The Ecclesiology of Karl Rahner* (Oxford: Clarendon Press, 1995).

am advocating here.[8] But while I think his work is more useful for contemporary theology if it is read less systematically, it is the more systematic Rahner that has been influential in ecclesiology. My thesis, anyway, applies to both readings, for I will argue that his ecclesiology, whether it is rigorously systematic or ad hoc and occasionalist, cannot be adequate to the present ecclesiological context.

Rahner fully acknowledged that the Spirit of truth is active outside as well as inside the church. At the same time, he always sought to maintain the uniqueness and superiority of the church against "ecclesiological relativism,"[9] and did so without turning to exclusivism. For him, the church is distinct from all other communal bodies, secular or religious, for it is "*the* way of salvation" (TI X, 31, his emphasis). Although it is sinful and finite, the church's orientation to Jesus Christ permits it to gain access to the truth about the world. This truth, although theological and thus never something conveyed by univocal propositions, is by no means simply just another religious perspective. Rather, it is the basis for the superiority of the church over all other religious bodies.[10] In avoiding a pluralistic perspectivalism, Rahner was following the teaching of his strand of the Christian tradition of inquiry, which since the middle of the nineteenth century has at various times warned against the dangers of ecclesiological relativism.[11]

As I noted in chapter 2, Rahner's ecclesiology is structured according to a sacramental model, and thus makes use of the twofold construal. His approach is grounded in his ontology, which is likewise bipartite. For him, "being is of itself symbolic, because it necessarily 'expresses' itself" (TI IV, 229). This ontological principle applies to "the basic structure of all Christianity" (TI IV, 252) and thus to the being of the church as well. As

---

8. I have argued that Rahner can be read coherently as an unsystematic, occasionalist and thoroughly pastoral theologian, in "Indirect Methods in Theology: Rahner as an Ad Hoc Apologist," *The Thomist* 56:4 (1992), 613–633. For more detailed arguments along not dissimilar lines, see Karen Kilby, "The Vorgriff auf esse: A Study in the Relation of Philosophy to Theology in the Thought of Karl Rahner" (PhD Diss., Yale University, 1994); and R. R. Reno, *The Ordinary Transformed: Karl Rahner and the Christian Vision of Transcendence* (Grand Rapids: Eerdmans, 1995). Fergus Kerr discusses Reno and Kilby's interpretations of Rahner favorably in the context of an analysis of Balthasar's criticisms of Rahner; see his *Immortal Longings: Versions of Transcending Humanity* (Notre Dame: University of Notre Dame Press, 1997), pp. 171ff.

9. See, for example, Rahner's discussion in "The New Image of the Church," *Theological Investigations*, vol. X (New York: Crossroad, 1977), especially p. 13, henceforth cited in the text as (TI volume, page). See also *Foundations of the Christian Faith* (New York: Seabury, 1978), pp. 352f.   10. *Foundations*, pp. 342f.

11. See Francis A. Sullivan, S. J., *Salvation Outside the Church?* (New York: Paulist Press, 1992), pp. 113f. for a sharply worded citation from Pius IX; for a rather different view from Paul VI, see pp. 185ff.

Rahner argues in *The Church and the Sacraments*,[12] the church is not only a hierarchical, juridical organization, though it is certainly also that, but *as* that organization, it is the "fundamental sacred sign or sacrament," or "the visible outward expression," of grace (CS 23, 34). Hence the church is not constituted by its human activity and institutions alone, but has a structure similar to the Incarnation. For the church is the "grace of God in the 'flesh' of an historical and tangible ecclesiastical embodiment" (CS 23) and as such, it is the presence of Christ within the history of humanity (CS 19).

The twofold, sacramental construal of the church is clearly in line with Rahner's ecclesiological agenda. Especially in his earlier work he was concerned to develop a way of reflecting upon the church that was more genuinely theological than that prevalent in Roman Catholicism at the time. Like the *Nouvelle Théologie* group who influenced him, Rahner sought to move beyond what they and he believed to be the one-sidedly juridical and quasi-sociological ecclesiology of neo-Scholasticism. Theologians working in the schools of the latter movement did not deny the theological aspects of the church. But they focused so heavily upon the institutional organization that it became difficult to discuss the constitutive activity of the Spirit. This difficulty was aggravated, and in part caused, by what Rahner and others saw as their too-rigid separation of nature and supernature.[13]

Rahner was also increasingly concerned to effect a better understanding of the relation between the church and the world. He thought it especially vital to bring the Roman church out of the defensive mentality it had fallen into since the Modernist crisis.[14] He combined an optimism about non-Christian cultural realities with a level-headed recognition of what he called the new diaspora situation of the church within modern secularized societies.[15] He believed that the dominance of Christianity within its various social and cultural environments is in such decline that

12. Karl Rahner, *The Church and the Sacraments* (New York: Herder, 1963). Cited here as (CS page).

13. See, e.g., Rahner's essay "Concerning the Relationship between Nature and Grace," TI I, 297–317. See also Reno, *The Ordinary Transformed*, pp. 57–133, for an insightful discussion of Rahner's Roman Catholic inheritance on this issue and his response to it.

14. Richard Lennan argues that Rahner moved from an organic ecclesiology to one that stressed the need for the church to engage the world; see Lennan's *Ecclesiology of Karl Rahner*, p. 9.

15. For Rahner's view of the church's diaspora situation see, e.g., his *The Christian of the Future* (London: Herder, 1967), and his essay, "On the Presence of Christ in the Diaspora Community According to the Teaching of the Second Vatican Council," TI X, 84–102; also Lennan, *Ecclesiology of Karl Rahner*, pp. 121ff. and 154–160.

Christians will in the future find themselves to be a poor and insignificant minority (TI X, 99). This need not be cause for alarm because non-Christian secular culture is impregnated by the grace of Christ and so is itself a vehicle of the Spirit's action. However, Rahner argued that the changed context does bring to the fore the question of the salvation of non-Christians, who now quite obviously make up the vast majority of humankind.

In response, Rahner's ecclesiology seeks to maintain three key principles: first, the traditional Christian doctrine that faith is necessary for salvation, and second, that there is no salvation outside the church. Together these two principles imply that faith is orientated necessarily towards the church. But they must be reconciled with a third principle, the doctrine of the universal salvific will (1 Tim. 2:4) strongly endorsed by Vatican II, which implied the availability of salvation to countless non-Christians. Rahner believed that these three principles indicate that "somehow all men must be capable of being members of the church" and thus there are "degrees of membership" (TI VI, 391). To show how this could be so, Rahner developed his concept of the supernatural existential along ecclesiological lines. The uncreated grace of God's self-communication is always present unthematically in the consciousness of every human being. Yet this transcendental offer of grace, God's saving self-offering, is not a natural attribute, but a truly gratuitous offer, "a unexacted, unmerited gift" beyond the gifts of creation (TI I, 310ff.). Thus there is a "holy mystery" at the heart of all human knowing and willing. All of our activity, religious or otherwise, is in some sense a response, for or against, to this offer. As a consequence it is possible to say that acceptance of God's offer occurs implicitly whenever "a person undertakes and lives the duty of each day in the quiet sincerity of patience, in devotion to his material duties and the demands made upon him by the persons under his care" (TI VI, 23). Rahner does not stop here, though, since this would imply a rather individualistic notion of salvation. According to him, the People of God, the biblical model of the church reaffirmed by Vatican II, "extends as far as humanity itself" (TI II, 83), for the presence of God's self-communication within the heart of all individuals creates "a unity" among them.[16] Rahner notes that the resulting "people" is not to be confused with an invisible church of those who have made a decision for God. For one thing, the people's unity is manifested in a "historically verifiable way" (TI II, 84) by monogenism, by original sin, and, most

16. Rahner, *The Theology of Pastoral Action* (New York: Herder, 1968), p. 26.

generally, in "the one history of the human race" (CS 12). Not that this means that it is possible to achieve salvation by means of a purely natural morality. Salvation is always a gift, and our positive response to God's self-offer, even if only implicit, is made possible only by the grace of Christ.

The People of God is, however, only a partial expression of the human acceptance of God's salvific offer. It presses forward, so to speak, to its full realization in the visible church. And so, because saving faith is so closely linked with the visible church, one must say that all of the People of God, whether they know it or not, and whether they are religious or not, are necessarily orientated towards the visible church. Even when people are members of non- or anti-Christian bodies, those who live well have an implicit desire to become members of the final expression of God's salvific offer (*votum Ecclesiae*). If, however, they genuinely (i.e., existentially rather than simply verbally or merely by their membership in other bodies) reject the visible church, they deny their membership in the People of God. And to deny one's membership in the People of God is in effect to reject one's salvation, since it is the same as rejecting the transcendental offer of Godself. In this way, then, Rahner can say that the membership in church is, in the intentionality of the believer at least, necessary for salvation (TI II, 83–88). But at the same time, those who do not reject their membership in the People of God are in a real sense members, though in a different degree, of the visible church through grace.

Rahner's twofold construal thus postulates, on the one hand, a primary reality, the People of God, which is a universal and largely implicit ecclesial form constituted by all those, non-Christian or Christian, who have accepted the transcendental offer of God's self-communication. On the other hand, there is the fuller expression of that reality, the visible church which makes explicit that offer and its acceptance. Rahner is clear that the order here is significant: the church is the expression of what is hidden and *already* present in the world, namely the salvific grace of God. Thus the concrete church is based upon the "prior reality" that is the People of God (CS 13), and this priority is both temporal and theological. He points out that this construal reverses Augustine's distinction between two kinds of Christians, both of whom are visibly members of the church: those who are true Christians (in their hearts, too: *corde*) and those who only go through the motions (*only* visibly: *corpore*). By contrast, for Rahner *all* people of goodwill are truly Christian in their heart and are therefore true members of the church, even if they are only anonymously rather than visibly Christian (TI X, 19). The visible church, in consequence, is "the concrete historical manifestation, in the dimension of a history that has acquired eschatological significance, and in the social dimension, of precisely that salvation which is achieved through the grace of God through the entire length and breadth of humanity" (TI X, 14). Rahner stressed that his notion of the anonymous Christian and his version of the model "People of God" was not meant to solve all problems, let alone undermine the importance of missions and preaching (TI VI, 397). It is likely that his theory was initially intended as an effort in internal rather than external apologetics. He saw it as a suitable way for the believer to consider the matter so as to "keep him from panic" about the salvific status of the many non-Christians he knows (TI VI, 396). It had the advantage, too, of promoting the church's new affirmation of modernity by stressing the fundamental unity of all humankind. The church now had a theoretical basis to support Vatican II's call to join with other religious and non-religious bodies in the various humanizing projects of the modern world.

Rahner's theory also appeared to many theologians to be a development of the tradition into a very useful form of external apologetics. His account of the church and its relation with the world is constructed from a realized-eschatological perspective. It describes who we – graced humanity as a whole – already secretly are in the light of our final redemption. Rahner contends that potentially, in the light of the goal to which every human being tends, we are all members of the church triumphant, whether or not we have any explicit connection with the concrete church. His theoretical reformulation of this belief made it difficult for those modern, agnostic Westerners who found his expressivist ontology congenial to ignore the gospel. If God is indeed closer than we are to ourselves, as Rahner seemed (with Augustine) to be saying, the question of God and the challenge of the church cannot be brushed aside as irrelevant to human endeavor. Thus Rahner's theory would be of major significance for those Roman Catholics who wanted to counter the belief that society had become so secularized that it could no longer find room for religious matters in the public domain.

Nevertheless, I want to suggest that while Rahner's systematic ecclesiology might have been suitable for his particular ecclesiological context, it is less than helpful or adequate for our own. The issues addressed by his theory can be better dealt with in a theodramatic horizon, and by a practical-prophetic form of ecclesiology. Moreover, significant ecclesiological problems follow as a consequence of the expressivist ontology and the twofold construal. We begin with internal apologetic issues, before turning later to problems with external apologetics.

Used inclusively and systematically, the twofold construal sets up an unnecessary dilemma. If one bifurcates the church in terms of an expressivist ontology, then one is perforce faced with a question: Is the church's primary reality unique to it? If, in the interest, say, of maintaining the church's witness, we say "yes," we fall into ecclesiological exclusivism. For all who use the twofold construal, exclusivists, pluralists and inclusivists alike, seem to agree that the primary reality must be salvifically significant. So to say "yes" is to deny the salvific significance of other religious bodies. Since most people no longer believe that exclusivism is a Christian possibility, they reply negatively to the question. But then we must more or less universalize the primary reality. And for us to be able to do that, it must be deep-spiritual enough to be a self-identical reality in spite of the evident pluralities of the concrete.

In Rahner's ecclesiologically inclusivist view, as we have seen, the twofold construal unites the church at a prethematic and spiritual level with what is not visibly or explicitly the church. The result is an epic notion of the People of God, highly spiritualized and encompassing everyone, for everyone has access to God's transcendental self-offer in grace. In spite of their membership in religious and non-religious bodies with diverse concrete identities, all people of goodwill, Buddhists and atheists, New Agers and Marxists, can be members of the People of God. The concept of people at work here is obviously unusual, since the customary usage involves the possibility of distinguishing, however vaguely, between one people and another. As a result of their members' acceptance of God's self-offer, other religious and non-religious bodies besides the church can be expressive of God's salvific offer (TI V, 121). To the extent that such bodies are good and right, Christ can be found therein, albeit to a lesser degree than in the church.[17] Both they and the church are constituted theologically, then, by the same thing: acceptance of God's salvific self-offer.

Again, this move is sufficiently reasonable on Christian grounds that it may well be appropriate in some contexts, possibly including Rahner's own, to make it. But in proportion as this universalizing and spiritualizing epic move is brought into ecclesiology as a system-structuring

---

17. See, e.g., *Foundations*, pp. 311ff. Admittedly Rahner says this only about *religious* bodies.

principle, it becomes harder to make the necessary dramatic counter-moves towards particularity and concreteness. In privileging the universal aspect and treating it as the normative origin of any particular realization, the realization, though certainly necessary, becomes less significant. The result is that the spiritual and universal are privileged theologically over the concrete and particular. One can stress how vital it is for the deep-spiritual to be expressed in visible form. But this is an insufficient move for particularity if one goes on to say that partial realizations can take concrete form in traditions as radically divergent as Buddhism and socialism, or Confucianism and Gnosticism. The distinctiveness of the concrete identities of the church's and the other traditions' embodiments are thereby relegated to secondary consideration.

Rahner himself, as I have noted, maintains the material as well as the formal distinctiveness of the church over against the world. He can do so, in part, I think, because of his rather *unsystematic* approach. His sacramental theology, for example, is a forceful theological description of the uniqueness of those aspects of the church's life. Yet he will also write things like this:

> However much a Christian and the church make individual statements, however much there is an ecclesial institution, and however much there are concrete sacraments, basically nevertheless a Christian and the church do not say something which others are against ... [T]he "yes" or the "no" of genuine competition cannot oppose the real essence of Christian existence, nor therefore of the church ... [A] Christian stands beyond all of the pluralistic confusion and hopes that in this beyond an ultimate "yes" is hidden in everyone who is of good will, a "yes" which cannot once again succumb to opposing opinions.[18]

We understand the point Rahner is making. But while it may have been possible for him in his own ecclesiological context to have achieved an appropriately tensive balance between universality and particularity, and between the spiritual and the concrete, it is unlikely that ecclesiological inclusivism can do so now. Either the context has changed significantly since Rahner's day or, more likely, he misread the context and its trajectory. The process of secularization and the loss of religious concern and activity once forecasted have instead taken a turn towards a rampant religiosity and perspectivalism. In many places the cultural environment has not got to the point at which it so secularizes the average individual that

18. Ibid., pp. 400f.

she has to be persuaded of the relevance of religion. Rather, it is just as likely that she will expend an appreciable amount of effort examining a comparatively broad range of competing religious traditions before selecting one.[19] Furthermore, at the theoretical level, the notion of a sharp contrast between theological and purely secular discourse has been strongly challenged. Theological or anti-theological claims are implicit in many supposedly neutral discourses and, as John Milbank has forcefully argued, the secular itself is a construct, not simply a given neutral background upon which competing ideologies are built.[20] The anti-theologies of the secular and the cultural pervasiveness of personal religious experimentation challenge the church, for they explicitly or implicitly deny its goal of glorying only in Christ crucified. If it is to perform its tasks within the contemporary ecclesiological context, the church needs to respond to such challenges by engaging in debate with their representative theoreticians and by fostering suitable counter-practices in its own communities. To postulate an underlying harmony between Christianity and the best forms of secular human endeavor is far too passive a response.

The changed context thus makes it harder to retain the subtle balance of Rahner's position. The twofold construal so identifies church and other bodies at their base that their particularities may now be understood as simply variant realizations within their respective cultural fields of what amounts to the same thing. The way is then opened up (though Rahner himself would certainly never take it) for treating the particularity of the church along pluralist lines, in largely cultural, sociological or psychological terms. The church's orientation to the truth of the world may indeed differentiate it from other religious bodies, but its distinctive shape can be explained as, for example, a social expression of a universal anthropological core. On such a view, the church displays the religious aspects of all that is best in its cultural environment, and Christianity becomes the religious ally of progressive Western humanism. The visible church and

19. For an argument against the earlier secularization thesis, see Robert Wuthnow, *The Restructuring of American Religion: Society and Faith since World War II* (Princeton: Princeton University Press, 1988); and less directly, Robert N. Bellah and associates, *Habits of the Heart: Individualism and Commitment in American Life* (New York: Harper and Row, 1985). The rise of religiosity or, less charitably and more theologically, neo-paganism, is not confined to the USA. See Nicholas Lash, "The Church in the State We're In," *Modern Theology* 13:1 (1997), 121–137.
20. John Milbank, *Theology and Social Theory: Beyond Secular Reason* (Oxford: Blackwell, 1990), p. 9. See also Peter B. Clarke and Peter Byrne, *Religion Defined and Explained* (New York: St. Martin's Press, 1993); and David Martin, *Reflections on Sociology and Theology* (Oxford: Clarendon Press, 1997), pp. 24, 35f.

its message can then be understood, as Walter Kasper has noted in his criticism of Rahner's eschatology, as "ultimately no more than the mere affirmation of what *is*, and what exists in principle, even without the church."[21] Distinctive practices such as the sacraments are reconfigured so as to reflect the church's religious function within society. But they can have no significance for life outside the visible church. For they are *religious* practices, unable to convey anything that is not already in existence or (implicitly, at least) known.[22]

Again, this is not Rahner's own position. Yet one can see how the way he privileges the universal and spiritual lays him open to such a pluralistic misreading of his work. The twofold construal makes it very difficult to close off such a reading. Peter Hodgson's critical comment, cited in chapter 4, that inclusivism is an intellectually indefensible "halfway house," seems to be near the mark, if only with regard to ecclesiological forms of inclusivism.[23] The force of Hodgson's comment, and the cogency of my suggestion that the systematic-ecclesiological kind of inclusivism tends to undermine the significance of the concrete and the particular, with deleterious consequences, can be seen if we look at some later theologians who use something like Rahner's approach.

As with Rahner, the liberation theologian Leonardo Boff's ecclesiological inclusivism is built upon his theological anthropology. There are, he says in his *Church: Charism and Power*, three stages by which religions arise. The first is the stage of the *homo religiosus*, in which the individual is called by the mystery of God at the heart of her being. The second stage is the response she makes to this call. The final, explicitly religious stage, occurs when the experience of mystery and its response is expressed in terms which are appropriated by the religious person from what is available to her in her culture.[24] According to this scheme, then, the experience of faith is a "reality that is more basic" than the church, one that lies at the heart of "every human community" (ECG 24). The originating element of the church is present among all people of goodwill and so we can say,

21. Walter Kasper, *Theology and Church* (New York: Crossroad, 1989), pp. 127f.

22. Thus even Rahner is open to Jeffrey Stout's criticism of academic theology, that it gives "the impression of saying nothing the atheists don't already know." *Ethics After Babel: The Languages of Morals and Their Discontents* (Boston: Beacon Press, 1988), p. 164.

23. Peter C. Hodgson, *Revisioning The Church: Ecclesial Freedom in the New Paradigm* (Philadelphia: Fortress Press, 1988), p. 94. S. Mark Heim argues, too, that "all theories of religion are either exclusivist or inclusivist in nature." *Salvations*, p. 152.

24. Leonardo Boff, *Church: Charism and Power: Liberation Theology and the Institutional Church*, trans. J. W. Diercksmeier (New York: Crossroad, 1992), ch. seven, esp. pp. 92ff.; cited henceforth as (CCP page). See also Boff's *Ecclesiogenesis: The Base Communities Reinvent the Church* (Maryknoll, NY: Orbis, 1986), p. 21; cited as (ECG page).

expanding and spiritualizing the meaning of the word 'church' accordingly, that "[n]o one is outside the church because there is no longer an 'outside,' because no one is outside the reality of God and the risen Christ" (CCP 152).

Thus we have here again a twofold construal of the church along inclusivist lines: a primary ecclesial reality that is universal, and its realization in various forms, the best of which is the church. Boff is usually quite clear in his witness to the church's orientation to the trinitarian God in and through Jesus Christ.[25] But at times one becomes less sure of this, especially when he stresses the universalism of the liberationist agenda. According to Boff, Vatican II contends that the universality of the church is not "founded on the specific nature of the Christian faith." Presumably by this he means that the church is not founded upon the universal significance of the particular person, Jesus of Nazareth. Rather it is founded upon "the universality of the historical aspirations of our current world, taken up and assumed by the church."[26] Church and world thus share not only a base, but a concrete goal, which is liberation or the establishment of just and peaceful community. The church must therefore work to strengthen "popular movements" as a "partner" of those who struggle for justice (CCP 129). The best form of the church is a combination of its "leaven" with the liberative praxis of those who are oppressed or who are in solidarity with the oppressed. Hence the primary reality of the church is best realized in the "authentic community" (ECG 6, 4) of the Basic Ecclesial Communities among the underclasses, which are "the correct expression of the church" (CCP 119).

While I do not find Boff's interpretation of Vatican II to be the most obvious or convincing one, it is evident (to me, anyway) that Boff's main concern is with the gospel, not with Marxism or an activism with a religious coating. "Liberation" is a concept in his hands which, while no doubt influenced by Marxist analysis, is one that conforms to the Scriptural precepts that require the church to work for a just and peaceful society and to privilege the poor and oppressed in all that it does. Yet it must be said that Boff's combination of universal goal (liberation) and universal base (by way of the twofold construal) leaves the church very little of its own to contribute. The way to the goal is liberative praxis, the norms for which are universally known, especially by the poor and oppressed. What, then,

25. See Boff's *Trinity and Society* (Maryknoll, NY: Orbis, 1988).
26. Boff, *Faith on the Edge: Religion and Marginalized Existence* (San Francisco: Harper and Row, 1989), p. 190.

can the church say of any significance about how to achieve liberation? Its primary function seems to be to provide religious motivation for liberative praxis, a motivation that might well be supplied by other religions or humanist philosophies.[27] Unless it can claim to have a distinctive conception of that to which liberative activity is orientated, the church's own practices lose much of their significance. They, and so the church itself, may be unique; but their uniqueness is not, finally, of much consequence. The specific practices and beliefs by which the primary, universal ecclesial core is realized in the visible church are of secondary importance compared with the question of their conformity to the universal norm of liberation. The construal thus seems to push Boff (against his express intent) towards a position where the church is not a necessary part of the means by which the goal is achieved.

One other example: the ecclesiology of Jean-Marie Tillard. Although he is by no means unsympathetic to the agendas of both Rahner and Boff, Tillard's is more of a restorationist ecclesiology, one that seeks to recover a neo-patristic and ecumenical way of being church. We noted earlier how he begins with the model of "communion." This is an analogical concept that refers primarily to the inner-trinitarian communion of the three divine persons and, secondarily, to its realization among us by means of our liturgical participation in that divine communion. It is when we celebrate the Eucharist that "the church is fully itself,"[28] and in a unique way (CoC 256). The eucharistic liturgy, which is "the central act of the community" (CoC 171), manifests "the profound being of the church of God" (CoC 169). Tillard then renders this twofold construal inclusive by remarking that "in its real depth, ecclesial *communion* goes beyond visible koinonia. ... [T]here exist those who are saved but ignorant of the fact that they are. And they belong to the *communion* of grace, which is for the Christian faith the essential value" (CoC 34f.). Thus communion, the essential element of the church, is shared by others of goodwill, indeed, by "[e]very upright being who has his conscience open to others." This is especially the case with "all those who adore God," for those who are "faithful to their religion or to their faith are spiritually united." There exists, according to Tillard, a "solidarity among believers," so that, "on a profound plane" a Muslim person at prayer and ourselves "become one" (CoC 35). Like Boff

27. See Vincent MacNamara, *Faith and Ethics: Recent Roman Catholicism* (Washington: Georgetown University Press, 1985) for a perceptive account of this recurrent problem in modern Roman Catholic theology.
28. Jean-Marie Tillard, O. P., *Church of Churches: The Ecclesiology of Communion*, trans. R. C. De Peaux, O. Praem. Collegeville: Glazier/Liturgical Press, 1992), p. 105; hereafter cited as (CoC page).

and Rahner, Tillard displays a laudable concern to avoid exclusivism. But to do so, again, his model of communion functions not only as universal basis but universal goal: "humanity is truly itself only in *communion*" (CoC 12). The goal is attainable through faith, but a faith that must be of a generic kind, it seems, if the goal is to be a genuinely universal possibility. Communion by a faithful attitude is thus achievable outside the church.

Tillard's inclusivist move lays open his rich trinitarian ecclesiology to expropriation by the pluralist religious sensibilities of our culture. The twofold construal and his emphasis upon the universal concrete goal of communion, taken together, render the concept of communion sufficiently analogical that it can be applied to virtually any kind of gathering in fellowship. Perhaps this is in some sense what should be said, for of course all social good is made possible by God's gracious presence. But by bringing all forms of communion together, the particularly Christian forms of it lose their distinctiveness. If communion is understood to be available outside the church, among those who do not explicitly gather in the name of Jesus Christ, to many people it may well be more obviously realized elsewhere than at the Eucharist. The warm, fuzzy feelings that indicate oneness are often much less evident at church than they are, say, among a group of *aficionados* at Bayreuth, or among a group of academics for whom baseball expresses something essential about the American experience, when together they attend a game of peculiar subtlety. Indeed, if true fellowship is the point of the church, can what one finds at church on Sundays ever measure up to the kind of communion found within a platoon on the front line in which each man is willing to sacrifice himself for the others?

Moreover, Tillard's inclusivist-ecclesiological move can promote the distortion of the church's concrete identity by privileging valuations and criteria from non-Christian analogues. The gatherings of people at the Eucharist become unhinged from their primary meaning as proleptic participations in the Trinity. The congregations lose the clear sense of work, service, and routine essential to liturgy, and their gatherings become celebrations of fellowship manifested in feelings of warmth and jollity. The point of coming together then becomes the gathering itself; the celebration of the Eucharist turns into a celebration of the community's spirit. Some consequences of this are described in the entertainingly exasperated book, *Why Catholics Can't Sing*, by Thomas Day. He writes of the narcissism of the Sunday gatherings in some Roman Catholic parishes in the USA, pointing out how the hymns now popular (among church leaders, at least) more frequently refer to the actions and feelings of the singing subject than to God. The music itself is like much bland popular material (Day calls it "reformed folk") rather than, as earlier, reflecting somewhat more distinctively Christian styles.[29]

None of this distortion is, needless to say, intended by Tillard. But he and Rahner and Boff do not close off such contextually prompted mis-readings by sufficiently strong counter-moves towards particularity and concreteness. The inclusivist use of the twofold construal, while it does not surrender as much as the pluralist, is similar enough to the latter to get easily confused with it. It seems to confirm what many people already know: the church, in spite of its claims to the contrary, is really just one among a plurality of religious bodies of roughly equal worth. When the ultimate goal of both church and world is believed by both to be the same, the assimilation of the church by the world becomes yet more troubling, for it introduces a normative element. The primary criterion by which to assess the church's concrete identity is how well it promotes that univer-sal humanistic goal, rather than the quality of its witness and disciple-ship. The latter become the secondary, particular means to the primary, universal end. The church is then understood to be a religious body that realizes what may be realized by other symbolic embodiments, and so it becomes finally dispensable. Without a complementary and system-wide basis for emphasizing the importance of the church's distinctiveness, these three ecclesiologies fail to clarify sufficiently for the present context the difference it makes to follow Jesus Christ. As a result, the expropria-tion of what were originally quite Christian-specific means and goals by the dominant cultural environment for its own use becomes all the easier. The church's witness is compromised, and the reasons for devoting one's life to Christian discipleship weakened.

Common to these otherwise fairly diverse ecclesiologies, then, is that they each in their own way identify the good with what is universal. The upshot in this context is that their work can too easily be read as if it iden-tifies the particular with what is secondary. In their use of the twofold construal, they privilege harmony and unity, or at least movement towards it. The modern horizon seems to have been influential here (even in Tillard in the area under discussion), as I suggested in chapter 2. And their theological styles are evidently more epic than theodramatic. This is particularly the case with Boff and Tillard, who present divergent system-atic models of the universal basis and goal of all humanity and blueprints

29. Thomas Day, *Why Catholics Can't Sing: The Culture of Catholicism and the Triumph of Bad Taste* (New York: Crossroad, 1995); on "reformed folk" music, see pp. 58ff.

for the ideal community. It is less the case with Rahner, for his systematic moves are always relativized by his stress upon the mystery that is our ultimate goal. His belief that theology and the Christian life is finally *reductio in mysterium* rather than a doctrinal system, together with his increasingly unsystematic ecclesiological reflections, leaves plenty of room for unanticipated turns in the plot. But he, like the other two, so stresses harmony and identity in his ecclesiology that he also insufficiently resists the pluralist reduction of particularity to perspectivalism.

Having looked at some of the internal-apologetic consequences of inclusivist ecclesiology, we now turn to external issues. An epic horizon is evident in the inclusivist assertion of deep-spiritual identity not only between the church and the world, but more generally among all religious and non-religious traditions of inquiry and their diverse concrete identities. It is here that the twofold construal most evidently undermines the church's responsibility to otherness. It does so by structuring the Christian metanarrative so that it loses its dramatic qualities. In discussing the neo-Nietzschean postmoderns in the previous chapter, I contended, in response to their rejection of all metanarratives, that Christianity has no choice but to work within one. The belief that God is active in creating, reconciling and redeeming the world requires us to think of things in terms of a beginning, a middle and an end. We quarrel over the details of the narrative, of course, and legitimately construe its shape in a number of different ways. But the only alternative to some version of it would seem to be to reduce our beliefs about the creative and redemptive activity of God to a set of metaphors about something else, something purely immanent or existential. Needless to say, to do that would not be consistent with Paul's rule. Furthermore, we cannot avoid making our Christian metanarrative more or less totalizing. We believe that the church is orientated towards the ultimate truth, towards the person who is recapitulating all things in himself. Thus if our narrative is true, as we claim, it must be capable of situating or absorbing all other narratives.[30] And to make that claim requires us, as I have argued, to engage in debate with those who would challenge it.

Yet clearly some forms of totalizing discourse are more harmful than

30. This is, of course, a form of inclusivism (though not of an ecclesiological sort), and one that overlaps in part with S. Mark Heim's proposals in his *Salvations*, especially ch. five. The notion of absorbing the world is found in George Lindbeck, *The Nature of Doctrine: Religion and Theology in a Postliberal Age* (Philadelphia: Westminster, 1984), p. 118. For a discussion and clarification see Bruce Marshall, "Absorbing the World: Christianity and the Universe of Truths" in *Theology and Dialogue: Essays in Conversation with George Lindbeck*, ed. Bruce Marshall (Notre Dame: University of Notre Dame Press, 1990), pp. 69–102.

others. My thesis is that the theodramatic version of the Christian meta-narrative permits us to bring the other within God's overarching play without harmful loss or occlusion of difference. The inclusivist-ecclesiological theory, in contrast, depends upon a more epic construal of the Christian narrative. As we have seen, it renders that narrative universally normative by treating it as if the church, the humanistic projects of modernity, and every religious body, are all fundamentally in harmony. It is true, of course, that the church has traditionally held that it knows and orientates itself to the one true goal of all humanity, namely participation in the trinitarian life of God in and through Jesus Christ. But it has not until recently been asserted that other religious and non-religious bodies in their spiritual depths implicitly do something much the same. Indeed, as the notion of conversion makes clear, the contrary seems usually to have been assumed. In becoming a Christian one radically reorientates oneself and rejects ("dies to") one's previous form of existence. The more recent claim for deep-spiritual harmony thus totalizes in a way that occludes otherness far more than the traditional claim need do. Inclusivist ecclesiology shares the modern view that genuine otherness cannot be a genuine good, but must be either the product of sin or ignorance, or else a temporary stage on the way towards the realization of the underlying essential harmony among all humanity. Tension and conflict among diverse traditions of inquiry and their respective embodiments are therefore to be overcome rather than used productively, for they undermine rational, humane and ultimately Christian action.

This epic move is not useful for any significant Christian purposes, especially in an ecclesiological context like the present. By denying genuine plurality among concretely diverse traditions of inquiry, inclusivist ecclesiology deprives the church of the possibility of engaging in debate with others who are genuinely different. And this presents problems for the church's witness, for it undermines its truth claims and the possibility of demonstrating the superiority of its orientation. As I argued in the previous chapter, it is not enough to present a theory that simply shows the coherence and reasonableness of the way we see things. To claim that one's beliefs are true it is necessary to seek out and engage with all those who would challenge them. Conflicting traditions are therefore a necessity for truth-seeking. A systematic inclusivist ecclesiology asserts on Christian and modern grounds that the church's goals are identical with those of humanity in general (recall the quotation from de Lubac, p. 130!). However, it fails to engage with the distinctive challenges of any particular tradition of inquiry except that of liberal modernism, to which it seems to be in thrall. Inclusivist ecclesiology implies, moreover, that to the extent that other religious or non-religious traditions disagree with the church's conclusions, they do not realize their true humanity. By not explicitly addressing the particularity and the humanity of other traditions of inquiry, the church fails to respond to them. Their otherness is occluded and, as a consequence, those traditions can readily and quite rationally dismiss the church's witness to its Lord.

Restricting the number of its debate partners to one is damaging not only to the church's witness, but also to its own quest for truth. The inclusivist theory permits the Spirit of truth to be received through only one form of external challenge. It is as if Christianity and liberal humanism together already possess the answer, or the outlines of it anyway, so that there is no need for the church to look any further in its quest for truthful discipleship. Such an epic (and parochial) implication does nothing to help Christian discipleship. We recall that a key concern of Rahner in developing his inclusivist ecclesiology was to prevent panic among Christians regarding the fate of their non-Christian friends and relatives. In the present cultural climate, "panic" about such matters is not a word that comes to mind. Rather, the difficulties Christians face may have more to do with the proposed solution. As many critics have noted, the inclusivist theory seems to impose upon others a view of themselves which may not be reconcilable with their own self-understanding.[31] The theory thus supports the prevalent notion that the church never listens to anyone but itself; that it is imperialistic and hubristic; and that its claims are irrational. As a consequence, it may appear to the disciple that he is faced with a dilemma. Either he follows the church in rejecting or ignoring otherness, or he is so embarrassed by the church's failed responsibility to otherness that he reinterprets its claims in a perspectivalist and relativist fashion.

For the remainder of this chapter the scope of the discussion expands beyond the inclusivist theory to consider the modern ecclesiological method more generally. I can now complete and summarize my case against its dominance and make some further theodramatic suggestions.

One suggestion is no doubt expected. I think it best to avoid using the twofold construal in any kind of systematic way within ecclesiology. It has a long history within the tradition, and it is evidently quite useful as a

---

31. Peter Hodgson is one such critic. See his *Revisioning the Church*, p. 94.

theologoumenon for certain issues. I suggested earlier that premodern ecclesiology used it unsystematically and in a restricted way to deal with one or two topics at a time; when they described our transformed existence as members of Christ's body, for example. With the increasingly systematic trend in modern ecclesiology and the newly arising concern about the fate of non-Christians, it was natural to turn to the twofold construal as a structuring principle. But, as I have tried to show, its use as a systematic device within modern ecclesiology is difficult to make consistent with the church's task of fostering genuine plurality. The construal not only undermines the church's responsibility to otherness, it inhibits its responsibility to act in ways that embody its witness to its Lord. One key element of responsible Christian action is the acknowledgment of the evident and not infrequent failure of the church to conform to the gospel. By privileging the spiritual, the construal makes it difficult to address that failure. This is despite the clear concern of at least one of the theologians whose work we have been examining. Rahner was one of the first Roman Catholic theologians to call for theological reflection upon the sinfulness of the church, and in doing so went considerably beyond the delicate sentences of Vatican II.[32] But he and others have been unable to develop this area adequately, in part because of their blueprint approach. Their attempts to present ideal and normative descriptions of the church abstract from its day-to-day messiness. By privileging the deep-spiritual, too, they seem unable to find room to discuss the sinfulness of the church in an appropriately theological way, for that would involve turning their full theological attention to the concrete. Material treatment of actual ecclesial sin thus would seem to be outside the scope of ecclesiology proper.

Generally, the treatment of ecclesial sin and error within a modern ecclesiological approach, whether inclusivist or not, seems to be limited to two related forms. One is a largely formal consideration of ecclesial sin as a distortion of the realization of its primary reality. The other is the criticism of the church that is implied by the blueprint description of its ideal realization. As I argued in chapter 2, one who writes an ecclesiology does so because he or she is concerned about some aspect of the church. Implicit within the ecclesiological proposals of all three ecclesiologies we have discussed here are judgments about the present state of the church

---

32. See Richard Lennan, *Ecclesiology of Karl Rahner*, pp. 28ff. for a good account of Rahner's conception of the church's sinfulness.

and where and how it is sinful or confused. Ecclesial existence, however, is far too conflictual and complex to be adequately analyzed by such indirect means. I noted earlier how such an abstract approach in Tillard's work seems to be behind some odd judgments about the concrete church. His almost exclusive emphasis upon unity, moreover, would seem to leave little room for the kind of prophetic, sometimes divisive kind of criticism that on occasion is a necessary part of discipleship. In Boff's work, too, a parallel issue surfaces. His discussion of Basic Ecclesial Communities omits proper consideration of the fact that even the homogeneously oppressed never realize truly authentic communion this side of the eschaton. The poor are also sinful and liable to division among themselves, whether or not they are oppressed; and those who are oppressed also oppress.

Reform of the church is not best done by offering competing blueprints of the ideal primary reality and treating ecclesial sin as its distortion. That approach deals too indirectly both with the church's problems as well as with the ecclesiological context. It leaves it up to someone else to draw out the implications for the church's concrete identity from the normative vision. Not, indeed, that such visions are in fact normative, since at best they can reflect only one of a number of legitimate construals of the Christian thing. Which construal is most suitable is a judgment made by the church with regard to its Scripture and the tradition of interpretation, and with regard to the appropriate practical-prophetic considerations. Accordingly, rather than the twofold construal and blueprint method of modern ecclesiology, it would be better to take a practical-prophetic approach. Ecclesiology helps the church perform its tasks by discerning and discussing specific failures to witness truthfully and specific sinfulness in its concrete identity. From there the church can turn to consider changes in how it embodies its witness.

A second key element of responsible Christian action is, of course, for the church to act in response to its Lord. That response, orientated as a whole to a particular ultimate goal, needs to be distinctively Christian if it is to be an effective form of witness. The twofold construal, however, undermines the distinctiveness of the response by privileging universality and deep-spiritual identity. If the church shares the same base and goal with other humanist bodies, it would be difficult for it to give good reasons why it should not act in conformity with those bodies. And for the individual disciple, it would be hard to see where being a Christian should make any significant difference to one's actions. Not that it is ever straightforward to describe exactly where the difference should lie, whether for a disciple or for the church as a body, as Vincent MacNamara's analysis of twentieth-century Roman Catholic ethical arguments makes clear.[33] He argues that Christian distinctiveness cannot depend directly upon following Scripture, nor upon a set of revealed Christian-specific principles and precepts. But neither can the church "simply farm out or subcontract morality to others and then re-invest it into faith."[34] Rather, the distinctiveness of Christian action depends upon the distinctively Christian education of church members. Living within the church for any length of time should so educate a disciple's desires that they become more and more orientated towards his ultimate goal. By adopting the social practices of the church, based *in*directly upon Scripture and the tradition of inquiry into its interpretation, the disciple acquires Christian virtues and dispositions. He thereby gains a "whole sustaining and enabling context" for the practical decisions of everyday life.[35] It is the task of practical-prophetic ecclesiology to help the church to function in this educative way. Hence ecclesiology cannot restrict its attention to the church's universal deep-spiritual essence, but should turn its critical and constructive attention to the church's concrete identity.

The turn to the concrete will be more fruitful, I suggest, if we make a further modification of ecclesiological method. The blueprint approach has proved to be helpful in describing the eschatological church of the saints who no longer can sin and whose lives together no longer need continual reformation. The eschatological church should continue to be the subject of theological inquiry since the pilgrim church proleptically participates in the eternal church and so an account of the latter bears upon what we say about the former. But the two forms of the church are not the same and cannot be treated in the same manner. An ecclesiological method that is appropriate for describing the ideal, eternal church is not broad enough to deal adequately with the church on earth. We must say far more about the church *in via* than about the heavenly church, and say it in a different and more complex way.

Hence my second proposal is that we shift from an epic to a theodramatic horizon in ecclesiology by making a sharper distinction, both substantive and methodological, between ecclesiology for the church

---

33. MacNamara, *Faith and Ethics*.   34. Ibid., p. 204.
35. Ibid., p. 200. MacNamara's proposals are similar to those of non-Roman theologians such as Gregory Jones and Stanley Hauerwas, discussed in ch. 1 above. On the indirect use of Scripture, see David H. Kelsey, *The Uses of Scripture in Recent Theology* (Philadelphia: Fortress Press, 1975), pp. 139–154.

triumphant and ecclesiology for the pilgrim church. Integrating explicit self-critical reflection into ecclesiology not only offers the possibility of improving the church's concrete identity, the theodramatic form of ecclesiology can also be a good form of witness. As an ecclesial social practice, it would embody the church's belief that all people and institutions, itself included, should humbly acknowledge their sinfulness, finitude and dependence upon the grace and mercy of God. We witness to our dependence upon the Other, upon God and his presence in others, by seeking out and listening to those, within and outside the church, who challenge the adequacy of our ecclesial action. When we need to, we contritely abandon a practice, or modify it or engage in bricolage to develop a better one. We offer arguments in support of those practices and beliefs we think we should maintain in spite of challenges. By seeking out or anticipating such challenges rather than dragging our ecclesial feet over such matters, we can take a little of the wind out of the sails of those who are quick to denounce the faults of the church. Thereby we get the chance to give our own account of why we have sinned and where we should make amends, setting the terms of the debate rather than fighting endless rearguard defenses. In this way, too, the church helps its members by providing them with theological support for their decision to devote their lives to Christian discipleship.

The distinction between the two forms of the church may also help resolve the problem of the salvation of non-Christians without reconstructing the dilemma of the twofold construal. We can follow Rahner and the tradition generally in claiming that salvation requires at least an orientation to the church; but we are not thereby obliged to understand this as an orientation to the church on earth. The church's concrete uniqueness can be maintained without compromise if we interpret the phrase *extra ecclesia nulla salus* as saying "outside the heavenly church, the completed Body of Christ, there is no salvation." In Rahner's language, we can say that an orientation to the church is indeed a necessary part of an implicit acceptance of God's universal salvific self-offer in grace. Such an orientation should in certain circumstances (though not in all) lead to membership in the visible church, although such circumstances are often lacking so that many reject the church for one reason or another. In doing so they really do not belong to that concrete body in any way at all. However, the plot of the theodrama requires a wide range of traditions and their embodiments in order that the quest for truth can be a genuine quest, rather than merely the epic realization in history of something preexistent or already known. Members of other traditions and their embodiments have been given their own distinctive parts to play within the theodrama. In pursuing and embodying their various goals, then, they may be viewed by Christians as actively involved in furthering God's will. It is therefore by virtue of their very diversity, rather than a deep-spiritual harmony, that they may be said to be orientated towards the eschatological Kingdom.

Furthermore, it may be that the inclusivist-ecclesiological theory, like the pluralist, is mistaken in assuming that there is a single form of salvation for all humanity. The shape of the heavenly church cannot be glimpsed from within the theodrama, for it is too far into the mystery that is the triune God. It may therefore be possible, as some have argued recently, to propose the theologoumenon of diverse "salvations."[36] We noted in chapter 4 how each religious tradition seems to have its own distinctive goal and the means to it, and thus its own understanding of human fulfillment. And if one takes the differences among these traditions of inquiry seriously, without perspectival reduction, it is difficult to reconcile them with one another. Buddhist Nirvana and Christian trinitarian salvation, for example, appear to be incompatible goals. But within a theodramatic horizon we can acknowledge that we do not know the shape of the end. So it may be possible to say that some at least of the goals towards which religious and non-religious bodies are working may be fulfilled within the overarching trinitarian mystery. The Kingdom of Heaven, the church triumphant, has many mansions, some of which may look quite different from one another. Thus one could account for religious diversity by means of a theodramatic doctrine of providence.[37]

The humanist might worry that this denies any hope for unity among the human race prior to the eschaton. Certainly, within a theodramatic horizon unity cannot be the ultimate goal, and it can only be rejected if it must come in the epic forms of a deep-spiritual harmony or a definable universal project. Pre-eschatological unity is not lost, however, but relocated away from ourselves into a center in God as the Director and chief player of the one overarching theodrama. Unity may therefore be

---

36. See Heim, *Salvations*, chs. five and six.
37. See DiNoia, *Diversity of Religions*, ch. three. DiNoia proposes that we make use of the doctrine of purgatory to resolve the issue of the salvation of those who have orientated their lives in such a way that they are rendered not immediately fit for union with the Blessed Trinity. The doctrine is used in Roman Catholicism with regard to less-than-perfect Christians and so, DiNoia suggests, it may be possible to apply it to certain non-Christians. See pp. 104ff. Obviously these proposals need to be explored further, but they do suggest some alternatives to modern ecclesiological inclusivism.

conceived in far broader terms than within the humanist horizon, for it also encompasses the non-human creation in all its diversity. All creatures may participate in the play; none is ignored or rejected by the Director. All are called to play their own distinctive parts within a theodrama the successful outcome of which is assured by the faithful and gracious activity of the triune God, not by human activity alone. We are unified in our diverse activities by our need for one another as debate partners, by our need for genuine others who can challenge us and thereby help us to receive and embody truth more adequately. We can come together to work on common projects, though we may each do so for different reasons and with different ultimate goals in mind. Evidently, we will carry on much as we have in the past, often sinfully or ignorantly rejecting or occluding the other at times. But action that is responsive to difference remains always a possibility, the condition of which is the Spirit of truth that guides the movement of the theodrama.

If the Christian metanarrative could be expanded along something like these theodramatic lines, it might be possible to show how it can situate all difference within itself without loss or occlusion of difference. Thereby it would demonstrate its responsibility to otherness as well as to action. And that would constitute the beginning of a rational and perhaps effective Christian response to some of the challenges of the ecclesiological context, especially the challenges of pluralism and neo-Nietzschean postmodernism. The church could then reasonably begin to make its case that the Christian tradition of inquiry is true and superior to those traditions. But it is likely that at some point the challenge would shift to focus upon the embodiment of the Christian tradition in the concrete identity of the church. How ecclesiology might anticipate and prepare for such a challenge, and how it can use it to improve the church's witness and discipleship, is the topic of the next chapter.

7

Practical-prophetic ecclesiology

In the foregoing chapters I have argued that ecclesiology can better perform its function if it is set within a theodramatic rather than an epic-modernist horizon. A theodramatic and traditioned understanding of religion and truth prompts the church to engage with other traditions of inquiry and their embodiments without domesticating their otherness. A theodramatic horizon provides the church with a framework within which it can develop self-critical responses to the various challenges and opportunities of the present ecclesiological context. It enables the church to argue forcefully that it is reasonable to witness to Jesus Christ as the ultimate truth, and that it is possible to embody that witness in truthful discipleship. Practical-prophetic ecclesiology assists the church in reforming its concrete identity to accord with Paul's rule, namely to glory (only) in Jesus Christ.

This final chapter makes a few suggestions about how ecclesiology might be expanded so as to draw upon the work of other disciplines, and how it might develop from those disciplines new theological approaches of its own. My suggestions are necessarily tentative and open-ended. Within a theodramatic horizon (at least), one cannot construct in purely theoretical terms a method guaranteed to produce successful concrete results; one can only present some approaches that will prove useful or not in the doing. There is no single right approach; other approaches may be more appropriate than the ones proposed within other contexts and particular denominations. My suggestions are related to my ecclesiological agenda which includes, we recall, a concern to develop ecclesiology into a social practice that reflects directly and theodramatically upon what modern ecclesiology often renders secondary, namely the church's concrete, *in via* identity. Practical-prophetic ecclesiology focuses theological attention upon the church's confused and sometimes sinful daily life and engages with other traditions of inquiry and their embodiments. This chapter discusses some of the ways in which ecclesiology may engage with some of the more significant of those disciplines that bear upon the concrete identity of the church, namely history, sociology and cultural analysis or ethnography.

The relation between the social sciences and theology is currently problematic. For some theologians, such as the pluralists (discussed in chapter 4 above), it seems that certain of the social sciences are normative for their own theological constructions. The practical theologians (noted at the end of chapter 2) contend that theology and social science should be on an equal footing. Other theologians, by contrast, view the social sciences with considerably greater suspicion. Some fear that the introduction of sociological or other empirical perspectives into ecclesiology will result in reductive, inadequately theological accounts of the church. And the more radical argument has been made that modern secular sociology is a form of inquiry based upon principles counter to those of Christianity. Fundamentally incommensurate with theology, secular sociology has nothing to add to a theological account at all; instead, the church should develop its own, theological forms of social science.[1] These varied and often conflicting views of the function of the social sciences within theology seem to be a product not only of different conceptions of theological method, but also, in part at least, of somewhat different conceptions of social scientific method, especially as it bears upon the analysis of religion and religious bodies. The position taken here will be theodramatic and informed by the traditioned notion of truth outlined in chapter 5. All forms of social science are useful, perhaps even necessary, for ecclesiology, including those thoroughly antagonistic to the church or to religious bodies generally. However, since they examine religious bodies in a variety of ways, they cannot be useful in quite the same way, and none of them is ever normative. My case for this position starts by developing some categories by which to distinguish among the range of ways in which the social sciences and history (and, indeed, any form of inquiry) approach religions and their embodiments.

In their helpful book, *Religion Defined and Explained*,[2] Peter B. Clarke

1. See John Milbank, *Theology and Social Theory: Beyond Secular Reason* (Oxford: Blackwell, 1990); David Lyon, *Sociology and the Human Image* (Downer's Grove, IL: InterVarsity Press, 1983).
2. Peter B. Clarke and Peter Byrne, *Religion Defined and Explained* (New York: St. Martin's Press, 1993).

and Peter Byrne discuss the classic modern theories of religion proposed by philosophers, sociologists, psychologists, and the like. Each theory takes one of four stances with regard to religion: atheist, agnostic, religious and theological; it is this fourfold typology of stances which will be adapted for the present discussion. The atheist stance is found in such theories of religion as those of Feuerbach, Marx, Freud and Durkheim. All of these take the view that the religions do not and cannot arise from a transcendent source since, they believe, the transcendent does not exist. The religions exist, however, and so a theory must be developed to account for them. Atheist theories seek to explain religion and religious bodies by redescribing them in terms that run directly counter to the descriptions of the participants themselves. The religions are illusions, fictive human constructions whose origins and development can be explained in terms of entirely non-religious facts about society or the individual. Religion is a human phenomenon the essence of which can be defined in psychological, sociological, economic, or anthropological terms. Thus every religion's true nature and function can be explained by radically recasting its members' false transcendent claims. The polar opposite of this perspective is the theological stance, in which a religion's claims about the transcendent, together with the categories used to make those claims, and their embodiment in a distinctive way of life, are all taken as normative. Clarke and Byrne give no examples of this type and do not discuss it, but much of the present work evidently exemplifies the theological stance.[3] Midway between these two extremes are the religious and the agnostic stances. We met the religious stance when we discussed the pluralist horizon in chapter 4 above. The religious theorist acknowledges the reality of the transcendent, but reworks the claims of particular religions so that they conform to a universal definition of religion.[4] Like the atheist, then, the religious theorist claims that an external view of religion is better than the participant view, even where the two views conflict. Clarke and Byrne devote most of their time to discussing the religious and atheist stances, since their concern is to argue that the fourth stance, the agnostic, is better than either of them. An agnostic

---

3. For those familiar with Hans Frei's typology of theology: any Type 3, 4 or 5 theologian takes a theological stance. See Hans W. Frei, *Types of Christian Theology*, ed. George Hunsinger and William C. Placher (New Haven: Yale University Press, 1992), esp. pp. 34–55. I avoid Type 5, however, and have at times come close to Type 2, e.g., during the discussion of MacIntyre in chapter 5.

4. Clarke and Byrne discuss John Hick's theory of religion as their example of this stance. See *Religion Defined*, pp. 79–97.

stance is one that respects the participant's language, but makes no assumptions either way about the veracity of the claims. Unlike both the atheist and the religious stances, agnostic description avoids reliance upon a theory of religion, and makes little systematic use of the distinction between description and explanation. Instead, it attempts to accumulate ever more detailed and accurate accounts of the various religions and their histories, with the understanding that its generalizations and conclusions must be continually revised in light of new results.

To be sure, these four stances cannot always be easily separated in practice. An agnostic stance may operate with humanist beliefs that bear upon descriptions of religious matters. Moreover, it may assume that by bracketing out the question of the veracity of religious claims, it provides a neutral account that is somehow more rigorous and scientific, just because it is acceptable to those who inhabit a secular horizon. John Milbank has argued forcefully that, on the contrary, the secular is as much a cultural construct as any other, and it is one that is informed by theological, and often anti-Christian, assumptions.[5] Nevertheless, if this overlapping is borne in mind, the distinctions between each category are sufficiently clear to be useful here. Each of these stances, including the atheist, can play a distinct and significant role in the church's self-reflection. While atheist theories of religion result in distorted or incorrect descriptions of religious bodies, they should not be ignored or ruled out as debating partners on that account alone, for they may formulate in theoretical terms a more general cultural perception which needs to be challenged by apologetic arguments. And it may be, too, that such theories offer helpful criticism of the church's concrete identity. Perhaps the church talks rather too frequently about the benefits of discipleship and avoids dwelling upon its hardships. It thereby opens itself up to a Feuerbachian critique of religion as wish-fulfillment, or to a psychological explanation of religion as a crutch for those whose personalities are not strong enough to face reality. In response, the church may find it appropriate to develop better descriptions of discipleship and to promote more effectively those practices which falsify the critique. With regard to the religious stance, the arguments of chapters 4 and 5 above have suggested that it is presently less than helpful to the church. Yet religious theorists clearly reflect cultural prejudices that challenge religious bodies like the church and need to be debated. And it is possible that in certain

5. Milbank, *Theology and Social Theory*, pp. 9ff.

ecclesiological contexts the church might find it appropriate to stress the similarities among religious bodies, and draw upon such theories to develop its own ways of doing so.

With these four categories in hand, we can now turn to discuss the use of some non-theological disciplines within ecclesiology and the development of new theological forms, beginning with history. Needless to say, historical analysis is essential to ecclesiology because the church's concrete identity is historical. The church's witness and discipleship are undertaken within changing ecclesiological contexts and in response to the ongoing movement of the theodrama. Moreover, every ecclesiology relies upon a (usually implicit) construal of the church's past for its conception of the church's present concrete identity and its future needs and opportunities. Practical-prophetic ecclesiology attempts to narrate that construal explicitly so that it may be assessed and debated. Within modern theology, however, church history is usually regarded as a discipline that operates according to different principles than systematic ecclesiology proper. It is assumed that, while ecclesiology must take a theological stance, church history must maintain an agnostic stance.[6] In order to preserve its credentials as a secular science, church history must operate "on the assumption," as John Macquarrie has put it, "that whatever events occur in the world can be accounted for in terms of other events that also belong within the world."[7] In practice, this methodological rule seems to permit other stances besides the agnostic; to take an atheist or religious stance may be regarded as quite respectable when writing histories of the church or other religious bodies. Classic among the atheistic histories is Gibbons' *Decline and Fall of the Roman Empire*, but the genre persists in various guises, including the neo-Nietzschean genealogy, which often displays anti-metaphysical and anti-religious beliefs.[8] An example of a religious-stance history is the unifying epic of religion by Wilfred Cantwell Smith, which makes explicit the narrative construal of world religious bodies of some pluralists.[9]

6. For a pertinent discussion of the place of history within modern theology, see John E. Thiel, *Imagination and Authority: Theological Authorship in the Modern Tradition* (Minneapolis: Fortress Press, 1991), esp. pp. 33–94.

7. John Macquarrie, *Principles of Christian Theology*, second ed. (New York: Scribners, 1977), p. 248, cited in Nicholas Wolterstorff, *Divine Discourse: Philosophical Reflections on the Claim that God Speaks* (Cambridge: Cambridge University Press, 1995), p. 124.

8. For a recent best-selling atheist history (religion as a humanist project) see Karen Armstrong, *A History of God: The 4,000-Year Quest of Judaism, Christianity and Islam* (New York: Ballantine Books, 1993).

9. Wilfred Cantwell Smith, *Towards a World Theology: Faith and the Comparative History of Religion* (Philadelphia: Westminster, 1981).

Thus it seems that the only form of history ruled out by everyone, including Christian historians and ecclesiologists, is the theological. Wolfhart Pannenberg has raised this issue recently, pointing out that: "In no other field has Christian theology given itself so unreservedly to a purely secular understanding of reality, detached from any connection with the reality of God, as in its handling of church history."[10] The result, he says, is "fatal" not only for theology, but for the life of the church. While the agnostic stance in church history is useful, even vital, it cannot be adequate for theological inquiry because, of course, theology operates with the conviction that Christian beliefs are true. Any account of reality that adopts an agnostic framework must bracket out the Director and key actor in the theodrama and consider the divine agent as merely an idea that is partly constitutive of the church's activities; hardly a neutral or adequate approach for ecclesiology. Pannenberg again: "A Christian theology of history must find its basis and norm in God's acts by election, sending, and judgment, not in the continuity of an earthly people or kingdom."[11] The church needs to be able to give an account of its historical identity in terms of its relation to the triune God, and thus from within a Christian horizon. Theologians already make implicit judgments about where the Spirit has been active within the church, and where the church has failed to respond to its call. Why not, then, make those judgments explicit, and argue for them by developing a theological-historical narrative? There are two main objections to doing so.[12]

The first objection concerns the church's responsibility to the other. Those who narrate the histories of any body, religious or otherwise, are often the powerful or their intellectual representatives. If histories of the church are written by its leadership, or by those who control the leadership, or by those who serve the interests of the powerful within the church or within its social environment, then those who are marginalized within the church or those who challenge its leadership may not be able to make known their conflicting construal of its history. As a

---

10. Wolfhart Pannenberg, *Systematic Theology*, vol. III (Grand Rapids: Eerdmans, 1998), p. 498.   11. Ibid., p. 515.

12. I take it that it is no longer necessary to consider objections to theological histories based upon the idea that to speak about God's acts within history is a category mistake, i.e., that a theological stance is illogical. Langdon Gilkey's classic article, "Cosmology, Ontology, and the Travail of Biblical Language," *Journal of Religion* 41 (1961), 194–205, raised the issue with regard to biblical theology. To my mind, one of the most convincing responses is that of Nicholas Wolterstorff, *Divine Discourse*, whose discussion is focused upon God's speech-acts. Pannenberg also (partly) addresses the issue in his *Systematic Theology*, vol. II (Grand Rapids: Eerdmans, 1994), pp. 1–58.

result, all those who do not fit the dominant account are likely to find themselves ignored, their difference occluded. This objection points to what is, without doubt, a significant difficulty, but it is one that afflicts any form of history, including the agnostic and, as I have argued, the religious. The best histories attempt to guard against ideological distortion by seeking out and responding to the construals of those who represent different interests, and clearly theological histories must do the same. Indeed, within a theodramatic horizon, there is greater reason to do so, for the purpose of theological histories is to further the church's quest for truthful witness and discipleship by seeking out the marginalized within the church, by debating with those whose theological position differs from one's own and with those who propose historical accounts developed within non-theological stances. Ironically, to deny a place for such inquiry within ecclesiology is in effect to occlude Christian difference.

A second objection – or set of objections – to theological history applies to a rather different discipline than that proposed here, to a theology of history or a theology of church history rather than to theological history. Among theologians who have considered the question,[13] some have expressed concern that histories which treat of the time of the church cannot produce normative accounts. Thus Karl Rahner, for example, uses the erstwhile common distinction between salvation history and profane history in a way that parallels the twofold construal, arguing that while the two histories are distinct, they are very difficult to tell apart except where God has distinguished them for us in the Scriptural histories of Israel and Jesus Christ.[14] In profane history there are only hints and signs of salvation history here and there that cannot be worked up into a full-fledged account. Behind Rahner's concern may be a worry that others such as Balthasar have expressed, namely that theologies of history may be developed in terms of categories alien to Scripture, like Hegel's epic grand narrative. Balthasar counters this by insisting, as does Rahner, that any theology of history remain centered upon the particular person, Jesus Christ.[15] The

---

13. Pannenberg discusses a fairly wide range of theologians on this issue in presenting his own proposal in his *Systematic Theology*, vol. III, pp. 498–526; his discussion informs my own in this paragraph.

14. See Karl Rahner, "History of the World and Salvation History" in *Theological Investigations* vol. V (New York: Crossroad, 1983), pp. 97–114, esp. p. 106.

15. Hans Urs von Balthasar, *A Theology of History* (New York: Sheed and Ward, 1963), esp. pp. 5–21. For a rather more theodramatic view, see Jean Daniélou, S.J., *The Lord of History: Reflections on the Inner Meaning of History*, trans. Nigel Abercrombie (London: Longmans, 1958), esp. pp. 14ff., 33, 197ff.

Protestant theologian, Wolfhart Pannenberg, is more sympathetic to the idea of a theology of church history. In response to these concerns, he suggests that a systematic theology of church history be constructed in terms of a central biblical theme such as election, and with a twofold construal of the church.[16]

The theological history proposed here is distinct from these systematic and normative theologies of history. Theological-historical inquiry within practical-prophetic ecclesiology describes and assesses the past practices, beliefs and valuations of the church in light of Paul's rule, in order that the church may better pursue its ongoing quest for more truthful discipleship and witness to its Lord and ultimate goal. Theological history neither celebrates the church (or a particular group within it) as an exemplary body or as a divinely given solution to the world's social problems; nor does it take a neutral stance, if neutral means simply presenting a series of events without judgment or as part of a humanist quest for meaning. Ecclesiology cannot rely upon agnostic histories to perform this function; it must do at least some of the work itself, for the questions it must ask are not those that belong within agnostic history. Such questions reflect the church's commitments and can therefore be addressed adequately only within a fully theological stance.[17] A theological history may well include a theology of (church) history but, as with all generalizations or conclusions within a theodramatic horizon, that theology must be continually reassessed in light of Scripture, tradition and developments in the ecclesiological context. (The theodramatic horizon is itself a kind of theology of history, of course.) Although generalizations may be possible, the primary concern is to focus attention upon the details of the church's concrete identity as it is produced by Christians through and against the Spirit over time. Further developments in the plot will give rise to further challenges and opportunities, and will require theologians to rework their previous understandings of our ecclesial response to the activity of God within history in light of new movements of the Spirit. All interpretations remain open to challenge; indeed, that is their point. Theological histories are written not in order to end inquiry, nor to structure all forthcoming inquiry, but to bring to light conflicting views and to

---

16. Pannenberg, *Systematic Theology*, vol. III, p. 509.
17. For a theologically astute discussion of this point with reference to Roman Catholic historiography, see Michael J. Baxter, CSC, "Writing History in a World Without Ends: An Evangelical Catholic Critique of United States Catholic History," *Pro Ecclesia* 5:5 (1996), 440–469. See also Stanley Hauerwas, *Sanctify Them In the Truth: Holiness Exemplified* (Nashville: Abingdon/T&T Clark, 1998), pp. 201–217, and 225.

stimulate debate. If ecclesiology fails to produce these histories, the church's concrete identity will be governed by unexamined construals of its history, which are more likely to be controlled by unacknowledged interests and assumptions.

One of the very few contemporary exercises in the genre of theological history is Ephraim Radner's *The End of the Church*.[18] Radner's profound account of the history of the post-Reformation church – an account too complex to do it justice in this brief summary – offers a genuine alternative to agnostic accounts, which he terms "socio-historical analyses of Western Christendom's evolution into ecclesial 'diversity'" (EC 6). Like the history of Israel in the Old Testament, and like the kind of theological history proposed here, Radner's history is "penitential," for it must dwell upon the church's rejection of its Lord, upon our failures in witness and discipleship. It seeks, according to his definition, to draw "into some kind of general coherence, bounded by what can be known of God's truth, the ecclesial phenomena of past, present and future as they pertain to faithfulness and unfaithfulness, and examines how this coherence reveals the humiliation of pride in the face of God's love and glory" (EC 8). By means of a figural exegesis of Israel and the church's concrete identity, Radner argues that although the church still retains the form of Christ's Body, the Spirit has abandoned the divided church. He discerns the absence of the Spirit in our inability to understand the Scriptures (EC 51ff.); in the hiddenness of true holiness (EC 132ff.); in our confusion over ordination and vocations; and above all, in our failure to discern our sinfulness and our need to repent of our "condition as a 'denominated' church" (EC 277).

Whether or not one agrees with Radner's historical-pneumatological thesis, his book represents a powerful challenge to the dominance of the agnostic stance in church history. It is to be hoped that by making explicit his theological judgments about the church's sinfulness, and by supporting these with sophisticated analysis of its concrete identity, Radner's work will stimulate other historians to engage with his account. One issue that can be raised here concerns the church's responsibility to justice and to otherness, in this case, to otherness within the church. While theological history is necessarily penitential, its primary concern, like that of individual confessional practice, is with the present and the future as it

18. Ephraim Radner, *The End of the Church: A Pneumatology of Christian Division in the West* (Grand Rapids: Eerdmans, 1998). Cited as (EC page).

makes possible more truthful witness and discipleship. It cannot forget that there are real distinctions between: an individual disciple confessing his sins; the church confessing its present communal sinfulness; and the church acknowledging the sinfulness of a past form of its concrete identity. Like Israel in the Old Testament theological history, the contemporary church is sufficiently self-identical that present members may acknowledge and ask forgiveness for a sinful past identity for which they had no personal or communal responsibility, such as the divisions that occurred at the Reformation (or the earlier Schism). Such a practice joins us to the church, for we adopt its past as constitutive of our present concrete identity and also witness in however slight a way to our Lord who freely bears the sins of others. However, the difference between confessing one's own guilt and acknowledging the sinfulness of one's community, past or present, needs to be maintained as part of our witness to a just God and to the seriousness of sin. It is not part of our witness to confess to what we have not done. The church is not such a monolith that all within it are responsible for all aspects of its sinful identity. Sinful practices have been promoted by various groups within the church, sometimes to the injury of other members. To "confess" the church's involvement in colonialism, for example, is perverse, since many of its present members may be descendants of those who had no means to challenge the policies of those in power or who were among those oppressed by those policies.[19] Apologies or confessions like this ring hollow and devalue true penitential practices, turning them into therapeutic exercises or moral self-congratulation rather than genuine prayers for mercy and forgiveness from our just and loving God.[20]

Theological histories may come in all shapes and sizes. Like Radner's, they may treat a broad segment of the church over centuries, or they may focus upon a particular parish or congregation over a single generation. They might take a particular theme, such as Radner's divided church; or, to note a few random examples, they might dwell on the church's responsibility to otherness, to the non-human environment, to its ministers or to its children. Theological histories could focus upon the reception of

19. The example is David Martin's; see "A Socio-Theological Critique of Collective National Guilt" in his *Reflections on Sociology and Theology* (Oxford: Clarendon Press, 1997), pp. 207–224.
20. See L. Gregory Jones, *Embodying Forgiveness: A Theological Analysis* (Grand Rapids: Eerdmans, 1995). Radner's conception of theological history provides him with ample means to address this issue.

Scripture, describing how interpretations of Scripture have shaped the church's concrete identity over time in particular regions or in the church as a whole.[21] Or they could follow the advice of John Milbank and construct a "counter-history" that "tells the story of all history from the point of view" of the emergence of the Christian community.[22] In all its forms, however, ecclesiological history needs to search out and debate with alternative accounts – including those developed within non-theological stances and non-Christian horizons – if it is to be an effective aid in the church's quest for truth. This requirement can be illustrated by a question that could be put to Radner's thesis concerning the link between the divided church and the absence of the Holy Spirit. David Martin's more agnostic stance (on this issue) permits him to question on socio-historical grounds the connection between church unity and the presence of the Spirit. He notes how spiritual renewals within the church are often attended by divisiveness, and argues that the Spirit seems to be associated more with "breakage of fellowship" than unity.[23]

A second discipline appropriate for practical-prophetic ecclesiology is sociology. Sociological analysis of religious bodies has taken both the atheist and the agnostic stances, and often its relation to theology is difficult to clarify.[24] Although both forms of inquiry are inadequate for ecclesiology, neither can be ignored or dismissed as discourse incommensurate with theology, even when they are founded upon anti-Christian principles, as I argued earlier. Rather, they should be welcomed as partners in debate who help the church in its quest for closer conformity to its Lord. Sociology can offer some useful checks upon theological claims, especially those made in areas subject to empirical verification. For example, theologians, religious theorists and humanist agnostics

21. See the article by Karlfried Froehlich, "Church History and the Bible," in Mark S. Burrows and Paul Rorem (eds.), *Biblical Hermeneutics in Historical Perspective* (Grand Rapids: Eerdmans, 1991), pp. 1–15. Here Froehlich argues for "the need to reclaim church history as a theological discipline" from the "imperialism of historical scholarship" (p. 3). The notion of reception history was first developed programmatically by Gerhard Ebeling in an early lecture of 1947, published later as "Church History Is the History of the Exposition of Scripture" in *The Word of God and Tradition: Historical Studies Interpreting the Divisions of Christianity*, trans. S. H. Hooke (Philadelphia: Fortress Press, 1968), pp. 11–31.
22. Milbank, *Theology and Social Theory*, p. 381.
23. David Martin, *Reflections*, p. 83. Martin also raises a theological question, noting that in the New Testament the Spirit seems to be defined as "inherently divisive," so that one shall be taken and one shall be left; see p. 86. Radner's thesis is sufficiently subtle to meet this challenge.
24. For some idea of the range of views on their relation, see David Martin, John Orme Mills and W. S. F. Pickering (eds.), *Sociology and Theology: Alliance and Conflict* (New York: St. Martin's Press, 1980).

sometimes claim that religion is necessary to human social well-being.[25] The sociologist can challenge this by noting that although the spiritual life of the Scandinavian countries is "singularly dormant," they display ample evidence of unified and flourishing communities.[26] And more constructively, both the agnostic and the atheist sociologist can provide data for ecclesiological reflection by analyzing the relations between the church and its social environment.

Yet while it may be that non-theological sociological analyses can be very useful for the church, they cannot replace theological analysis, as an example shows. Nancy Ammerman's *Congregation and Community* is a fascinating and informative sociological study of church life at the end of the twentieth century in the USA.[27] She and her associates analyze from an agnostic stance the resources, the structures of authority and the cultural patterns of twenty-three congregations or parishes located in diverse "communities" (i.e., social environments) scattered across the nation. Their research is concerned to discover how each congregation responds to changes in its environment. The analyses are nicely detailed and may well have significant implications for the church in the USA, offering, for example, convincing evidence against one element of the secularization thesis, namely the assumption that the rise of cities will inevitably lead to a decline in church membership (CC 348ff., 353). Ammerman's conclusions present a stimulating challenge to the church as a whole as well as to those particular congregations.

The limits of the agnostic stance taken in this study can be seen in the influence of unsupported beliefs and principles upon its analyses. It displays, for example, what might be termed a civic-humanist concern for the community-forming function of religion (CC 3, 367ff.). It uses the metaphor of ecology to describe the competition among congregations as they seek to serve the religious needs of Americans; apparently only the fittest and most adaptable congregations survive (CC 346). Perhaps this is not unreasonable, but it raises some obvious ecclesiological questions which the study bypasses: What relation pertains, or should pertain,

25. See, for example, Robert N. Bellah and associates, *Habits of the Heart: Individualism and Commitment in American Life* (New York: Harper and Row, 1985), pp. 282ff.; and Peter C. Hodgson, *Revisioning the Church: Ecclesial Freedom in the New Paradigm* (Philadelphia: Fortress Press, 1988), p. 94.
26. The example is from David Martin, *Reflections*, p. 86.
27. Nancy Tatom Ammerman, with Arthur E. Farnsley II and others, *Congregation and Community* (New Brunswick, NJ: Rutgers University Press, 1997). Cited in the text as (CC page).

between the concern for survival and for strengthening the ties of the larger society on the one hand, and the concern for following Paul's rule to glory only in the Cross of Jesus Christ, on the other? Is the notion of "meeting religious needs" (which plays a significant role in the analysis and its conclusions) theologically appropriate for assessing the church's performance of its task of schooling its discipleship? Are there some religious "needs" that should *not* be met by the church? What kind of construal of the ecclesiological context warrants calling the congregation's social environment the "community"? Does the conclusion, that "theological and other ideological factors" do not well explain how congregations adapt to changes in their social environments (CC 343), suggest in itself something for the church to consider?

To answer such questions would evidently be the task of a theological rather than an agnostic sociology, for they bear upon matters that pertain directly to the church's witness and discipleship. It would be a mistake to ask Ammerman to deal with such questions; she and her colleagues rightly operate in this work as agnostics, whatever their religious convictions may be. Agnostic sociology of this kind should indeed be appropriated by ecclesiology, but it can be used only indirectly, since it requires theological assessment and modification before it can become part of an ecclesiological proposal. In contrast to the agnostic, thin-theoretical approach, a theological form of social analysis describes and assesses the church's concrete identity in light of Scripture, the tradition of its interpretation, and the ecclesiological context, with a view to practical reforms. It will make use of non-theological analyses and construals of the ecclesiological context as it does so, but will subject these to the same criteria. Thus, for example, it cannot assume that congregations should work for the flourishing of the social environment within which they are situated, for the inquiry may conclude that they should challenge or even reject their social environment through counter-practices and through apologetic engagement with conflicting beliefs and practices. The church's survival in the midst of change is not the point of the inquiry; the point is to discern the movement of the Spirit in our midst so as to improve our witness and discipleship. The theologian therefore undertakes her work in an engaged, even prayerful manner, rather than with the disinterested objectivity or humanist agenda of the academic agnostic sociologist.

A theological form of sociology is thus necessary if the difference involved in being members of the church is not to be occluded. John

Milbank is correct to call for a form of "Christian sociology," as an analysis that adopts the concerns and agenda of the church.[28] But Milbank's claim that the church is a distinct society seems too strong. The church may be a society in the minimal sense that it is a group of people who share a distinctive goal, but the membership of the church live out much of their lives within a society that is not Christian, as do many other religious bodies, and they are influenced by their society as least as much as they influence their society as Christians. Theological sociology may indeed prove useful within ecclesiology as a means to analyze these mutual influences according to Christian principles, provided, again, that it engages with other forms of inquiry. But it is difficult to see how Christians share enough social practices and structures to constitute a more or less independent society. Whether or not they ought ideally to do so, in fact for most of their time most Christians live as members of non-Christian societies.[29] It may therefore be more useful for ecclesiology to describe and assess the church using the tools of a discipline that attends rather more to the details of the church's concrete identity, and is less concerned to generalize and compare (or contrast).[30] The church's identity is constituted by a wide range of elements, all of which are on the move: by the actions of the Holy Spirit; by the beliefs, valuations, feeling and experiences of its members; by the relations between its members and both the church collective and the non- or anti-Christian societies around them; by social practices, rituals and institutions the church has developed in the course of its history; by the power structures, the financial considerations, the external constraints and opportunities that the church faces in diverse times and places; and so on. The functions of the concrete church are likewise various. It is an institution dedicated to handing on a set of beliefs (the "deposit of faith") from one generation to the next; it is also a moral guide and teacher and – something not quite the same – a forum for moral inquiry; it is a community within which its members are socialized, less or more successfully, into various forms of

---

28. Milbank, *Theology and Social Theory*, p. 380f.

29. In the same work Milbank claims that Christianity "implies a unique and distinctive structural logic for human society" (p. 406). The historical evidence suggests otherwise, in terms of social forms at least. See Gillian Rose's criticisms of Milbank's spiritualized ecclesiology in her "Shadow of Spirit" in *Judaism and Modernity: Philosophical Essays* (Oxford: Blackwell, 1993), pp. 35–51; also Kathryn Tanner, *Theories of Culture: A New Agenda for Theology* (Minneapolis: Fortress Press, 1997), p. 97.

30. Naomi Schor argues that the concern for detail goes back to Scripture and reflects an anti-idealist move that counters what she calls the "hegemony of the sublime" found within classicism. See her *Reading in Detail: Aesthetics and the Feminine* (New York: Methuen, 1987), esp. p. 147.

its distinctive way of life; it is a place where religious experience of one kind or another is made possible; it is a force for peace and justice in the world as well as a force for much less laudable things; it is a communal experiment in following Jesus Christ which sometimes succeeds, at other times fails; and so on.

My proposal is that practical-prophetic ecclesiology describe and assess these elements in their detailed interrelations using the tools of a third discipline besides history and sociology, namely ethnography or cultural analysis. The idea that religions embody their distinctive orientations and convictions in cultural forms has been discussed by George Lindbeck in his book, *The Nature of Doctrine*.[31] We begin with his proposal, which is that:

> [A] religion can be viewed as a kind of cultural and/or linguistic framework or medium that shapes the entirety of life and thought.... [I]t is a communal phenomenon that shapes the subjectivities of individuals ... and just as a culture has both cognitive and behavioral dimensions, so it is also in the case of a religious tradition. Its doctrines, cosmic stories or myths, and ethical directives are integrally related to the rituals it practices, the sentiments or experiences it evokes, the actions it recommends and the institutional forms it develops.

The suggestion, then, is that ecclesiology reflect upon the church's concrete response to its Lord using the metaphor of culture.[32] The church, of course, is not reducible to cultural terms. In fact, it is not a culture in the modern sense at all; and only some aspects of it are describable in theological-cultural terms. Thus "culture" cannot be a model of the church in the way that "Body of Christ" or "*Creatura Verbi*" are; it cannot be mistaken for a basic systematic principle or a description of the church's primary reality. It is simply a metaphor that permits some useful ways of approaching the church's production of webs of social practices, beliefs and valuations. As such, it has about the same force as the metaphor of "institution," though it may prove to be considerably more useful. My proposal is thus fairly simple: it is useful for ecclesiology to regard the *in via*, concrete Body of Christ as if it were, in some significant respects,

---

31. George A. Lindbeck, *The Nature of Doctrine: Religion and Theology in a Postliberal Age* (Philadelphia: Westminster, 1984), p. 33.
32. David H. Kelsey is correct to insist that "culture" should be used of the church only metaphorically. See his essay on Lindbeck's proposal, "Church Discourse and Public Realm," in Bruce D. Marshall (ed.), *Theology and Dialogue: Essays in Conversation with George Lindbeck* (Notre Dame: University of Notre Dame Press, 1990), pp. 7–30.

something like a culture, a culture that necessarily engages with other religious and non-religious bodies similarly conceived as something like cultures.

The cultural aspects of the church and other religious bodies have long been analyzed by cultural anthropologists and ethnographers who take a non-theological stance.[33] All three stances may be useful even where they distort or are mistaken; but again, none of them is adequate for practical-prophetic ecclesiology because they fail to ask the necessary theological questions relating to the church's tasks and its goal. Thus the church needs to introduce its own, theological form of cultural analysis, which we can call ecclesiological ethnography. To make this suggestion, though, is to raise a host of issues, for the word "culture" is used in a variety of ways, not all of which are suitable for theological appropriation. Moreover, Lindbeck's own cultural-linguistic theory has come under some heavy criticism. James Gustafson has argued that Lindbeck's (and Stanley Hauerwas's) concern to maintain the distinctiveness of Christianity and its "historic identity" has led them to succumb to "a sectarian temptation."[34] Significantly, Gustafson uses "sectarian" to refer not so much to a splinter group within Christianity, as traditional usage has it, but to a splinter group within society conceived as a whole.[35] The danger in thinking of the church as the cultural embodiment of the distinctively Christian tradition of inquiry is that it separates the church from its social environment. Lindbeck's theological appropriation of cultural-anthropological categories protects the church's (and other religious bodies') claims and their embodiment from the influence and criticism of other stances and disciplines. As a result, Christianity becomes a closed and rigid system, "isolated from the critical currents of the [larger] culture."[36] Were Christians to adopt Lindbeck's cultural-linguistic approach, they would abandon their concern for truth in witness and discipleship,

33. The atheist stance is rare among ethnographers except insofar as the agnostic stance commonly takes such an immanentist approach that it amounts to a denial of religious claims. The religious stance is found, e.g., in the theories of Micea Eliade, or the treatment of myth popularized by Joseph Campbell. The agnostic stance is pervasive among the ethnographers discussed below; it can also be seen in Lindbeck's definition just cited.
34. James M. Gustafson, "The Sectarian Temptation: Reflections on Theology, the Church, and the University," *Proceedings of the Catholic Theological Society of America* 40/1985, 83–94. Stanley Hauerwas has responded to Gustafson's criticisms in the introduction to his *Christian Existence Today: Essays on Church, World and Living In Between* (Durham, NC: Labyrinth Press, 1988), pp. 1–21.
35. A point made by Arne Rasmusson, *The Church as Polis: From Political Theology to Theological Politics as Exemplified by Jürgen Moltmann and Stanley Hauerwas* (Notre Dame: University of Notre Dame Press, 1995), p. 233.   36. Gustafson, "The Sectarian Temptation," p. 85.

renege on their responsibility to the other, and retreat into a ghetto-like existence. Other critics of Lindbeck's theory have challenged his assumption that one can delineate clear boundaries between the church and other traditions of inquiry. They have also argued that he simplifies the ambiguities of Christian existence and the complexities of the church's relation with the world, and overlooks otherness and conflict by asserting too great a uniformity within each tradition of inquiry.[37]

Whether or not these criticisms are fairly made of Lindbeck and Hauerwas,[38] they do not apply to an ecclesiological ethnography developed within a theodramatic horizon and in terms of a traditioned understanding of truth. To repeat: truth is discerned through engagement with those who are other than "we" are: with the Spirit, with those Christians with whom we disagree; and with those outside the church. To be a disciple and to witness to Jesus Christ requires one to practice engaged inquiry and responsibility to the other. The church's quest for truth is ongoing; debate cannot be ended by epic accounts of the church or the world or their relation. The pre-eschatological church needs the religious and non-religious bodies of the world to be genuinely different from itself, and different from one another, in order for it to play its own role within the theodrama and construct its concrete identity through ecclesial bricolage.[39] But the boundaries between church and world are never clear. The church is sinful and "worldly," and the Spirit acts throughout creation; so "church" and "world" may often be more prescriptive than descriptive categories within a theodramatic horizon.

It seems likely that some of the concern about the use of the cultural metaphor within theology is due to certain assumptions about what cultures are. It is important to be clear on this issue since, as Kathryn Tanner has pointed out, theological use of cultural studies has often hitherto been rather intuitive and thus open to considerable misunderstanding.[40] The following is a very brief account of the development of the modern

---

37. See, e.g., Robin Gill, *Moral Leadership in a Postmodern Age* (Edinburgh: T&T Clark, 1997), p. 65; Milbank, *Theology and Social Theory*, p. 386; Tanner, *Theories of Culture*, pp. 140ff. and 159.
38. Arne Rasmusson, *The Church as Polis*, argues in support of Stanley Hauerwas by bringing to light some of Gustafson's misleading background assumptions. Bruce Marshall has helped to clarify Lindbeck sufficiently to suggest that Gustafson misses his mark there, too. See Marshall's "Aquinas as a Post-liberal Theologian," *The Thomist* 53 (1989), 353–402.
39. As Aidan Kavanaugh notes, even such a distinctively Christian practice as baptism "has always been a compound act absorbing cultural patterns into itself; it has taken on definite shape in various cultures, shaping those cultures in turn." *The Shape of Baptism: The Rite of Christian Initiation* (New York: Pueblo, 1978), p. xiv.
40. Tanner, *Theories of Culture*, p. x.

concept of culture. According to Renato Rosaldo,[41] the modern, anthropological concept of culture arose in the period leading up to about 1920, during which the job of the "Lone Ethnographer" was to go boldly into "distant" lands to find and describe examples of pure culture. The description was to be objective; with "detached impartiality" the observer would gather "data" from the "utterances" of the "natives," and then go home to the metropolis with his collection of "primitive facts"[42] in order to write up a "definitive" account of that particular culture (CT 30ff.). The assumption of this period was that cultures are primitive, homogeneous entities. Internally consistent and thus without conflict, they remain virtually unchanged throughout history. In their monumental timelessness they reflect the earliest stages of humankind's evolution. This "heroic" period of ethnography gave way to a second, "classic" period, lasting, according to Rosaldo, (with "mock precision," CT 32) from 1921 to 1971, during which Durkheim was especially influential. Retained from the previous period was "a complicity with imperialism, a commitment to objectivism and a belief in monumentalism" (CT 31). What distinguished the work of this period from that of the previous one was an increased concern to discover the patterns and structures of cultures, understood as largely autonomous, internally consistent systems. The idea was to analyze the bits and pieces of a culture so as to develop a consistent, scientific view of the whole; from there a cross-cultural view would attempt to build a general theory of culture. As a consequence of its theoretical concern, the work of this period tended to ignore or rule out as irrelevant whatever did not fit the cultural system. Thus, for example, individuals were treated as if their behavior was wholly determined by the cultural system within which they lived.

To adopt either of these modern understandings of culture as the analogy for ecclesiological reflection would presumably require us to describe the church as an instance of a pure culture, as a closed, internally consistent system. To do so would be to place ecclesiology back within a thoroughly epic horizon in which it seeks to describe the concrete church tidily and undramatically as an internally coherent system of practices and beliefs. Since the church is independent of other systems, there need be no reference to the shifting ecclesiological context. And since it is a

---

41. Renato Rosaldo, *Culture and Truth: The Remaking of Social Analysis* (Boston: Beacon Press, 1989). Cited as (CT page).
42. The phrase "primitive facts" is from Clifford Geertz, *The Interpretation of Cultures* (New York: Harper Torchbooks, 1973), p. 16.

"monumental" and homogenous system, it would appear reasonable to describe it by means of normative blueprints that apply to all times and places. Normative claims for one's blueprint would be encouraged by the "impartial observer" status claimed by modern ethnographers and adopted by modern ecclesiologists. The theologian might think that one could reflect upon the church without preunderstanding, horizon or agenda, so as to write the "definitive" description of the church as an integrated system. This, of course, is but an extreme version of the modern ecclesiological method I argued against in chapter 2 above.

It is likely, moreover, that this approach would eliminate any sense of the struggle involved in the pilgrim church's attempts to witness and care for its discipleship within ever-shifting ecclesiological contexts. Such an epic view would suggest too forcefully for theological safety that the church's center lies within itself, as a secure self-possession. Change in the church's patterns could be explained as a distortion of its true being, either by inadequate socialization of its membership, or by pollution from contact with another system. The only positive form of change could be organic, whereby the internally consistent church developed into fuller realizations of its essential being in accordance with its own principles. Contact with other systems could not be considered fruitful since each system is a self-contained entity with its own principles and conception of rationality. The church would have no reason to consider others as anything more than raw material for conversion. The church's incommensurability with regard to other religious and non-religious bodies would protect its witness from external critique, but would also undermine the possibility of making genuine truth claims and engaging with competing traditions. Gustafson-like criticisms would thus be reasonably made of a modern form of ecclesiological ethnography, for it would be likely to treat the church as if it were a community of fideistic disciples, a "sect" or an exclusivist religious body. Clearly such a concept of culture has no place within a theodramatic horizon. While it is true that the church draws upon a number of rules (the *regula fidei*) to regulate its life, how these rules should be applied in concrete cases is always subject to debate, the church being both the forum of that debate and its product. The church's concrete identity is never static; as the embodiment of a tradition that is inherently conflictual it is constructed over time by way of argument about bricolage and by experimentation and reform, as the church engages with its various challengers, internal and external, and as it is led by the Spirit towards the Father through the Son. Both as a human activity and as a body dependent upon trinitarian activity, it is far too complex to be described by means of a systems-theoretical approach.

Moreover, if the modern concept of culture were applied to the church, it would permit the church to be reductively redescribed according to theories developed within atheist or religious stances. This is immediately evident with the systems-theoretical approach. The analyst moves from particular cultural systems, among which is the concrete church, to a general theory of cultures. The church's distinctive cultural patterns are then explained in terms of general religio-social laws. The problem of reductive redescription is less obvious, perhaps, but not on that account less dangerous for ecclesiology, within more recent kinds of ethnography. Clifford Geertz has noted how ethnography has become in recent years (in part due to his influence), "not an experimental science in search of law, but an interpretive one in search of meaning."[43] A culture is now viewed not as a power, as if it were "something to which social events, behaviors, institutions, or processes can be causally attributed." Rather, it is a taken-for-granted "context for meaningful thought and action and thus something which can be intelligibly – that is, thickly, described."[44] While this interpretive concept of culture may be more amenable for ecclesiological purposes, it is often located within a horizon that conflicts in part with Christianity, namely a humanistic metanarrative. Cultures, on this view, are the product of the universal human quest for meaning; they are particular answers to the questions we face in all societies. The point of describing cultures is not to evaluate them, since one could do so only according to one's own cultural criteria, which would be an ethnocentric error. Rather, the function of cultural analysis is to further a larger "humanistic project of social criticism."[45] By getting to know other cultures we learn alternative ways of dealing with issues that we also face, thereby gaining some critical leverage upon our own culture and enabling us to develop a freer and more rational society. Something like this has been the approach of a number of theologians, especially among the pluralists, as we have seen.[46] But seen from within a theodramatic horizon, the humanist project would distort the point of cultural analysis within ecclesiology. It is not the primary task of the church to contribute to the development of rational and free society, even though that may be a very significant secondary concern. The church knows that it cannot heal itself or save its social environment; it can only try as best it can to play its

43. Ibid., p. 5.   44. Ibid., p. 14.   45. Tanner, *Theories of Culture*, p. 37.
46. For a critical discussion of Kaufman's cultural approach, see ibid., pp. 63–68.

part within the theodrama. Ecclesiological ethnography within a theo-dramatic horizon must be critical, carefully assessing our ecclesial culture and the cultural patterns of other traditions of inquiry in an effort to render the church's witness and discipleship more truthful. Such critical theological evaluation draws not upon some general notion of rationality but upon our orientation in the Holy Spirit to Jesus Christ crucified, in and through whom we receive meaning and truth. Otherwise there is little point in engaging with other cultural patterns or in describing our own.

Concern about using a modern concept of culture within ecclesiology is thus quite reasonable. However, many elements of the modern concept have come under sustained attack in recent years from postmodern eth-nographic theorists, who retain the interpretive aspect of cultural analy-sis but reject the humanist metanarratives. It is from this more postmodern concept that a theodramatic concept of culture can be devel-oped to apply to the church. Contemporary postmodern ethnography (of the kind useful to ecclesiology, at any rate)[47] has abandoned the earlier view of culture as a timeless, self-sufficient entity. As Rosaldo notes, "[i]n the postcolonialist world, the notion of an authentic culture as an auton-omous internally coherent universe no longer seems tenable" (CT 217). Cultures are not static things; they evolve, and their evolution cannot be explained simply as an organic development, as an independent unfold-ing or expression of an essential core. Cultural changes occur as a result of internal conflict and by engagement with surrounding cultures. Cultural boundaries, though, are never clear; cultures overlap one another, sharing many elements, so that many people may be at home in more than one. Cultural identity is thus not "essential", the product of some core principle or belief that sharply defines the shape of a particular way of life. Rather, to use James Clifford's term, it is "conjunctural" (PC 11), the product of engagement and bricolage. This is not to say that a culture cannot have a distinctive identity, only that its "sense of difference or dis-tinctiveness can never be located solely in the continuity of a culture or tradition." Since conflict and dissonance, both internal and external, are inherent in any cultural tradition, "[a]nalysts no longer seek out harmony and consensus to the exclusion of difference and inconsistency" (CT 28).

---

47. There is, of course, no such thing as "the" postmodern view of cultural analysis. In light of my theological agenda, I have found it useful to draw especially from Rosaldo's *Culture and Truth*, and from James Clifford, *The Predicament of Culture: Twentieth Century Ethnography, Literature, and Art* (Cambridge, MA: Harvard University Press, 1988), cited as (PC page).

Hence, as Geertz notes, "coherence cannot be the major test of validity for a cultural description."[48]

This postmodern concept of cultural identity as "a hybrid, relational affair, something that lives between as much as within cultures,"[49] is clearly far more amenable to appropriation within a theodramatic horizon than the modern concept. The church's cultural products are constructed in engagement with the other: with those others who lived earlier in the tradition; with other Christians who may not agree with me or with the authorities as to what it means to follow Jesus Christ; with other traditions of inquiry and their members; and with the condition of the possibility for all such engagement to be fruitful, the Holy Other. Ecclesial cultural identity is constructed as a struggle, not to preserve some essential identity, but to construct and reconstruct that identity in light of an orientation to what it alone seeks, the truth revealed in the person and work of Jesus Christ. That identity is constructed by experimentation, by bricolage and by retrieval of earlier forms. Conflict, error and sin are inherent aspects of the concrete church, and so self-criticism is a necessary element in its further construction. The prophetic and practical function of a theodramatic ecclesiological ethnography is thus, as Kathryn Tanner notes of postmodern ethnography generally, to open up our constructed identity to ongoing reassessment. One vital way it performs this self-critical function is "by uncovering and giving sense to the internal contestations of a culture, by disputing the homogeneity and consistency of a culture, by resisting the temptation to assume unified cultural totalities."[50]

It is evident, too, that this postmodern view of culture supports the theodramatic critique of the correlation method. The church cannot be correlated with "the" culture, for neither church nor world can be reduced to clearly defined positions. The modern view of culture as more or less isomorphic with society is not only misleading, it undermines our responsibility to otherness. To develop a normative description of putatively society-wide cultural patterns is to abstract from the cultural diversity concretely present within that society; it is to gloss over those who, either as individuals or as members of less powerful or noted cultural groups, do not share the same cultural norms as "we" do or who are marginalized by that society. "Our" culture, so described, is likely to be the universalization of a particular group within society; such a move lends

48. Geertz, *Interpretation of Cultures*, p. 17.   49. Tanner, *Theories of Culture*, p. 57f.
50. Ibid., p. 58.

itself to ideological distortion. To make this point, however, is not to rule out correlation as such, but to suggest that it is better done in very piecemeal, ad hoc fashion. If we say, for example, that the project of Schleiermacher is an exercise in correlation theology, it is not unreasonable to describe it as an effort to translate Christianity into categories that helped to make it make sense for the "cultured despisers" of his time. That is, he construed Christianity in such a way that, while less than adequate (in view of his doctrine of the Trinity, for example), he enabled a small and rather self-important group within his society to overcome their culturally induced errors and inhibitions and take Christianity seriously.[51] Thereby he opened up the possibility that one or two of them might be converted; they might find the orientation embodied in the church to be superior to their despising culture, and so transfer their allegiance. If they did so, they would find it necessary to translate and redescribe back in the other direction, to absorb the despising culture into the categories and framework provided by the church.[52] One could do the same thing for other groups, especially for those who are less powerful. That project, however, is quite different from another reading of Schleiermacher's work, namely as the model of a theological method whereby one correlates a set of non-theological, universal (or at least society-wide) norms and principles with a single, normative account of Christianity. For those living within postmodern and theodramatic horizons such a move appears naive at best.

Contemporary postmodern ethnography has largely abandoned the earlier notion of an "impartial observer" whose description of a culture is understood to be definitive because it is objective and unprejudiced. To describe a culture requires imagination, both in trying to understand it and in trying to portray it. As James Clifford remarks, "the imposition of coherence on an unruly textual process is now inescapably a matter of strategic choice" (PC 54). And as a "positioned subject" (CT 207), the interpreter's imagination is itself culturally informed. Ethnography therefore now privileges the voices of the insiders, of those who are at home in the

51. The issue, of course, is whether Schleiermacher distorted Christianity by mediating it to its cultured despisers. One might argue that in his *On Religion: Speeches to its Cultured Despisers* (New York: Harper and Row, 1958), Schleiermacher adopted more of a religious stance than the theological one more in evidence in his later *The Christian Faith* (Edinburgh: T&T Clark, 1976).
52. One could argue that Schleiermacher thereby contributed to the Christian tradition of inquiry, positively as well as negatively, as I think Barth would agree (with massive reservations, no doubt). For a reading of Schleiermacher along these lines, see Hans Frei, "Ad Hoc Correlation" in his *Types of Christian Theology*, pp. 70–91.

culture. But even among insiders there may be a wide range of perspectives on cultural identity. Some participants may have higher status than others; some may live more on the "cultural borderlands" (CT 28) while others live more at the center of the culture. In listening to the marginalized voices as well as those of the center, the observer recognizes that any culture is "an open-ended, creative dialogue of sub-cultures, of insiders and outsiders, of diverse factions" (PC 46).

The question of who should undertake the task of practical-prophetic ecclesiology is thus by no means insignificant in view of the church's responsibility to otherness. I argued in chapter 2 that all ecclesiology is conditioned by the theologian's agenda, horizon, place in society and church, and suchlike. All who do theology are "positioned subjects." None of our construals of Christianity or the shape of the church's concrete identity is normative, though certainly some may be far better than others, and some may be plainly wrong. This suggests that theological reflection upon the concrete church should be done by more than just a few authoritative churchpeople, perhaps more as a collaborative project of the church as a whole. Too often, books on ecclesiology are produced, like this one, by theologians or pastors working virtually alone, more or less independent of much of the Christian community. Perhaps (though I think not) they are the only churchpeople who care enough about the church to do such work; possibly they are the only ones who have the necessary doctrinal and ecclesiastical expertise. It is true that any reflection on the church, in whatever form – descriptive, critical or constructive – must be governed by theological considerations, and so those who are most familiar with the Christian tradition of inquiry will find it easiest to make a convincing theological case for their views. Nor is the church a liberal-democratic institution, to be governed by the will (or the manipulated emotions) of the majority. Its goal is to correspond to its Lord rather than to be tolerant of any and all kinds of religious expression. That said, however, professional theologians and pastors may often have a different perspective upon the church than many of its other members, a difference due not simply to their expertise. Other churchpeople usually have to spend much more of their time involved with non-church issues. They live, accordingly, more at the cultural borderlands, at those places where the Christian tradition must engage with other forms of inquiry and their embodiments. They are less encumbered by the sometimes distracting theoretical apparatus taught to the experts. Laypeople, women, majorities and minorities of various kinds may be marginalized within some

forms of the Christian church. They may not only have a different perspective upon the church and its interaction with other traditions, they
may have clearer insights into its sinfulness and inadequacies, into the
challenges it faces, and perhaps as to how it should be reformed. Ecclesiological ethnography, then, would benefit from as inclusive a theological
assessment of the church body by its membership as possible. Thereby it
would attempt to respond to the entire spectrum of challenges made
from within the church to its present form, and become more aware of
external challenges.

The suggestion that ecclesiology become a church-wide social practice
of communal self-critical analysis bears upon the issue of Christian formation, and may reveal one of the limits of the culture metaphor, modern
or postmodern. It is sometimes said that a disciple of Jesus Christ must
give herself over to the church so entirely that, faced with two courses of
action, she need not make a decision but simply act in the way in which
she has become habituated. Stanley Hauerwas sometimes talks a little
like this, especially when he advocates cultural Christianity and what he
calls "peasant Catholicism."[53] Hauerwas's stress upon formation is reasonable, but his own practice would suggest that he would likely agree
that the church's function is not to coerce its membership into acting in
accordance with a uniform or centralized way of being Christian. The
church's function is to serve the individual who, in turn, is to serve the
church. It serves its discipleship by socializing them into the Christian
life. But this does not mean that it should try to produce a set of people
who play only the parts given them by the church, such as layperson,
priest, bishop, or nun.[54] The church does not cause individuals to become
Christians; that is the work of the Spirit. Each of us is called by the Spirit
of Christ to our own unique roles by which we receive our particularity as
persons. The church only mediates that call, co-operating in the work of
the Spirit or obstructing it. Within a theodramatic horizon, one cannot
say that one's salvation is proportionate to one's conformity to a particular
ecclesial culture, for that culture is pre-eschatological, the product of a

53. See, e.g., Stanley Hauerwas, "The Sanctified Body: Why Perfection Does Not Require a
'Self'" in his *Sanctify Them*, pp. 77–91. The phrase "peasant Catholicism" is obviously a
rhetorical ploy intended to upset liberal Roman Catholics. That Hauerwas does not
advocate uniformity is evident from a later chapter in the same book, "Characterizing
Perfection," pp. 123–142.

54. Miroslav Volf rightly criticizes a notion of personhood developed along these lines in
John D. Zizioulas, *Being as Communion: Studies in Personhood and the Church* (Crestwood, NY:
St. Vladimir's Seminary Press, 1985); see Volf, *After Our Likeness: The Church as the Image of the
Trinity* (Grand Rapids: Eerdmans, 1998), pp. 109ff.

very mixed body that is dependent upon other bodies. As I noted in an earlier chapter, it may well be that the more a Christian grows into her unique role, the more she will find herself having to challenge certain ecclesial cultural patterns, even if she has no leadership role. Of course, discerning whether prophecy is true or false is sometimes extremely difficult, but such difficulties cannot be avoided; they are an inherent part of the dramatic struggle that constitutes Christian ecclesial existence. Hence the church is not the kind of collective that demands the individual give herself over to the group without remainder; nor is the purpose of ethnographic ecclesiology to foster an ecclesial culture for its own sake. Rather, it does so only to serve the church's witness and to enable each of its members to play their parts in the theodrama. Those two tasks will indeed require a strong and complex ecclesial culture, but the test of that culture lies in whether it produces strong and complex disciples.

Before we leave postmodern ethnography behind, it is worth noting a couple of the tools it has developed which may be useful in building up a well-rounded ecclesiology for the pilgrim church. Unlike earlier forms of the discipline, postmodern ethnography recognizes the need to analyze the interplay of feelings, emotions, and will with cultural beliefs and practices. Accordingly the notion of cultural "force" has been proposed by Geertz and developed further by Rosaldo (CT 2). This refers to the thoroughness with which a given cultural form is internalized, whether, that is, it is central or marginal in the lives of individuals within a given culture. Within the Christian social body a particular practice may be stressed by teaching and preaching, yet it may have little force within the affective lives of Christians. And the contrary may obtain: there may be a remarkable amount of emotion generated within an individual or group without it being linked to a specific social practice or belief. With the notion of force in mind, ecclesiological ethnography might analyze how far the belief in the sacramentality of marriage in the lives of married Catholics has been internalized. Or how far does biblical language bear upon the everyday decisions and emotions of those Christians for whom bible-reading is claimed to be a central practice? How forceful is the image of "light," so often stressed in rituals such as the Easter Vigil, in a time when light seems so ordinary by comparison to earlier centuries?

The postmodern conception of culture has moved firmly away from the modern idea that cultures display patterns that can be adequately described in synchronic ways alone. Time should be considered in all forms of cultural analysis, whether internal or in relation to other cultures. Ethnographic descriptions are to show "how ideas, events and institutions interact and change through time," an approach that is sometimes called "processual analysis" (CT 92f.). To describe adequately any given social pattern we cannot simply describe its present form, but must analyze the process by which it arrived at that form. In a rather different sense of time, there is now a greater appreciation of the temporal dynamics within a given culture. The practices of everyday life have a certain "tempo" (CT 105ff.) which must be adhered to for them to be done well. A church service that is too quickly or slowly recited, too short or long-winded a sermon – such mistakes in tempo are likely to unsettle a congregation, whether for good or ill. Tempo is also an important factor in church reform. Some commentators have suggested that the changes to the Roman liturgy following Vatican II were too rapid. And every pastor knows that she or he must proceed with caution in introducing new elements in Sunday worship.

The postmodern concept of culture is evidently more useful as a metaphor for the church than the modern, but it is not, of course, a theological concept; it must be modified if it is to be used within a theological stance. Not only must the theological concept of culture have a much stronger notion of truth than is often the case in postmodern forms, it must be thoroughly absorbed into a Christian horizon. Ecclesiological ethnography shares with the postmodern theorists the concern to describe cultural patterns "thickly," with rigorous attention to detail, nuance, process and relationship. But it cannot adopt a "thin" agnostic theory for doing so, especially if that theory is brought in normatively from another tradition of inquiry (though certainly it must engage with such theories and their analyses). Instead, it adopts the "thick" theory that is the ongoing, self-critical Christian tradition of inquiry.[55]

Ecclesiological ethnography may reflect critically upon the church in a wide variety of ways and at all levels, from a single congregation to the worldwide church.[56] Although a few theologians, such as Karl

---

55. I cannot address here the important and complex question of the kind of exegesis suitable for an ethnographic and theodramatic ecclesiology. But see, for example, Frances M. Young, *Biblical Exegesis and the Formation of Christian Culture* (Cambridge: Cambridge University Press, 1997); Stephen E. Fowl, *Engaging Scripture: A Model for Theological Interpretation* (Oxford: Blackwell, 1998); Francis Watson, *Text, Church and World: Biblical Interpretation in Theological Perspective* (Edinburgh: T&T Clark, 1994). Interestingly, in a discussion of the use and authority of Scripture, N. T. Wright has used the metaphor of a five-act play, the last act of which must be worked out by us. See his *The New Testament and the People of God* (Minneapolis: Fortress, 1992), pp. 140–143.

56. I say "worldwide" because the more customary "universal" would presumably include the eschatological church which, needless to say, is not patient of ethnographic analysis.

Rahner[57] and David Kelsey,[58] have discussed the possibility of parish or congregational ecclesiology, such work has rarely been attempted, perhaps in part because it must be so focused upon the concrete.[59] This is a surprising and, I think, unwarranted restriction of the scope of ecclesiology. Every congregation or parish has its own quite distinctive way of being church, which can be the subject of ecclesiological-ethnographic reflection. The work of James Hopewell and other sociologists shows that, although most members of a congregation do not usually mingle very much with one another outside their Sunday gatherings, yet by meeting once a week or so to worship, they "communicate with each other sufficiently to develop intrinsic patterns of conduct, outlook, and story."[60] They build up a "complex network of signals, symbols, conventions" that constitutes the distinctive identity of their particular congregation.[61] Although many of their practices and beliefs are shared by other Christian congregations and by society at large, the configuration of these is the congregation's own. That configuration is the embodiment of that congregation's effort to contribute to the tradition of inquiry into how to correspond to Jesus Christ in its particular time and place, and constitutes its attempt to witness and foster the discipleship of its members.

The configuration of a parish is constructed over time, by processes that include internal and external bricolage. As Christians come together over the years they experiment with different ways of thinking and acting. They sift through the resources of the various cultures and subcultures in which their members live, rejecting certain possibilities, modifying, privileging or down-playing others so as to make them serve the tasks of witness and discipleship. They do something similar with the various practices and beliefs of Christianity, too, though with considerably less freedom if they are to remain truly a Christian community. Building up a parish's cultural configuration – we could call it the

57. See Karl Rahner, "Zur Theologie der Pfarre" in *Die Pfarre: Von der Theologie zur Praxis*, ed., Hugo Rahner, (Freiburg im Breisgau: Lambertus Verlag, 1956), pp. 27–39. Some idea of how the parish has been understood within Roman Catholicism can be gathered from a brief historical and doctrinal overview by James A. Coriden, *The Parish in Catholic Tradition: History, Theology, and Canon Law* (Mahwah, NJ: Paulist Press, 1997). For a critical analysis of some of the key issues, see Joseph Komonchak, "The Local Church and the Church Catholic: The Contemporary Theological Problematic," *The Jurist* 52 (1992), 416–447.
58. See David H. Kelsey, *To Understand God Truly: What's Theological About a Theological School* (Louisville: Westminster/John Knox Press, 1992), chapter seven.
59. Some of Stanley Hauerwas's essays could be understood as exercises in congregational ecclesiology; see e.g., Stanley Hauerwas and William H. Willimon, *Resident Aliens: Life in the Christian Colony* (Nashville: Abingdon Press, 1989), pp. 112–143.
60. James F. Hopewell, *Congregation: Stories and Structures* (Philadelphia: Fortress, 1987), p. 13.
61. Ibid., p. 7.

congregation's "character" – is usually accomplished without much explicit reflection; indeed, such congregational decisions are often made implicitly, by something like a communal taste. Certainly, the self-understanding of the regional and worldwide church is often normative (depending upon polity, of course) and has a great deal of influence upon the formation of that character, as does the regional body and, where appropriate, the diocese. However, no two congregations are exactly the same, nor are their characters analyzable simply as expressions of a diocesan or regional norm. In seeking to play its part in the theodrama within a particular place, the parish or congregation produces cultural forms, some of which may be quite idiosyncratic, all of which have a significant bearing upon the quality of its witness.

Thus it seems reasonable that ecclesiological ethnography turn its attention to particular congregations. Their often unreflectively constructed identities may well contain less than suitable elements, or those that are less than fitting for their ecclesiological contexts. Lack of self-reflection may also result in a congregation's failing to take advantage of an opportunity for better discipleship, perhaps by engaging more directly with another tradition of inquiry or by retrieving one of its practices that has fallen into disuse. A congregational form of ecclesiological ethnography could be an ecclesial practice undertaken by the congregation itself. It might be possible, for example, to complement the confession of congregational sinfulness by some discussion, on a more informal occasion, of precisely where that sinfulness is manifested, and what opportunities are available to the congregation for suitable reforms. The congregation, in effect, would engage in an examination of its collective conscience (metaphorically speaking) by means of a critical inquiry into its cultural patterns. By developing its penitential history, it would try to discern the movements of the Spirit in its past, and by ethnographic and sociological ecclesiology discern and develop proposals about the opportunities and failures in its present concrete identity. Its membership would come together to try to make explicit their goals and ambitions as a congregation in order to assess their fittingness for witness and discipleship in their particular ecclesiological context. Congregations may be able to do quite a lot of this by themselves, but at some point they will need some outside help. They may seek the fraternal insights (and, if need be, correction) of representatives of other congregations or of the regional or diocesan authorities. They may engage with representatives of other traditions of inquiry or with analyses done according to non-theological stances in order to gain further insight into their congregation's concrete identity and the effectiveness of its witness. It is likely, too, that more rigorous analyses by suitably trained observers would be useful, especially in trying to situate the particular congregation in its ecclesiological context.[62]

Ecclesiological ethnography cannot, of course, be restricted to congregations; to serve the church it is necessary to analyze the cultural patterns of regional churches and, indeed, the church worldwide. Avery Dulles has rightly contended that to acknowledge the cultural variations among congregations or dioceses does not imply that there should not be many cultural elements in common throughout the church.[63] Developing broader analyses may help to promote such a common Christian culture, while also bringing to light significant experiments at the more local level, and assessing them before proposing them for more general adoption. Ecclesiological ethnography should not be restricted to a social scientific style either. William T. Cavanaugh's *Torture and Eucharist*,[64] which we noted briefly in chapter 2, is a model of an ecclesiological ethnographic form which, in examining two conflicting sets of cultural patterns, relies rather less upon thick description than upon thick theological analysis. A brief summary, while not doing justice to the work, will give some idea of the approach. Cavanaugh's study is, one might say, a theological history of the conflict between the cultural patterns of the church and the state in Chile during the Pinochet regime. The opposition is embodied in its most extreme form in the state's practice of torture versus the church's eucharistic practice. The former makes concrete an imagination of violence, while the latter is an imagination of what really is, namely the peaceful Kingdom of God (TE 279). The former is a "kind of perverse liturgy" (TE 16), creating isolated individuals who lose their very souls to the state. The practice of torture is thus not simply a denial of the rights of individuals; it denies the reality of the church. And, as Cavanaugh shows, this is in part the church's fault, for it relied upon an overly epic form of ecclesiology which the bishops took a remarkably long time to unlearn, during which time they could do little or nothing for their discipleship (TE 82). That

---

62. For an insightful discussion of this, see Stanley Hauerwas, "The Ministry of a Congregation" in his *Christian Existence Today*, pp. 111–131.
63. Avery Dulles, *The Catholicity of the Church* (Oxford: Clarendon Press, 1985), p. 176; and Dulles, *The Reshaping of Catholicism: Current Challenges in the Theology of Church* (San Francisco: Harper and Row, 1988), pp. 45ff.
64. William T. Cavanaugh, *Torture and Eucharist: Theology, Politics, and the Body of Christ* (Oxford: Blackwell, 1998), cited as (TE page).

ecclesiology assumed a fundamental harmony and division of labor between nation state and church, following a Maritainian "distinction of planes" in which the state would take care of things political, while the church would care for the "soul" of the nation (TE 151ff.). This blueprint ecclesiology contributed to the distortion of the church's concrete identity in Chile at that time, for it was inappropriate (at best) in its ecclesiological context. Its failure to acknowledge the theodramatic aspect of Christian existence inhibited the church's leadership from performing their task of witness and pastoral care. Their concern for harmony overwhelmed their call to boast only in Jesus Christ crucified.

While ecclesiological ethnography should direct much of its effort to developing similarly rigorous forms of analysis, there is room for less carefully documented forms. It might be possible, for instance, to portray an ecclesial culture imaginatively and therefore with greater force than purely scholarly accounts can. An example is David Lodge's *Souls and Bodies*.[65] While Lodge is not attempting critical ecclesiology, and adopts a critically agnostic stance, he presents a fascinating account of the cultural patterns of Roman Catholicism in Britain in the 1960s and 70s. He presents a suitably caustic narrative about a group of young Roman Catholic Londoners who deal with the conflicts between their sexuality and their religious commitments during the years just prior to and following Vatican II. Similar narratives could be developed within a theological stance by those suitably gifted. Another, similarly unscientific example worth noting is Thomas Day's *Why Catholics Can't Sing*, mentioned in an earlier chapter, which describes parish life in North American Roman Catholicism in terms of its liturgical music.[66] Day's book is an enjoyable read; it offers few statistics, relying instead upon a vigorous anecdotal style. The style is deceptively lightweight, though, for the book is a significant processual analysis of some contemporary liturgical styles and practices, tracing them back to their origins in Irish Catholicism. And his analyses and criticisms, while no doubt partly informed by his musical tastes, are ultimately governed by a theological stance, and show how discipleship suffers and witness becomes distorted when a community adopts practices that foster a tendency to glory in itself rather than in its Lord.

Whatever forms are selected as appropriate for the task in hand, eccles-

65. David Lodge, *Souls and Bodies* (New York: Penguin Viking, 1990).
66. Thomas Day, *Why Catholics Can't Sing: The Culture of Catholicism and the Triumph of Bad Taste* (New York: Crossroad, 1995).

iological ethnography, as well as theological history and theological sociology, should be ongoing theological practices. Effective critical self-reflection by the church is often episodic, done only when things get obviously bad, when discipleship and witness have suffered and reforms have to be drastic. Practical-prophetic reflection upon the concrete church seeks to anticipate and forestall the need for such drastic measures, seeking out error and sin as early as possible, as well as discerning new opportunities. It is somewhat analogous to the older idea of confession in the Roman church. One went every week or so, not necessarily because one was a particularly egregious sinner; usually quite the contrary. Confession was understood as an ongoing self-critical practice, a continuing effort to reorientate oneself anew to Jesus Christ. I suggest that it is the function of ecclesiology to do something similar for the church, bearing in mind the stipulations about penitence noted earlier with regard to theological history.

Of course, no ecclesiological approach will preempt any and all deviation from the church's orientation to its Lord; within a theodramatic horizon, such a notion is absurd. But ecclesiological forms of history, sociology and ethnography, in debate with parallel non-theological disciplines, may help the church live more truthfully by drawing critical theological attention back to the confusions and complexities of life within the pilgrim church. Practical-prophetic ecclesiology acknowledges that Christian existence is never stable or resolvable in terms of purely theoretical constructions, but is ever-moving, always struggling along within the theodrama. It acknowledges, too, that the church must engage with other traditions of inquiry and their embodiments not only for their sake, but for its own, in order that it may on occasion hear the Spirit of our Lord in their midst. It acknowledges the church's sinfulness and errors, not only when it is obliged to do so by others, but by actively seeking out and bringing to light anti-Christian practices and beliefs and by proposing suitable reforms. It responds to ever-shifting ecclesiological contexts by means of occasionalist and experimental practical and theoretical responses that seek to push the tradition of inquiry along a little further. It thus provides a way for theological inquiry to focus as much upon the details of Christian ecclesial existence as upon its more general patterns, so that it may help the church pursue its quest of glorying in Jesus Christ in everything it does.

Bibliography

Ammerman, Nancy Tatom, with Arthur E. Farnsley II and others. *Congregation and Community*. New Brunswick, NJ: Rutgers University Press, 1997.

Apczynski, John V. "John Hick's Theocentricism: Revolutionary or Implicitly Exclusivist?," *Modern Theology* 8:1 (1992), 39–52.

Aquinas, Saint Thomas. *Summa Theologiae*. Turin: Marietti, 1962.

Armstrong, Karen. *A History of God: The 4,000-Year Quest of Judaism, Christianity and Islam*. New York: Ballantine Books, 1993.

Augustine, Saint. *Augustine: Later Works*, trans. John Burnaby. Philadelphia: Westminster Press, 1955.

    City of God, trans. H. Bettenson. London: Penguin, 1972/1984.

Avis, Paul D. L. *The Church in the Theology of the Reformers*. Atlanta: John Knox, 1981.

Balthasar, Hans Urs von. *A Theology of History*. New York: Sheed and Ward, 1963.

    Theo-Drama: Theological Dramatic Theory, vols. I–V, trans. Graham Harrison. San Francisco: Ignatius Press, 1988–1998.

    Explorations in Theology II: Spouse of the Word. San Francisco: Ignatius Press, 1991.

Barth, Karl. *Church Dogmatics*, trans. G. W. Bromiley. Edinburgh: T&T Clark, 1956–1975.

Baxter, Michael J., CSC. "Writing History in a World Without Ends: An Evangelical Catholic Critique of United States Catholic History," *Pro Ecclesia* 5:5 (1996), 440–469.

Bechert, Heinz. "The Buddhist Community and Its Earlier History" in Hans Küng, *et al.*, *Christianity and the World Religions: Paths of Dialogue with Islam, Hinduism and Buddhism*. New York: Doubleday, 1986.

Bellah, Robert N., and associates. *Habits of the Heart: Individualism and Commitment in American Life*. New York: Harper and Row, 1985.

Bettenson, H. (ed. and trans.) *Documents of the Christian Church*. New York: Oxford University Press, 1943.

Black, C. Clifton. "Serving the Food of Full-Grown Adults: Augustine's Interpretation of Scripture and the Nurture of Christians," *Interpretation* 52:4 (1998), 341–353.

Boff, Leonardo. *Ecclesiogenesis: The Base Communities Reinvent the Church*. Maryknoll, NY: Orbis, 1986.

    Trinity and Society. Maryknoll NY: Orbis, 1988.

    Faith on the Edge: Religion and Marginalized Existence. San Francisco: Harper and Row, 1989.

Church: Charism and Power: Liberation Theology and the Institutional Church, trans. J.W. Diercksmeier. New York: Crossroad, 1992.

Bonhoeffer, Dietrich. *The Communion of Saints: A Dogmatic Inquiry into the Sociology of the Church*. New York: Harper and Row, 1960.

Letters and Papers from Prison, revised edition. New York: Macmillan, 1967.

Bouwsma, William J. *John Calvin: A Sixteenth Century Portrait*. Oxford: Oxford University Press, 1988.

Brown, Raymond. *The Churches the Apostles Left Behind*. New York: Paulist Press, 1984.

Browning, Don S. *A Fundamental Practical Theology: Descriptive and Strategy Proposals*. Minneapolis: Fortress Press, 1991.

Browning, Don S. (ed.) *Practical Theology: The Emerging Field in Theology, Church and World*. San Francisco: Harper and Row, 1983.

Brueggemann, Walter. "Rethinking Church Models Through Scripture,'" *Theology Today* 48:2 (1991), 128–138.

"'In the Image of God' . . . . Pluralism,'" *Modern Theology* 11:4 (1995), 455–469.

Brunner, Emil. *The Misunderstanding of the Church*. London: Lutterworth, 1952.

Burrows, Mark S. and Rorem, Paul (eds.). *Biblical Hermeneutics in Historical Perspective*. Grand Rapids: Eerdmans, 1991.

Calvin, John. *Institutes of the Christian Religion*, ed. John T. McNeill. Philadelphia: Westminster, 1960.

Carter, Stephen L. *The Culture of Disbelief*. New York: Basic Books, 1993.

Cavanaugh, William T. *Torture and Eucharist: Theology, Politics, and the Body of Christ*. Oxford: Blackwell, 1998.

Chardin, Pierre Teilhard de. *Science and Christ*. London: Collins/Harper and Row, 1968.

Chenu, M.-D., O.P. *Toward Understanding St. Thomas*. Chicago: Regnery, 1964.

Christian, William A., Sr. *Doctrines of Religious Communities: A Philosophical Study*. New Haven: Yale University Press, 1987.

Clarke, Peter B. and Byrne, Peter. *Religion Defined and Explained*. New York: St. Martin's Press, 1993.

Clifford, James. *The Predicament of Culture: Twentieth Century Ethnography, Literature, and Art*. Cambridge, MA: Harvard University Press, 1988.

Coleridge, S. T. *Aids to Reflection* (London, 1825).

Congar, Yves. "The Church: The People of God" in *Concilium*, vol. I. New Jersey: Paulist Press, 1964, pp. 11–37.

L'Église: De Saint Augustin à l'époque moderne. Paris: Cerf, 1970.

Coriden, James A. *The Parish in Catholic Tradition: History, Theology, and Canon Law*. Mahwah, NJ: Paulist Press, 1997.

Daniélou, Jean, S.J. *The Lord of History: Reflections on the Inner Meaning of History*, trans. Nigel Abercrombie. London: Longmans, 1958.

Day, Thomas. *Why Catholics Can't Sing: The Culture of Catholicism and the Triumph of Bad Taste*. New York: Crossroad, 1995.

D'Costa, Gavin. *Theology and Religious Pluralism: The Challenge of Other Religions*. Oxford: Blackwell, 1986.

John Hick's Theology of Religions: A Critical Evaluation. Lanham, MD: University Press of America, 1987.

Deane, Herbert A. *The Political and Social Ideas of Saint Augustine*. New York: Columbia University Press, 1963.

Derrida, Jacques. *Writing and Difference*. London: Routledge and Kegan Paul, 1978.

  Dissemination, trans. Barbara Johnson. Chicago: University of Chicago Press, 1981.

  Pysché: Inventions de l'autre. Paris: Galilée, 1987.

  Limited Inc. Evanston, IL: Northwestern University Press, 1988.

  A Derrida Reader: Between the Blinds, ed. Peggy Kamuf. New York: Columbia University Press, 1991.

Dickens, William T. "The Doctrine of Scripture in Hans Urs von Balthasar's *The Glory of the Lord: A Theological Aesthetics*," PhD Diss., Yale University, 1997.

Dingemans, Gijsbert D. J. "Practical Theology in the Academy: A Contemporary Overview," *Journal of Religion* 76:1 (1996), 82–96.

DiNoia, J. A., O.P. *The Diversity of Religions: A Christian Perspective*. Washington: Catholic University of America, 1992.

Dulles, Avery, S.J. *Models of the Church*, expanded edition. New York: Doubleday, 1974/1987.

  A Church To Believe In: Discipleship and the Dynamics of Freedom. New York: Crossroad, 1982/1987.

  The Catholicity of the Church. Oxford: Clarendon Press, 1985.

  The Reshaping of Catholicism: Current Challenges in the Theology of Church. San Francisco: Harper and Row, 1988.

  "From Symbol To System: A Proposal for Theological Method," *Pro Ecclesia* 1:1 (1992), 42–52.

Dunn, James D. G. *Unity and Diversity in the New Testament*, second edition. London: SCM Press, 1990.

Eagleton, Terry. *The Illusions of Postmodernism*. Oxford: Blackwell, 1996.

Ebeling, Gerhard. "Church History Is the History of the Exposition of Scripture" in *The Word of God and Tradition: Historical Studies Interpreting the Divisions of Christianity*, trans. S. H. Hooke. Philadelphia: Fortress Press, 1968, pp. 11–31.

Elshtain, Jean Bethke. *Augustine and the Limits of Politics*. Notre Dame: University of Notre Dame Press, 1995.

Erikson, Robert P. *Theologians Under Hitler*. New Haven: Yale University Press, 1985.

Eusebius, *The Ecclesiastical History*, trans. Kirsopp Lake. Cambridge, MA: Harvard University Press, 1926.

Fiorenza, Elisabeth Schüssler. "Missionaries, Apostles, Co-workers: Romans 16 and the Reconstruction of Women's Early Christian History," *Word and World* 6:4 (1986), 420–433.

  Discipleship of Equals. New York: Crossroad, 1993.

Fiorenza, Francis S. *Foundational Theology: Jesus and the Church*. New York: Crossroad, 1985.

Flannery, Austin, O.P. (ed.) *Vatican Council II: The Conciliar and Post Conciliar Documents*. Northport, NY: Costello, 1975/1986.

Foucault, Michel. *Madness and Civilization*. New York: Pantheon, 1965.

  Discipline and Punish: The Birth of the Prison, trans. Alan Sheridan. New York: Vintage Books, 1977.

  The Foucault Reader, ed. Paul Rabinow. New York: Pantheon, 1984.

Fowl, Stephen E. *Engaging Scripture: A Model for Theological Interpretation*. Oxford: Blackwell, 1998.

Frei, Hans W. *The Eclipse of Biblical Narrative*. New Haven: Yale University Press, 1975.

  Types of Christian Theology, ed. George Hunsinger and William C. Placher. New Haven: Yale University Press, 1992.

Froehlich, Karlfried. "Church History and the Bible" in Mark S. Burrows and Paul Rorem (eds.), *Biblical Hermeneutics in Historical Perspective*. Grand Rapids: Eerdmans, 1991, pp. 1–15.

Garrigou-Lagrange, Reginald, O. P. *Christ the Savior: A Commentary on the Third Part of St. Thomas's Theological Summa*. St. Louis: Herder, 1950.

Geertz, Clifford. *The Interpretation of Cultures*. New York: Harper Torchbooks, 1973.

Gethin, Rupert. "The Resurrection and Buddhism" in Gavin D'Costa (ed.), *Resurrection Reconsidered*. Oxford: One World, 1996.

Gilkey, Langdon. "Cosmology, Ontology, and the Travail of Biblical Language," *Journal of Religion* 41 (1961), 194–205.

Gill, Robin. *Moral Leadership in a Postmodern Age*. Edinburgh: T&T Clark, 1997.

Grabowski, Stanislaus J. *The Church: An Introduction to the Theology of St. Augustine*. St. Louis: Herder, 1957.

Griffiths, Paul J. *An Apology for Apologetics: A Study in the Logic of Interreligious Dialogue*. Maryknoll, NY: Orbis, 1991.

   Religious Reading: The Place of Reading in the Practice of Religion. New York: Oxford University Press, 1999.

Gunton, Colin E. *The Promise of Trinitarian Theology*, second edition. Edinburgh: T&T Clark, 1991/1997.

   "A Rose by Any Other Name? From 'Christian Doctrine' to 'Systematic Theology,'" *International Journal of Systematic Theology* 1:1 (1999), 4–23.

Gustafson, James M. *Treasure in Earthen Vessels: The Church as a Human Community*. Chicago: University of Chicago Press, 1961.

   "The Sectarian Temptation: Reflections on Theology, the Church, and the University," *Proceedings of the Catholic Theological Society of America* 40 (1985), 83–94.

Gutiérrez, Gustavo. *The Power of the Poor in History*, trans. R. R. Barr. Maryknoll, NY: Orbis, 1983.

Gutting, Gary (ed.). *The Cambridge Companion to Foucault*. Cambridge: Cambridge University Press, 1994.

Habermas, Jürgen. "Taking Aim at the Heart of the Present" in David Couzens Hoy (ed.), *Foucault: A Critical Reader*. Oxford: Blackwell, 1986, pp. 103–108.

Hall, Pamela, M. *Narrative and the Natural Law: An Interpretation of Thomistic Ethics*. Notre Dame: University of Notre Dame Press, 1994.

Hardy, Daniel W. *God's Ways with the World: Thinking and Practising Christian Faith*. Edinburgh: T&T Clark, 1996.

Hardy, Daniel W. and Sedgwick, P. H., (eds.). *The Weight of Glory: A Vision and Practice for Christian Faith: The Future of Liberal Theology. Essays for Peter Baelz*. Edinburgh: T&T Clark, 1991.

Hauerwas, Stanley. *A Community of Character: Toward a Constructive Christian Social Ethic*. Notre Dame: University of Notre Dame Press, 1981.

   Christian Existence Today: Essays on Church, World and Living In Between. Durham, NC: Labyrinth Press, 1988.

   Sanctify Them In the Truth: Holiness Exemplified. Nashville: Abingdon/T&T Clark, 1998.

Hauerwas, Stanley and Pinches, Charles. *Christians Among the Virtues: Theological Conversations with Ancient and Modern Ethics*. Notre Dame: University of Notre Dame Press, 1997.

Hauerwas, Stanley and Willimon, William H. *Resident Aliens: Life in the Christian Colony*. Nashville: Abingdon Press, 1989.

Hays, Richard B. *Echoes of Scripture in the Letters of Paul*. New Haven: Yale University Press, 1989.

Healy, Nicholas M. "Indirect Methods in Theology: Karl Rahner as an Ad Hoc Apologist," *The Thomist* 56:4 (1992), 613–633.

"The Logic of Karl Barth's Ecclesiology: Analysis, Assessment and Proposed Modifications," *Modern Theology* 10:3 (1994), 253–270.

"Communion Ecclesiology: A Cautionary Note," *Pro Ecclesia* 4:4 (1995), 442–453.

Hegel, G. W. F. *Aesthetics: Lectures on Fine Art*, 2 vols., trans. T. M. Knox. Oxford: Clarendon Press, 1975.

Heim, S. Mark. *Salvations: Truth and Difference in Religion*. Maryknoll, NY: Orbis, 1995.

Hibbs, Thomas S. *Dialectic and Narrative in Aquinas: An Interpretation of the Summa Contra Gentiles*. Notre Dame: University of Notre Dame Press, 1995.

Hick, John. *An Interpretation of Religion: Human Responses to the Transcendent*. New Haven: Yale University Press, 1989.

The Metaphor of God Incarnate: Christology in a Pluralistic Age. Louisville, KY: Westminster/John Knox Press, 1993.

Hick, John, and Knitter, Paul F. *The Myth of Christian Uniqueness: Toward a Pluralistic Theology of Religions*. Maryknoll, NY: Orbis, 1987.

Hodgson, Peter C. *Revisioning the Church: Ecclesial Freedom in the New Paradigm*. Philadelphia: Fortress Press, 1988.

Hopewell, James F. *Congregation: Stories and Structures*. Philadelphia: Fortress Press, 1987.

Hoy, David Couzens. "Power, Repression, Progress; Foucault, Lukes, and the Frankfurt School" in Hoy, David Couzens (ed.). *Foucault: A Critical Reader*. Oxford: Blackwell, 1986, pp. 123–147.

Hunsinger, George. *How To Read Karl Barth: The Shape of His Theology*. New York: Oxford University Press, 1991.

Interdicasterial Commission. *Catechism of the Catholic Church*. Liguori, MO: Liguori Publications, 1994.

Jaki, Stanley. *Cosmos and Creator*. Edinburgh: Scottish Academic Press, 1980.

Jameson, Frederic. *Postmodernism, or the Cultural Logic of Late Capitalism*. Durham: Duke University Press, 1991.

Jeanrond, Werner G. *Call and Response: The Challenge of Christian Life*. Dublin: Gill and Macmillan, 1995.

Jenson, Robert W. *Systematic Theology: Volume I: The Triune God*. New York: Oxford University Press, 1997.

Jones, L. Gregory. *Transformed Judgement: Toward a Trinitarian Account of the Moral Life*. Notre Dame: University of Notre Dame Press, 1990.

Embodying Forgiveness: A Theological Analysis. Grand Rapids: Eerdmans, 1995.

Jones, Serene. *Calvin and the Rhetoric of Piety*. Louisville, KY: Westminster/John Knox Press, 1995.

Journet, Charles. *Théologie de l'Église*. Paris: Desclée de Brouwer, 1958.

Kasper, Walter. *Theology and Church*. New York: Crossroad, 1989.

Kaufman, Gordon D. *An Essay on Theological Method*. Atlanta: Scholars Press, 1990.

In Face of Mystery: A Constructive Theology. Cambridge, MA: Harvard University Press, 1993.

God, Mystery, Diversity. Minneapolis: Augsburg Fortress, 1996.

Kavanaugh, Aidan. *The Shape of Baptism: The Rite of Christian Initiation*. New York: Pueblo, 1978.

Kelsey, David H. *The Uses of Scripture in Recent Theology*. Philadelphia: Fortress Press, 1975.
   "Church Discourse and Public Realm" in Bruce D. Marshall (ed.), *Theology and Dialogue: Essays in Conversation with George Lindbeck*. Notre Dame: University of Notre Dame Press, 1990, pp. 7–30.
   To Understand God Truly: What's Theological About a Theological School. Louisville: Westminster/John Knox Press, 1992.
Kenneson, Philip D. and Street, James L. *Selling Out the Church: The Dangers of Church Marketing*. Nashville: Abingdon Press, 1997.
Kerr, Fergus, O. P. *Immortal Longings: Versions of Transcending Humanity*. Notre Dame: University of Notre Dame Press, 1997.
Kilby, Karen. "The Vorgriff auf esse: A Study in the Relation of Philosophy to Theology in the Thought of Karl Rahner," PhD Diss., Yale University, 1994.
   Karl Rahner. London: Fount/Harper Collins, 1997.
Knitter, Paul F. *One Earth, Many Religions: Multifaith Dialogue and Global Responsibility*. Maryknoll, NY: Orbis, 1995.
   Jesus and the Other Names: Christian Mission and Global Responsibility. Maryknoll, NY: Orbis, 1996.
Komonchak, Joseph. "The Local Church and the Church Catholic: The Contemporary Theological Problematic," *The Jurist* 52 (1992), 416–447.
Küng, Hans. *The Church*. New York: Image Books, 1976.
Lakeland, Paul. *Postmodernity: Christian Identity in a Fragmented Age*. Minneapolis: Augsburg Fortress, 1997.
Lash, Nicholas. *Believing Three Ways in One God*. Notre Dame: University of Notre Dame Press, 1993.
   The Beginning and the End of 'Religion.' Cambridge: Cambridge University Press, 1996.
   "The Church in the State We're In," *Modern Theology* 13:1 (1997), 121–137.
Lennan, Richard. *The Ecclesiology of Karl Rahner*. Oxford: Clarendon Press, 1995.
Lindbeck, George A. *The Nature of Doctrine: Religion and Theology in a Postliberal Age*. Philadelphia: Westminster, 1984.
   "The Story-Shaped Church: Critical Exegesis and Theological Interpretation" in G. Green (ed.), *Scriptural Authority and Narrative Interpretation*. Philadelphia: Fortress Press, 1987, pp. 161–178.
   "Dulles on Method," *Pro Ecclesia* 1:1 (1992), 53–60.
   "Atonement and the Hermeneutics of Social Embodiment," *Pro Ecclesia* 5:2 (1996), 144–160.
   "The Gospel's Uniqueness: Election and Untranslatability," *Modern Theology* 13:4 (1997), 423–450.
Lodge, David. *Souls and Bodies*. New York: Viking Penguin, 1990.
Lonergan, Bernard J. F. *Method in Theology*. New York: Seabury, 1972.
Lossky, Nicholas, *et al.*, (eds.). *Dictionary of the Ecumenical Movement*. Geneva: WCC Publications/Eerdmans, 1991.
Loughlin, Gerard. *Telling God's Story: Bible, Church and Narrative Theology*. Cambridge: Cambridge University Press, 1996.
Lovibond, Sabina. *Realism and Imagination in Ethics*. Minneapolis: University of Minnesota Press, 1983.
Lubac, Henri de, S. J., *Catholicism: A Study of Dogma in Relation to the Corporate Destiny of Mankind*, trans. Lancelot C. Sheppard. New York: Sheed and Ward, 1958.
   The Motherhood of the Church. San Francisco: Ignatius Press, 1982.

Lyon, David. *Sociology and the Human Image*. Downer's Grove, IL: InterVarsity Press, 1983.

Lyotard, Jean-François. *The Postmodern Condition: A Report on Knowledge*, trans. G. Bennington and B. Massumi. Minneapolis: University of Minnesota Press, 1984.

MacIntyre, Alasdair. *After Virtue: A Study in Moral Theory*, second edition. Notre Dame: University of Notre Dame Press, 1984.

  Whose Justice? Which Rationality? Notre Dame: University of Notre Dame Press, 1988.

  Three Rival Versions of Moral Enquiry: Encyclopedia, Genealogy, and Tradition. Notre Dame: University of Notre Dame Press, 1990.

Mackey, Louis. *Peregrinations of the Word: Essays in Medieval Philosophy*. Ann Arbor: University of Michigan Press, 1997.

MacNamara, Vincent. *Faith and Ethics: Recent Roman Catholicism*. Washington: Georgetown University Press, 1985.

Macquarrie, John. *Principles of Christian Theology*, second edition. New York: Scribners, 1977.

Markus, R. A. *Saeculum: History and Society in the Theology of St. Augustine*, revised edition. Cambridge: Cambridge University Press, 1970.

  "Church History and Early Church Historians" in *From Augustine to Gregory the Great*, vol. II. London: Variorum Reprints, 1983, pp. 1–17.

  The End of Ancient Christianity. Cambridge: Cambridge University Press, 1990.

Marshall, Bruce D. *Christology in Conflict*. New York: Blackwell, 1987.

  "Aquinas as a Post-liberal Theologian," *The Thomist* 53 (1989), 353–402.

  "'We Shall Bear the Image of the Man of Heaven:' On the Concept of Truth," *Modern Theology* 11:1 (1995), 93–118.

  "What Is Truth?," *Pro Ecclesia* 4:4 (1995), 404–430.

  "Christ and the cultures: the Jewish people and Christian theology" in Colin E. Gunton (ed.), *The Cambridge Companion to Christian Doctrine*. Cambridge: Cambridge University Press, 1997.

Marshall, Bruce D. (ed.) *Theology and Dialogue: Essays in Conversation with George Lindbeck*. Notre Dame: University of Notre Dame Press, 1990.

Martin, Dale B. *The Corinthian Body*. New Haven: Yale University Press, 1995.

Martin, David. *Reflections on Sociology and Theology*. Oxford: Clarendon Press, 1997.

Martin, David, Mills, John Orme, and Pickering, W. S. F. (eds.). *Sociology and Theology: Alliance and Conflict*. New York: St. Martins Press, 1980.

McCormack, Bruce L. *Karl Barth's Critically Realistic Dialectical Theology*. Oxford: Clarendon Press, 1995.

Meeks, Wayne. *The Origins of Christian Morality: The First Two Centuries*. New Haven: Yale University Press, 1993.

Megill, Allan. *Prophets of Extremity: Nietzsche, Heidegger, Foucault, Derrida*. Berkeley: University of California Press, 1985.

Mersch, Emile. *The Whole Christ*. Milwaukee: Bruce, 1938.

Midgley, Mary. *Science As Salvation*. London: Routledge, 1992.

Milbank, John. *Theology and Social Theory: Beyond Secular Reason*. Oxford: Blackwell, 1990.

Molnar, Paul D. "Myth and Reality: Analysis and Critique of Gordon Kaufman and Sallie McFague on God, Christ, and Salvation," unpub. paper.

Myrdal, Gunnar. *An American Dilemma*. New York: Harper, 1944.

Niebuhr, H. Richard. *Christ and Culture*. New York: Harper and Row, 1951.

Norris, Christopher. *Derrida*. Cambridge, MA: Harvard University Press, 1987.

  "'What Is Enlightenment?': Kant According to Foucault" in Gary Gutting (ed.), *The Cambridge Companion to Foucault*. Cambridge: Cambridge University Press, 1994.

Oakes, Edward T. *Pattern of Redemption: The Theology of Hans Urs von Balthasar*. New York: Continuum, 1994.

O'Donovan, Leo, S.J. "A Changing Ecclesiology in a Changing Church: A Symposium on Development in the Ecclesiology of Karl Rahner," *Theological Studies* 38 (1977), 736–762.

Pannenberg, Wolfhart. *Systematic Theology*, vols. II and III. Grand Rapids: Eerdmans, 1994+.

Pelikan, Jaroslav. *The Christian Tradition: 1 The Emergence of the Catholic Tradition*. Chicago: University of Chicago Press, 1971.

Perrone, Ioannes, S.J. *Praelectiones Theologicae*. Augustae Taurinorum, 1877.

Pesch, Otto Hermann, O.P. *Theologie der Rechtfertigung bei Martin Luther und Thomas von Aquin: Versuch eines Systematisch-theologischen Dialogs*, 2 Aufl. Mainz: Matthias Grünewald, 1967/1985.

Pickstock, Catherine. *After Writing: On the Liturgical Consummation of Philosophy*. Oxford: Blackwell, 1998.

Placher, William C. *The Domestication of Transcendence: How Modern Thinking about God Went Wrong*. Louisville, KY: Westminster/John Knox Press, 1996.

Polkinghorne, John. *The Faith of a Physicist: Reflections of a Bottom-Up Thinker*. Minneapolis: Fortress Press, 1996.

Porter, Jean. *Moral Action and Christian Ethics*. Cambridge: Cambridge University Press, 1993.

Quash, J. B. "'Between the Brutally Given, and the Brutally, Banally Free': Von Balthasar's Theology of Drama in Dialogue with Hegel," *Modern Theology* 13:3 (1997), 293–318.

Radner, Ephraim, *The End of the Church: A Pneumatology of Christian Division in the West*. Grand Rapids: Eerdmans, 1998.

Rahner, Karl, S.J. *Die Pfarre: Von der Theologie zur Praxis*, ed. Hugo Rahner, S.J. Freiburg im Breisgau: Lambertus Verlag, 1956.

　Theological Investigations. New York: Crossroad, 1961+.

　The Church and the Sacraments. London: Herder, 1963.

　The Christian of the Future. London: Herder, 1967.

　The Theology of Pastoral Action. New York: Herder, 1968.

　Foundations of the Christian Faith. New York: Seabury, 1978.

　Karl Rahner In Dialogue, ed. and trans. Harvey Egan. New York: Crossroad, 1986.

Rasmusson, Arne. *The Church as Polis: From Political Theology to Theological Politics as Exemplified by Jürgen Moltmann and Stanley Hauerwas*. Notre Dame: University of Notre Dame Press, 1995.

Rawls, John. *A Theory of Justice*. Cambridge, MA: Harvard University Press, 1971.

Reno, R. R. *The Ordinary Transformed: Karl Rahner and the Christian Vision of Transcendence*. Grand Rapids: Eerdmans, 1995.

Rikhof, Herwi. *The Concept of Church: A Methodological Inquiry into the Use of Metaphors in Ecclesiology*. London: Sheed and Ward, 1981.

Rogers, Eugene F., Jr. *Thomas Aquinas and Karl Barth: Sacred Doctrine and the Natural Knowledge of God*. Notre Dame: University of Notre Dame Press, 1995.

Roof, Wade Clark. *A Generation of Seekers*. New York: HarperCollins, 1993.

Rorty, Richard. *Contingency, Irony, and Solidarity*. Cambridge: Cambridge University Press, 1989.

　Achieving Our Country: Leftist Thought in Twentieth-Century America. Cambridge, MA: Harvard University Press, 1998.

Rosaldo, Renato. *Culture and Truth: The Remaking of Social Analysis*. Boston: Beacon Press, 1989.

Rose, Gillian. *The Broken Middle: Out of Our Ancient Society*. Oxford: Blackwell, 1992.
Judaism and Modernity: Philosophical Essays. Oxford: Blackwell, 1993.

Rosenau, Pauline Marie. *Post-Modernism and the Social Sciences: Insights, Inroads, and Intrusions*. Princeton: Princeton University Press, 1992.

Sabra, George. *Thomas Aquinas' Vision of the Church: Fundamentals of an Ecumenical Ecclesiology*. Mainz: Matthias Grünewald, 1987.

Schleiermacher, Friedrich. *On Religion: Speeches to its Cultured Despisers*. New York: Harper and Row, 1958.
The Christian Faith. Edinburgh: T&T Clark, 1976.

Schor, Naomi. *Reading in Detail: Aesthetics and the Feminine*. New York: Methuen, 1987.

Segundo, Juan Luis, S. J. *The Liberation of Theology*, trans. John Drury. Maryknoll, NY: Orbis, 1982.

Smith, Wilfred Cantwell. *Towards a World Theology: Faith and the Comparative History of Religion*. Philadelphia: Westminster, 1981.

Soskice, Janet Martin. *Metaphor and Religious Language*. New York: Oxford University Press, 1985.

Soulen, Kendall R. *The God of Israel and Christian Theology*. Minneapolis: Fortress Press, 1996.
"YHWH the Triune God," *Modern Theology* 15:1 (1999), 25–54.

Stout, Jeffrey. *Ethics After Babel: The Languages of Morals and Their Discontents*. Boston: Beacon Press, 1988.

Sullivan, Francis A., S. J. *Salvation Outside the Church?* New York: Paulist Press, 1992.

Sykes, Stephen. *The Identity of Christianity: Theologians and the Essence of Christianity from Schleiermacher to Barth*. Philadelphia: Fortress Press, 1984.

Tanner, Kathryn. *God and Creation in Christian Theology: Tyranny or Empowerment?* Oxford: Blackwell, 1988.
The Politics of God. Minneapolis: Fortress Press, 1992.
Theories of Culture: A New Agenda for Theology. Minneapolis: Fortress Press, 1997.

Taylor, Charles. *Sources of the Self: The Making of the Modern Identity*. Cambridge, MA: Harvard University Press, 1989.

Taylor, Mark C. *Erring: A Postmodern A/Theology*. Chicago: University of Chicago Press, 1984.

Thiel, John E. *Imagination and Authority: Theological Authorship in the Modern Tradition*. Minneapolis: Fortress Press, 1991.

Thils, G. *Les Notes de l'Église dans l'Apologétique Catholique depuis la Réforme*. Paris: Desclée, no date.

Thompson, William M. *The Struggle for Theology's Soul: Contesting Scripture in Christology*. New York: Crossroad, 1996.

Tillard, Jean-Marie, O. P. *Church of Churches: The Ecclesiology of Communion*, trans. R. C. De Peaux, O. Praem. Collegeville: Glazier/Liturgical Press, 1992.
"Was the Holy Spirit at Canberra?" *One In Christ* 29:1 (1993), 34–64.

Tillich, Paul. *Systematic Theology*, vol. III. Chicago: Chicago University Press, 1963.

Torrance, Alan J. *Persons in Communion: An Essay on Trinitarian Description and Human Participation*. Edinburgh: T&T Clark, 1996.

Torrance, Thomas F. *Divine and Contingent Order*. Oxford: Oxford University Press, 1981.

Tracy, David. *The Analogical Imagination: Christian Theology and the Culture of Pluralism.* New York: Crossroad, 1981.

Unger, Roberto Mangabeira. *Social Theory: Its Situation and Its Task.* Cambridge: Cambridge University Press, 1987.

Vacek, E., S.J. "Development within Rahner's Theology," *Irish Theological Quarterly* 42 (1975), 36–49.

Vatican Commission for Religious Relations with the Jews. "We Remember: A Reflection on the 'Shoah,'" *Origins* 27:40 (1998), 669–675.

Ven, Johannes van der. *Ecclesiology in Context.* Grand Rapids: Eerdmans, 1996.

Volf, Miroslav. *After Our Likeness: The Church as the Image of the Trinity.* Grand Rapids: Eerdmans, 1998.

Vroom, Hendrik. *No Other Gods: Christian Belief in Dialogue with Buddhism, Hinduism, and Islam,* trans. Lucy Jansen. Grand Rapids: Eerdmans, 1996.

Wainwright, Geoffrey. *Doxology: The Praise of God in Worship, Doctrine and Life.* New York: Oxford University Press, 1980.

Walzer, Michael. *Spheres of Justice.* New York: Basic Books, 1983.

Watson, Francis. *Text, Church and World: Biblical Interpretation in Theological Perspective.* Edinburgh: T&T Clark, 1994.

Webster, John. *Barth's Ethics of Reconciliation.* Cambridge: Cambridge University Press, 1995.

   Barth's Moral Theology: Human Action in Barth's Thought. Edinburgh: T&T Clark, 1998.

Werpehowski, William. "Ad Hoc Apologetics," *Journal of Religion* 66 (1986), 282–301.

White, Stephen K. *Political Theory and Postmodernism.* Cambridge: Cambridge University Press, 1991.

Williams, Rowan D. "Between Politics and Metaphysics: Reflections in the Wake of Gillian Rose," *Modern Theology* 11:1 (1995), 3–22.

Wolterstorff, Nicholas. *Divine Discourse: Philosophical Reflections on the Claim that God Speaks.* Cambridge: Cambridge University Press, 1995.

Wright, N. T. *The New Testament and the People of God.* Minneapolis: Fortress Press, 1992.

Wuthnow, Robert. *The Restructuring of American Religion: Society and Faith since World War II.* Princeton: Princeton University Press, 1988.

Wylie, Amanda Berry. "The Exegesis of History in John Chrysostom's 'Homilies on Acts'" in Mark S. Burrows and Paul Rorem (eds.), *Biblical Hermeneutics in Historical Perspective: Studies in Honor of Karlfried Froelich on His Sixtieth Birthday.* Grand Rapids: Eerdmans, 1991, pp. 59–72.

Yeago, David. "The New Testament and Nicene Dogma" in Stephen E. Fowl (ed.), *The Theological Interpretation of Scripture: Classic and Contemporary Readings.* Oxford: Blackwell, 1997.

Yoder, John Howard. *For The Nations: Essays Public and Evangelical.* Grand Rapids: Eerdmans, 1997.

Young, Frances M. *Biblical Exegesis and the Formation of Christian Culture.* Cambridge: Cambridge University Press, 1997.

Zizioulas, John D. *Being as Communion: Studies in Personhood and the Church.* Crestwood, NY: St. Vladimir's Seminary Press, 1985.

Index